Alexander Balmain Bruce

St. Paul's conception of christianity

Alexander Balmain Bruce

St. Paul's conception of christianity

ISBN/EAN: 9783743329676

Manufactured in Europe, USA, Canada, Australia, Japa

Cover: Foto ©Lupo / pixelio.de

Manufactured and distributed by brebook publishing software (www.brebook.com)

Alexander Balmain Bruce

St. Paul's conception of christianity

ST. PAUL'S CONCEPTION OF CHRISTIANITY

PRINTED BY
MORRISON AND GIBB LIMITED,
FOR
T. & T. CLARK, EDINBURGH.

LONDON : SIMPKIN, MARSHALL, HAMILTON, KENT, AND CO. LIMITED.
NEW YORK : CHARLES SCRIBNER'S SONS.
TORONTO : THE WILLARD TRACT DEPOSITORY.

ST. PAUL'S CONCEPTION

OF CHRISTIANITY

BY

ALEXANDER BALMAIN BRUCE, D.D.

PROFESSOR OF
NEW TESTAMENT EXEGESIS IN THE FREE CHURCH COLLEGE, GLASGOW

AUTHOR OF
"APOLOGETICS; OR, CHRISTIANITY DEFENSIVELY STATED" "THE KINGDOM OF GOD"
"THE TRAINING OF THE TWELVE" "THE HUMILIATION OF CHRIST"
ETC. ETC.

EDINBURGH
T. & T. CLARK, 38 GEORGE STREET
1896

PREFATORY NOTE

THIS book on *St. Paul's Conception of Christianity* is a companion volume to my work on *The Kingdom of God*, published five years ago. I have in view to issue a similar work on *The Epistle to the Hebrews* as soon as I can command the necessary leisure.

The note at p. 184 on the book recently published by Professor Everett of Boston, entitled *The Gospel of Paul*, is the substance of a review which appeared in the pages of *The Christian World*. It is reproduced here by the kind permission of the publishers.

A. B. BRUCE.

GLASGOW 1st *September* 1894.

CONTENTS

CHAPTER I
THE SOURCES

	PAGE
Chief Sources — Epistles to Galatian, Corinthian, and Roman Churches	2
These the controversial group	4
Contain all the leading ideas of Paulinism	4
Even of the Christological Epistles	5
Was there a growth in St. Paul's theology?	6
A priori possible	8
No proof of the fact	9
Epistles to the Thessalonians no proof	10
These the Primer-Epistles	15
Analysis of their teaching	17

CHAPTER II
ST. PAUL'S RELIGIOUS HISTORY

Important bearing on his theology	26
Autobiographical hints	27
Conversion of Saul of Tarsus	31
Not so sudden as it seems	32
Significance of the conversion	35
Confirmatory notices in Galatians i.	37
His universalism dates from his conversion	45
Religious intuitions and theological formulations	46
Apologetic elements the latest growth	47

CHAPTER III

THE EPISTLE TO THE GALATIANS

	PAGE
Origin of the controversy with the Judaists	49
Phases of the controversy	51
Epistle deals with first phase—perpetual obligation of the Law	52
The earliest of the four	53
Occasion of the writing	55
Analysis of the Epistle	56
Main body of the Epistle	59
Postscript	70

CHAPTER IV

THE EPISTLES TO THE CORINTHIANS

Second phase of the controversy—attack on St. Paul's apostolic standing	71
Little about it in the First Epistle	72
Yet leading points of St. Paul's apology indicated	75
These worked out in the Second Epistle	75
First line of defence—He has seen the Lord	76
Second line—The success of his work	79
Third line—He has suffered in the cause	84
Last four chapters	85

CHAPTER V

THE EPISTLE TO THE ROMANS—ITS AIM

An occasional writing, not a theological treatise	91
Deals with the last phase of the Judaistic controversy, the prerogative of Israel	93
Temper of the Judaists to be dealt with	94
Baur's view of the Epistle	97
Who were the foe?	99
Was the Roman Church mainly Jewish or mainly Gentile?	102
Influence of missionary plans	104
And of the letter being addressed to Rome	105

CHAPTER VI

THE EPISTLE TO THE ROMANS—THE TRAIN OF THOUGHT

Theme of the first eight chapters, salvation through faith	107
The sin section	108
Gentile sins	109
Jewish sins	111

	PAGE
Paganism and Judaism both failures	112
"A righteousness of God"	114
Support to the doctrine	115
The historical argument	116
The argument from experience	117
The Adam-Christ section	118
Apologetic train of thought,	119
Triumphant conclusion	122
The problem of the election (chapters ix.-xi.)	123

CHAPTER VII

THE DOCTRINE OF SIN

Embraces four particulars	125
(1) General prevalence of sin	125
(2) Connection with Adam	127
Universal prevalence of death	128
Imputation of Adam's sin	130
Doctrine of the Talmud	134
(3) Sinful proclivity of the flesh	137
Source of this proclivity	141
(4) The Law's action on the flesh	143

CHAPTER VIII

THE RIGHTEOUSNESS OF GOD

A righteousness given to faith	147
Essential significance of the doctrine	147
Specific aspects of the doctrine	151
Functions of faith	152
Conflicting theological types	155
What St. Paul meant to teach	157
Justification and Christ's resurrection	160
Theory of Ménégoz	161

CHAPTER IX

THE DEATH OF CHRIST

Christ's doctrine and St. Paul's	165
Pauline *logia* on the subject	166
ἱλαστήριον	167
The principle of redemption	171
Romans viii. 3.	172
Objective and subjective	175

x CONTENTS

	PAGE
Subjective identity	178
Vicar, Representative, Brother	181
Professor Everett's theory	184

CHAPTER X
ADOPTION

No formal doctrine of the Fatherhood of God	188
Sonship in the teaching of Christ and St. Paul	189
Adoption as St. Paul understood it	190
Objective aspect	191
The filial spirit	192
Privileges of the filial state	193
Liberty	194
The Spirit of His Son	197
Heirship	204

CHAPTER XI
WITHOUT AND WITHIN

The Pauline apologetic, topics involved	207
Two aspects of his soteriology	208
Connection between them, various theories	209
True view of the matter	213
The mystic element in St. Paul, its source	216
The *faith-mysticism* his own	219
Subjective righteousness in *Romans* and *Galatians*	221

CHAPTER XII
THE MORAL ENERGY OF FAITH

Faith a guarantee for holiness	225
Faith good for all purposes	227
Faith energetic in all spheres of life	229
"Faith alone" tested by religious history	230
Faith establishing fellowship between the believer and Christ	233
Weiss' view as to faith	235
Function of baptism	237

CHAPTER XIII
THE HOLY SPIRIT

Apologetic setting of the theme defended	242
Holy Spirit in the primitive Church	243
His influence chiefly charismatic	245

CONTENTS xi

	PAGE
Charisms and grace divorced	247
St. Paul's view of the Spirit's influence ethical	248
Transcendent action of the Spirit intermittent	251
Immanent action constant	253
Acts through our rational powers and idea of Christ	254
St. Paul did not neglect the history of Christ	256

CHAPTER XIV

THE FLESH AS A HINDRANCE TO HOLINESS

"Body" and "Flesh"	263
St. Paul experienced the hindrance	264
What is meant by the "Flesh"?	267
Hellenistic theory	268
Not held by St. Paul	269
Difficulties of Pauline anthropology	273
An ethical dualism taught by the apostle	276

CHAPTER XV

THE LIKENESS OF SINFUL FLESH

Romans viii. 3.	279
Different views as to the meaning of	280
Does St. Paul decide the question as to Christ's flesh being the same as ours?	283
Theory of Atonement associated with doctrine of identity of Christ's flesh with ours	286
Criticism of the theory	288
Sacramentarianism involved in the theory	290

CHAPTER XVI

THE LAW

The Law in *Galatians* and *Romans*	293
St. Paul's view of the Law	295
Three questions as to St. Paul's view of the Law	295
Is it in accordance with the view of the Law in the Old Testament?	295
Are the functions St. Paul ascribes to the Law real?	302
Is St. Paul's view of the Law exhaustive?	305
St. Paul's view and that of the Epistle to the Hebrews compared	307

CHAPTER XVII
THE ELECTION OF ISRAEL

	PAGE
Third topic in the Pauline apologetic	310
The problem dealt with in two ways (*Romans* ix., x., xi.).	311
Hypothesis of a cancelled election	312
Was the election really cancelled?	317
St. Paul's idea of election	321
Figurative expression of it	322
Relativity of biblical utterances	324
Last word on the subject	325

CHAPTER XVIII
CHRIST

Why taken up at so advanced a stage	327
Doctrine of Christ and doctrine of Redemption	328
Redemption by self-humiliation	329
Involves a step out of time into the Eternal	329
Pre-existence	330
Raises three questions	331
Christ's relation to man	331
Christ's relation to the universe	335
Christ's relation to God	336
Has St. Paul called Christ God?	339

CHAPTER XIX
THE CHRISTIAN LIFE

Beginning of Christian life	344
A new creation	346
St. Paul's view compared with our Lord's	349
Does St. Paul recognise the idea of growth?	350
Hints of it in earlier letters	353
Result	357
Salient features of the Christian life	358
Place of love	359

CHAPTER XX
THE CHURCH

Church and Kingdom in Gospels and Pauline Epistles	362
The Church idealised by St. Paul	366
Church fellowship	368
At first all on a level	370
Differentiation ensues	371

Rulers	371
Teachers	372
The Christian ministry	373
A "learned ministry"	377

CHAPTER XXI
THE LAST THINGS

Modern views and ancient contrasted	379
Salvation eschatologically conceived	380
St. Paul expected the παρουσία soon	381
Change of mind	383
Does St. Paul teach a universal resurrection?	385
Physical and ethical resurrection	387
Mr. Matthew Arnold on St. Paul's idea of the resurrection	388
Kabisch on the same	391
The resurrection body	392
Chiliasm	394
1 *Corinthians* xv.—its value religious not theological	395

SUPPLEMENTARY NOTE
THE TEACHING OF ST. PAUL COMPARED WITH THE TEACHING OF OUR LORD IN THE SYNOPTICAL GOSPELS

Summary of results	397
Views of Dr. Wendt stated	398
Chief point of contrast refers to Atonement	400
The question raised vital	402
Self-salvation and salvation by another	403
Adjustment of Atonement to the natural order	403
Faith in the teaching of our Lord and St. Paul	404

ST. PAUL'S CONCEPTION OF CHRISTIANITY

CHAPTER I

THE SOURCES

Two important questions may be asked concerning St. Paul's Christian theology: Where did he get it? and, Whence do we obtain our knowledge of it? It is with the latter of these questions that we are now to be occupied. By "sources" is here meant the literary materials available for becoming acquainted with the great Gentile apostle's characteristic way of thinking on the leading themes connected with the Christian faith.

If we wanted to know, as far as is possible, all that St. Paul thought on any topic relating to the faith, we should have to regard all his extant Epistles as our sources, and our first task would be to ascertain to the best of our ability how many of the separate writings ascribed to him in the New Testament are authentic. If, on the other hand, our aim be, as it is, to determine the nature of the distinctively Pauline type of Christianity.

to make ourselves acquainted with what St. Paul called his gospel,[1] or what, in modern phrase, we call *Paulinism*, it is really not necessary to do more than study carefully four of the reputedly Pauline Epistles, those, viz., to the Galatian, Corinthian, and Roman Churches respectively. This limitation of the field to be studied, while reducing the subject to manageable dimensions, may be justified by other considerations possessing more weight than can attach to reasons of personal convenience.

Among these considerations a foremost place is due to the fact that the four Epistles referred to are generally recognised by biblical critics of all schools as indubitably genuine.[2] Apart altogether from personal convictions, even though one may have little or no doubt as to the authenticity of any one of the thirteen letters,[3] it is due to the actual state of critical opinion that in a scientific attempt to ascertain the nature of St. Paul's Christian teaching, primary importance should be attached to the

[1] *Rom.* xvi. 25.

[2] There is a school of critics possessing hardihood enough to call in question the genuineness of even these Epistles. Its best-known representative is Rudolf Steck, who has expounded his views in a work recently published on the Epistle to the Galatians (*Der Galaterbrief nach seiner Echtheit untersucht*, 1888). The assumption which underlies his criticism is, that the sharp opposition to Judaistic Christianity revealed in the Epistle did not really exist in St. Paul's time, but came much later, as the result of a gradual development which reached its culminating point about the time of Marcion. On this new criticism, which I cannot bring myself to take seriously, see some remarks of Lipsius in the introduction to his Commentary on Galatians, etc., in the *Hand-Commentar zum Neuen Testament*. This school of New Testament criticism corresponds in character to that of Vernes and Havet in the Old Testament, who make the prophets post-exilian.

[3] Of course the Epistle to the Hebrews is left out of account.

Epistles which command a general, if not quite universal, consensus of critical approval. Other Epistles may legitimately be cited by any writer on Paulinism who has no doubt as to their genuineness, but even in that case, if he is to pursue a strictly scientific method, only in the second place, and by way of parallels. It will be understood, of course, that in a homiletic use of Scripture this distinction between primary and secondary may be disregarded.

The four Epistles in question have the advantage of being more or less controversial in their nature. This is, it must be owned, not advantageous in all respects. A polemical origin is in some ways prejudicial to the quality and value of a writing. Controversy readily leads to the placing of an undue emphasis on some aspects of truth to the neglect of others not in themselves unimportant. It involves an unwelcome descent from the serene region of intuition to the lower and stormier region of argumentation. The *rôle* of the prophet or seer is replaced by that of the theological doctor. On both accounts the quality of temporariness is apt, in some measure, to characterise all controversial writings. When the occasion is past the one-sidedness to which it gave rise ceases to satisfy. Arguments which told at the time when the controversy raged lose their cogency, though the truths they were employed to defend possess perennial importance. Yet, on the other hand, the literature of a great debate, which formed a crisis in the religious history of the world, must possess an exceptional and imperishable worth. The thoughts of men at such a time are clear, for they define themselves against those of opponents. We have a twofold clue to their meaning: their own words, and the views of those against whom they contend. Then the deepest thoughts of men's minds are brought to light at such a crisis. Conflict sets their hearts on fire, and stimulates to the uttermost their intellectual powers; they say, therefore, what is dear to them as life, and they say all in the most energetic manner.

These remarks have their full application to the four Epistles which we may conveniently distinguish as the *controversial* group among the Pauline writings. The issue involved is clear; we have no difficulty in knowing what were the views of those against whose evil influence the apostle sought to fortify the churches to which he wrote. In other Epistles, such as that to the Colossians, we can only guess what were the unwholesome tendencies the writer desired to counteract. The issue is also vital. The controversy concerns nothing less than the nature and destination of Christianity. Here therefore, if anywhere, we may expect to learn what St. Paul deemed central and essential in the Christian faith; to get to the very bottom of his mind and heart as a believer in Jesus, all the more that the foes he fights are not only the men of his own house, but the very impersonation of his former self. They advocate what he once held, they represent religious tendencies which formerly made him a determined enemy of Christianity, and a relentless persecutor of all who bore the Christian name. With what passion, yes and with what pathos, he must throw himself into such a quarrel! We may expect to find in what he writes bearing thereon not merely much fresh original thought trenchantly expressed, but here and there autobiographical hints, involuntary self-revelations, the man unveiled alongside of the theologian. It will be our own fault if in our hands these writings become dry scholastic productions.

Even in reference to what is specific or peculiar in later Epistles, we may find a sufficient indication of St. Paul's view in the controversial group. So, for example, in the case of what are called the *Prison* Epistles, whose special characteristic is the prominence given to Christology, on which account they are sometimes distinguished as the *Christological* group.[1] There is quite enough Christology in the four great controversial Epistles to show us what St. Paul thought concerning the great Object of the Christian's faith and reverence. The Christological Epistles contain interesting and valuable statements concerning the Lord Jesus which repay earnest study, but the Christ-idea of these Epistles embraces little, if anything, essential in advance of what can be gathered from the relative texts in the controversial Epistles. The person of Christ is more prominently the theme of the former as compared with the latter, but the doctrine taught is not pronouncedly higher, though it is applied in new directions.

Besides these two groups of Epistles, there are other two containing respectively the earliest and the latest of St. Paul's reputed writings, preserved in the New Testa-

[1] This group includes the Epistles to the Ephesian, Philippian, and Colossian Churches; also the Epistle to Philemon, which, however, possesses no doctrinal significance. Of the Christological Epistles the authenticity of *Philippians* is least doubted, that of *Ephesians* most.

ment, the one consisting of the two Epistles to the church of Thessalonica, the other of the two to Timothy and the one to Titus, called from their leading subject-matter the *Pastoral* Epistles. Neither of these groups yields a contribution of importance to *Paulinism*, if we use that term to denote not what St. Paul wrote casually on any subject whatever connected with the Christian faith, but the distinctively Pauline system of thought on essential aspects of the faith. In the former are to be found no definite specific formulations of belief, but only general and elementary statements of truth; while the latter, in so far as they refer to matters of faith, but repeat familiar Pauline ideas as commonplaces, their proper occasion and specialty being to supply directions with reference to ecclesiastical organisation.

These four groups of letters, written at different times, the earliest separated from the latest by a period of some sixteen years, naturally suggest a question which may here be briefly touched on. Was there any growth in St. Paul's mind in relation to Christianity, or must we conceive of his system of Christian thought as the same at all stages of his history, poured out at the first in one gush, so to speak, and setting thereafter into an unchangeable rigid form? On this question opinion is greatly divided. Sabatier, *e.g.*, earnestly contends for growth, and makes it his business to prove and exhibit it by analysis of the different groups of Epistles, beginning with the Epistles to the Thessalonians, called the *mission* group, and supposed to show the apostle's way of thinking before the great controversy arose, and passing in succession through the controversial and the Christological groups to the pastoral.¹ Pfleiderer, on the other hand, inclines to the other alternative.² The difference between these two authors, however, does not consist in this, that the one affirms and the other denies the existence of traces of advance, development, or modification of view within the range of the Epistles ascribed to St. Paul. The point of difference is, that the one holds that the growth was in St. Paul's own views and teaching, and the other that the growth was not in St. Paul, but in *Paulinism*, that is in the conception of Christianity which took its origin from St. Paul, and in its main features was adopted by a section of the Church, and in the hands of his followers underwent expansion and modification. The facts founded on in the maintenance of the two rival hypotheses are much the same. They are such as these, that in the Epistle to the Colossians, for example, a somewhat higher view of the Person of Christ is presented than in the four undisputed Epistles, that Christ's work is there regarded from a somewhat novel point of view, that a less purely negative attitude towards the law is therein assumed than that which characterises the controversial Epistles, and that the whole subject of Christianity is contemplated in a metaphysical way *sub specie æternitatis*, rather than in the

¹ *Vide* his *L'Apôtre Paul*, translated into English, and published by Messrs. Hodder & Stoughton; a most suggestive and helpful book, whatever one may think of his theory as to the development of doctrine in the mind of the apostle.

² *Vide* his *Der Paulinismus*. Ménégoz (*Le Péché et La Redemption d'apres Saint Paul*, 1882) speaks of these two works by Sabatier and Pfleiderer as best indicating the present state of thought on Paulinism.

historical manner of the earlier Epistles. The use made of the facts is very different. One says: "Having regard to such facts, it is evident to me that St. Paul's mind underwent a process of vital growth as years passed, and new circumstances arose to stimulate that ever active powerful intellect to fresh thought on the great theme which engrossed its attention." The other says: "Having regard to these phenomena, I have no hesitation in affirming that this Epistle to the Colossians is not of Pauline authorship, though I am sure it proceeded from the Pauline school, for the affinities between it and the undoubted writings of St. Paul are very marked."

In presence of such contrariety of opinion, and considering the importance of the issues involved, it is necessary to come to some sort of conclusion as to this question of growth. Now, there is no *à priori* objection to the hypothesis of development as applied to St. Paul's personal apprehension of the significance of Christianity. Growth in knowledge as in grace is the law of ordinary Christian life, and there is no stringent reason why we should regard an apostle as an exception. Inspiration is no such reason. Inspiration was compatible with its possessor knowing in part and prophesying in part, for St. Paul predicates such partiality of himself.[1] But if inspiration be compatible with knowing in part at the best, it is also compatible with knowing less at one time than at another. We know, moreover, that it was not God's way to reveal all truth at one time to the agents of revelation. He spoke in many parts and in many modes by the prophets to the fathers. Why should He

[1] 1 *Cor.* xiii. 2.

not follow the same method with the apostles: not communicating to them at once a full understanding of the Christian faith in all its bearings, but simply providing that their insight should keep pace with events, so that they should always be able to give the Church such guidance as was required? The mere fact, therefore, that one of St. Paul's reputed Epistles contains teaching on any subject in advance of that found in admittedly Pauline Epistles is not of itself any proof that that Epistle is not also Pauline. Questions of genuineness must be settled on independent grounds.[1]

Thus far as to the *à priori* aspect of the question. But how now as to the matter of fact? Is there any reason to believe, *e.g.*, that St. Paul had a much clearer and deeper insight into the nature and destination of Christianity when he wrote the controversial Epistles, than at the time of his conversion some twenty years before, or at least during the earlier years of his missionary activity? The supposition is in itself reasonable and credible, and the burden of proof may seem to lie on those who deny it. Much depends on the way in which we conceive the conversion and what it involved. For some that event signifies very little, for others it means almost everything characteristic in Pauline Christianity. I shall

[1] Ménégoz admits not only the possibility but the reality of a development in St. Paul's thought. But he holds that whatever development there was took place before the writing of the Epistle to the Galatians, which, he thinks, came next in the order of time to the Epistles to the Thessalonians. In the other Epistles, from *Galatians* onwards, he finds no advance in thought. It cannot be proved, he thinks, that the Christology of *Romans* is behind that of *Colossians*, though Christology is not its specialty, as it is of the latter. *Le Péché et la Redemption*, pp. 7, 9.

have occasion to state my own view in the following chapter, and must not anticipate what I have to say there. Leaving over the psychological aspect of the question till then, I can now only refer to what may be supposed to make for the hypothesis of growth in the extant Pauline literature.

The two Epistles to the Thessalonians have been supposed to furnish indisputable evidence that, previous to the great controversy, St. Paul's way of thinking was of a simpler, less developed type than is found in the controversial group. Along with the reports of Pauline discourses in the Book of Acts, they have been regarded as a source of knowledge concerning what is called *Primitive Paulinism*, understood to signify not merely what St. Paul thought it fitting to teach to infant churches, founded in the course of his missionary journeys, but his own way of conceiving the gospel antecedently to the great anti-Judaistic controversy. Now, that these Epistles do present to our view what we may call a rudimentary gospel, interesting to note,' and, as will hereafter appear, justifying an important inference, is beyond doubt. But it by no means follows that that rudimentary gospel represents all the apostle then knew, and that all the great deep thoughts found in the four controversial Epistles lay as yet beneath his mental horizon. To satisfy ourselves of this we have only to reflect when the Epistles in question were written, and what had happened before they were penned. It is not necessary to inquire into exact dates; it is enough to say that the Thessalonian letters presuppose a Thessalonian *Church*, and could not have been written before that Church was founded, and until it had had some experiences calling for such instruction and counsel as the letters contain. Turning now to the memoirs of St. Paul's missionary activity in *Acts*, what do we find? That St. Paul's visit to Thessalonica is placed after the Council in Jerusalem, at which the critical question of circumcision was discussed and provisionally settled. That is to say, the cleavage between the Apostle of the Gentiles who appeared at that Council as the enthusiastic champion of Gentile liberties, and those who took a narrow, conservative view of the question at issue, had taken place at least a year or two before the letters to the Thessalonian Church could possibly have been written. How keenly alive to the issues at stake St. Paul was at the time when the Council met, we learn from his own memoranda preserved in his Epistle to the Galatians, where in language thrilling with passion he refers to "false brethren unawares brought in, who came in privily to spy out our liberty, which we have in Christ Jesus."[1] If the apostle had not thought out his gospel before, here was a crisis to set him thinking, and to stimulate a very rapid theological development. It may be taken for granted that by the time he wrote his Epistles to the Thessalonians, during his long sojourn in Corinth,[2] all his most characteristic ideas had taken their place in his system of religious thought. Indeed, there is every reason to believe that he had by that time already given expression to them, if not in writing, at

---

[1] *Gal.* ii. 4.
[2] Such is the general opinion of critics. Paul, Silvanus, and Timothy are named together in the salutations. Vide *Acts* xviii. 5.

least in vigorous, incisive speech. The encounter with Peter at Antioch referred to in the Epistle to the Galatians is not recorded in the Book of Acts, but its proper historical place, doubtless, falls within the period of St. Paul's stay in Antioch before setting out on the long mission tour, which had for its eventful result the extension of Christianity from Asia into Europe.[1] In that memorable interview, the apostle for the first time, so far as we know, gave utterance to his distinctive conception of the Christian faith. In *Galatians* ii. 14–21 we have the Pauline gospel *in nuce*; not the supposed primitive Paulinism of a yet undeveloped Christian consciousness, but the fully formulated Paulinism of the controversial letters, which contain nothing clearer, more definite, or more characteristic than is to be found in that remarkable utterance. But that speech to Peter was uttered many months before the Thessalonian Epistles were written.[2]

If, therefore, we are to find in these Epistles the faint outlines of a rudimentary Pauline gospel, forming the Christian creed of the apostle before he understood the implications of the faith, we must disregard the historical notices of *Acts*, and relegate their composition to a period antecedent to the rise of the dispute about circumcision and the meeting of the Jerusalem Conference.[3]

[1] Vide *Acts* xv. 35, 36.
[2] The bearing of the above-mentioned facts on the question of a primitive Paulinism, supposed to be exhibited in the Epistles to the Thessalonians, is very forcibly brought out by Holsten. Vide *Das Evangelium des Paulus*, Vorwort, p. viii.
[3] So Ménégoz, who thinks the Epistles to the Thessalonians the most doubtful of all Paul's reputed writings, and that ex-

THE SOURCES

The hypothesis of a primitive Paulinism escapes in that case from the control of fact and the hazard of authoritative contradiction. Not altogether indeed, even on that gratuitous supposition; for, from the statement St. Paul makes in his Epistle to the Galatians, that he did not meet with any of the apostles till three years after his conversion, it may very reasonably be argued that, even at that early period, his conception of Christianity was well defined. Such an inference harmonises with the aim of the statement. But of this more hereafter.

So far, then, as the earliest letters of St. Paul are concerned, there is no evidence to support the theory of a slow, gradual growth of his system of Christian thought. The phenomena they exhibit can neither prove, nor be explained by, that theory. But how, then, are they to be accounted for? Accounted for in some way they must be, for their existence cannot be denied. It is evident to every attentive reader that the statements in these early letters concerning the Christian faith are of the most elementary character. The most likely suggestion is, that the Epistles to the Thessalonian church show us the form

---

pressly on the ground that the views of the gospel they present are so unlike what we find in the other Epistles. His idea is, that if they were really Paul's, they must have been written long before the others, at a time when Paul's particular tendency was not yet accentuated, and his system not yet in course of formation. Vide *Le Péché et la Redemption d'apres Saint Paul*, p. 4. On the historical value of the narrative in *Acts* xv., and its true place in the course of events, *vide* Spitta, *Die Apostelgeschichte*, 1891, and Weizsäcker's *Apostolic Age*, pp. 200-216. Both these writers are of opinion that the author of *Acts* has antedated the decree of the Jerusalem Council, and that it belongs to a later time, later than the encounter between Peter and Paul at Antioch.

in which St. Paul judged it fitting to present the gospel to nascent Christian communities; when he had in view merely their immediate religious needs and capacities, and had no occasion to guard them against errors and misconceptions. This view sets the apostle's character in an interesting light. It makes him appear a Paulinist, so to speak, against his will. He preached Paulinism, that which was most distinctive in his way of apprehending the faith, under compulsion; when free from the constraint of false and mischievous opinions, he taught the common faith of Christians in simple, untechnical language. This point is worth emphasising at the commencement of this study, as helping us at once to appreciate the wisdom of the apostle, and to put the proper value on the developed system of thought contained in his controversial Epistles. Why is it that the earliest Epistles are not to be reckoned among the sources of what we call Paulinism? Not because Paulinism was yet unborn, but because its author kept it in its proper place. St. Paul distinguished between religion and theology, between faith and knowledge; and while he spoke wisdom to them that were perfect, and theology to them that needed it and could make a good use of it, he practised reserve or self-restraint in speaking to babes in Christ, and in teaching them carefully avoided the use of abstruse ideas and technical terms.

This is the important inference referred to on a previous page as deducible from the rudimentary gospel contained in the earliest Epistles. And in view of that inference it becomes important to inform ourselves as to the precise character of St. Paul's rudimentary or missionary gospel. It is what he deemed sufficient to salvation, though not to a full comprehension of Christianity. One cannot but desire to know what so great a master reckoned essential; and as his early letters are not available for the study of his developed theology, one may well be excused for lingering at the threshold to glance over their pages before entering on the more arduous task. The controversial Epistles are to be our text-book, but let us look for a little at those simple, childlike Epistles to the Thessalonian Church as a kind of Christian primer. We shall be none the worse qualified for mastering the text-book, and understanding its true meaning, that we carry the lessons of the primer along with us.[1]

The use of these Epistles as a primer is justified by the writer's own way of expressing himself as to the purpose of his writing. Careful readers must have noticed the frequent recurrence of such phrases as "ye remember," "ye know." Baur utilises this feature as an argument against the genuineness, asking in effect: "To what purpose this repetition of matters admitted to be familiar to the readers, and not of old date, but of quite recent occurrence?"[2] The obvious reply is, that the writer wished to impress upon his readers the importance of the things alluded to, his aim in writing being not to

---

[1] The two Epistles do not stand on a level critically, as many critics accept the first who dispute the authenticity of the second. But the characteristics commented on here are common to both, and may be used in the present connection without discrimination of source.

[2] *Vide* his *Paulus der Apostel Jesu Christi*, ii. 95.

give new instruction, but to make a fresh impression by recapitulating old instructions, and by recalling to mind facts of didactic significance. Thus when he says, "Knowing, brethren, beloved of God, your election of God,"[1] his purpose is, by reminding them of their election to salvation, to suggest a valuable source of comfort and strengthening amid present tribulation. It is as if he had said, "Think of your election, and what it implies— a sovereign love of God which will not forsake you, a divine purpose which shall surely be fulfilled." Again, when he says, "Yourselves know our entrance in unto you, that it was not in vain; but even after that we had suffered before, and were shamefully entreated, as ye know, at Philippi, we were bold in our God to speak unto you the gospel of God amid much opposition,"[2] he manifestly means: "As we did not allow our purpose in coming to Thessalonica to be frustrated by opposition, but resolutely preached the gospel, refusing to be intimidated, so do ye resolve that persecution shall not make your reception of the gospel vain, and persevere in faith in spite of all that evil men may do." When once more he reminds them of his way of life among them, alluding to his engaging in manual labour for his own support, to his nurse-like gentleness, to his perfect sincerity, to the purity and exemplariness of his whole behaviour, as things perfectly well known to them all,[3] he means to suggest that they should make his conduct, of which a vivid image remained in their minds, a pattern for their own. In a word, the apostle treats the Christians of Thessalonica as children who need to hear

---

[1] 1 *Thess.* i. 4.   [2] *Ibid.* ii. 1.   [3] *Ibid.* ii. 5-12.

the same things over and over again, not so much that they may know them, as that they may duly lay them to heart. And as he evidently does so in the instances cited, it is fair to assume that he does so throughout, and that all his statements, and in particular those referring to the Christian faith and life, are reminiscences and repetitions of what he had been accustomed to teach persons whom he regarded as spiritual children.

Let us then collect, in brief summary, the elements of gospel truth contained in the few pages of this Christian primer.

1. The name employed by St. Paul, as by Jesus Himself, to denote the message of salvation is the *gospel*, more definitely the *gospel of God*, an expression used repeatedly in the First Epistle,[1] but occasionally replaced by such phrases as "our gospel,"[2] "the gospel of Christ,"[3] "the word of God."[4]

2. The substance of the message thus variously named, is the proclamation of a way of escape from "the wrath to come."[5] Salvation, that is to say, is regarded chiefly from the *eschatological* point of view. Judging from the manner of expression pervading these Epistles, the apostle, in addressing heathen audiences, was wont to speak of a coming day of judgment, when the Lord Jesus would be revealed from heaven to inflict punishment on them that know not God, and to tell them that by believing on Jesus they should escape the doom of the impenitent, and become partakers of all the

---

[1] 1 *Thess.* ii. 2, 8, 9.
[2] *Ibid.* i. 5 ; 2 *Thess.* ii. 14.
[3] 1 *Thess.* iii. 2 ; 2 *Thess.* i. 8.
[4] 1 *Thess.* ii. 13.
[5] *Ibid.* i. 10.

joys of the kingdom of God.¹ It may be noticed in passing that it is just after this fashion that St. Paul is represented in the book of *Acts* as addressing the Athenians on Mars' Hill.² This is one of several instances in which the accounts of his preaching given in *Acts* correspond with the idea of it suggested by the language of these early letters.

3. As the substance of the gospel is contemplated from an eschatological point of view, so Christ, the author of salvation, is regarded under the same aspect. The great object of Christian trust appears not so much as Jesus the crucified, but rather as Jesus exalted into heaven, and about to come thence again for the destruction of sinners and the salvation of believers. The purchase of salvation by Christ's death falls into the background, and prominence is given to the final accomplishment of salvation by Christ glorified. This characteristic comes out in the description of the Thessalonian Christians as persons who have turned from idols to the living God, and who now "wait for His Son from heaven."³ Their relation to Christ is one of expectancy. Only once is Christ's death referred to as a means of salvation, and that in the most general terms. "For," writes the apostle in the text referred to, "God hath not appointed us to wrath, but to obtain salvation by our Lord Jesus Christ, who died for us, that, whether we wake or sleep, we should live together with Him."⁴ Here it is plainly implied that Christ's death took place for our salvation, salvation being here, as always in the

---

¹ 2 *Thess.* i. 5-9. ² *Acts* xvii. 30, 31.
³ 1 *Thess.* i. 10. ⁴ *Ibid.* v. 10.

two Epistles, regarded from the eschatological viewpoint; but there is no indication how Christ's death contributed to that end. If we were left with no other means of determining that question than these Epistles we might conclude that Christ's death was saving, not by itself, but because it was followed by His resurrection. This might not unnaturally appear to be the import of another text referring to the death of Jesus: "If we believe that Jesus died and *rose again*, even so them also which sleep in Jesus will God bring with Him."[1] It would not be right, even on the primer-hypothesis, to infer that St. Paul had never made any more definite statements than these to the Thessalonian Church, seeing that they both manifestly owe their form to the connection of thought in which they occur. The purpose in both cases is to comfort the members of the Church in reference to deceased friends, also believers, by assuring them that death before the coming of the Lord would not, as they seem to have imagined, cut them off from a share in the joys of the kingdom. The comfort given is: Christ Himself died, and afterwards rose; and Christians who have died will also rise and partake in the bliss of those who shall be for ever with the Lord. Furthermore, Christ died in our behalf, for the very purpose that we might obtain salvation; therefore it does not matter whether we sleep with the dead, or wake with the living at His coming. God's end in His Son's death will not fail; we shall all live together with Him. It may be assumed that, over and above this, the apostle in his missionary preaching

[1] 1 *Thess.* iv. 14.

indicated at least in a general way that Christ's death had reference to *sin*. This assumption has good foundation in the summary which he gives of what he had been accustomed to teach the Corinthian Church: "I delivered unto you first of all that which I also received, how that Christ died for our sins, according to the Scriptures; and that He was buried, and that He rose again the third day, according to the Scriptures."[1] It may be taken for granted that St. Paul, like all the other apostles—for he gives it as the common gospel[2] —kept in view the points indicated in this summary, not only in Corinth, but wherever he went on his evangelising mission. Still it is remarkable that in these two letters to a young Christian community no express mention is made of the first article in the summary; especially if the design of the writer was to rehearse the leading points of instruction, to recall to the recollection of the readers what he had taught them when he was present with them. It implies this, at least, that the apostle was not accustomed in his mission-addresses to enter with much fulness or exactness of statement into the doctrine of redemption by Christ's death. And here, again, there is a correspondence between what we infer from the Epistles, and what we learn from the book of *Acts*. The reports of St. Paul's mission-addresses in that book correspond closely to the summary of his preaching given by himself in his Epistle to the Corinthians. There is, in the first place, careful

---

[1] 1 *Cor.* xv. 3, 4.
[2] *Ibid.* xv. 11: "Whether it were I or they, so we preach, and so ye believed."

detailed proof from Scripture of the truth of his leading positions. Then the points chiefly insisted on are just those indicated: Christ's death for sin, and His resurrection. The former, however, curiously enough, is the less prominent, being rather implied than plainly expressed. The words referring to this topic in the first and longest of the missionary speeches by St. Paul reported in *Acts* are these: "Be it known unto you, therefore, men and brethren, that through this Man is preached unto you the forgiveness of sins; and by Him all that believe are justified from all things from which ye could not be justified by the law of Moses."[1]

4. In the sentence just quoted, the word "justified"[2] occurs. No such word occurs in our two Epistles. But two other words are found, suggestive of cognate ideas, and sufficient to show that St. Paul's way of presenting the gospel in mission sermons was the same in *essence* as it appears in the controversial Epistles, the only difference being that in the one we have the religious kernel, in the other the theological form. These words are *Faith* and *Grace*; trite words now, but great words then, and profoundly significant as to the character of the religion of which they were the watchwords. The

[1] *Acts* xiii. 38, 39. Hausrath thinks that the type of St. Paul's preaching is to be found in the Epistle to the Romans—that the apostle writes to that Church which he had never visited as he preached to the Churches he himself founded. Vide *Neutest. Zeitgeschichte*, ii. 514, 515. This opinion is based on prejudice against *Acts* as a non-reliable source of information as to St. Paul's preaching, not on a just view of the Epistle to the Romans, which, as we shall see, was a special writing meant to serve a special purpose.

[2] δικαιωθῆναι δικαιοῦται.

terms are not used in any sharply defined dogmatic sense, but in a practical popular way. Christians are called believers—"you who believe."[1] God is represented as the object of faith.[2] Faith is not sharply opposed to works, but is itself a work.[3] The word "grace" occurs less frequently, and chiefly in connection with sanctification. In the superscriptions the apostle wishes for his readers, already believers, grace and peace, and in the superscription of the Second Epistle these are represented as having their source in God the Father and the Lord Jesus Christ. The grace thence emanating is viewed as the means by which believers are enabled to glorify the name they bear, and are themselves fitted for future glory.[4] In both Epistles the writer closes as he begins, with the prayer that Christ's grace may be with his readers, as if that were all that was needful both for holiness and for happiness. It looks as if the writer knew something of the earthly life of Him who dwelt among men "full of grace," whose sermons were "words of grace," whose gracious love drew the sinful and sorrowful to Him, and sent them away into purity and peace.

5. By what titles does St. Paul name Jesus in these primer-Epistles? He calls Him *the Son of God*, and *the Lord*. The former title occurs in the text where the Thessalonians are described as having turned to the true God, and as waiting *for His Son* from heaven;[5] a connection of thought which gives to the designation much

---

[1] 1 *Thess.* ii. 13.   [2] *Ibid.* i. 8.
[3] *Ibid.* i. 3; 2 *Thess.* i. 11.   [4] *Ibid.* i. 12.
[5] 1 *Thess.* i. 10.

significance. The honour and prerogative of the only true God are jealously guarded against the injury done to them by idolatrous worship, and yet in the same sentence in which this is virtually done Jesus is spoken of as a Son of the living and true God, and as one whose present abode is in heaven. What impression could such language produce on men who had been worshippers of gods many but that Jesus was divine? The other title, "Lord," points in the same direction of a high doctrine respecting the author of the faith. It is St. Paul's favourite title for Christ in his controversial Epistles, and it may be regarded as a result of this fact that the same title is frequently used in the Gospel of Luke (eminently Pauline in spirit) in places where the other Synoptists use the name Jesus. The designation occurs repeatedly in the two Epistles now under consideration, sometimes with the effect of identifying Jesus in the Christian consciousness with God; as, *e.g.*, in the expression, "the day of the Lord,"[1] corresponding to the expression, "the day of Jehovah," in the Old Testament, and meaning the day when the $\pi\alpha\rho o\upsilon\sigma\iota a$ of the Lord Jesus Christ shall take place.

'6. Mention is made in these primer-Epistles of the Holy Spirit, and in the specifically Pauline sense as the *Sanctifier*. Opportunity will occur hereafter for considering at length St. Paul's doctrine of the Spirit, and in connection therewith for adverting to the distinction between the Spirit as transcendent, and the Spirit as immanent; as the former, the source of charisms or preternatural gifts, as the latter, the source of Christian

[1] 1 *Thess.* v. 2 ; 2 *Thess.* ii. 2.

sanctity. I simply remark here that it is from the immanent, ethical point of view that the Spirit is regarded in these Epistles, at least chiefly, if not exclusively.[1] God gives His Holy Spirit to Christians,[2] and for the purpose of *sanctification*.[3] For while salvation, as already stated, is regarded from an eschatological point of view, present sanctification is strongly insisted on as a necessary preparation for the future salvation. "Chosen unto salvation in or by sanctification," is the programme. The apostle reminds his readers that when he was with them he had charged them to walk worthily of the God who had called them to His kingdom and glory.[4] He now tells them that God's will is their sanctification, that God had not called them to uncleanness, but to holiness,[5] and that he who practically forgets this is guilty of despising God, who gave the Spirit for this very end.[6] He sets before them as their great aim the sanctification of the whole man—spirit, soul, and body.[7] They must cultivate purity; also unworldliness, so as to be free from all suspicion of covetousness, taking their teacher as their example. They must resolutely fight against every form of evil—drunkenness, impurity, greed, revenge, and all other sins of flesh and spirit, as Christian soldiers fully armed for the conflict, with faith and love for breastplate, and the hope of salvation for helmet.[8] The interest of the writer in real Christian

---

[1] The other aspect may be implied in the exhortation, "Quench not the Spirit," 1 *Thess.* v. 19.
[2] *Ibid.* iv. 8.
[3] 2 *Thess.* ii. 13.
[4] 1 *Thess.* ii. 12.
[5] *Ibid.* iv. 7.
[6] *Ibid.* iv. 8.
[7] *Ibid.* v 23.
[8] *Ibid.* v. 8.

goodness is intense and unmistakable; and it inspires us with confidence that whatever Paulinism may mean, it will not be found to imply indifference to ethical ideals, and their embodiment in right conduct. We may expect to discover in the literature of Paulinism anything rather than a divorce between religion and morality; if, perchance, at any point the author's conception of Christianity may seem to compromise ethical interests, he will be sure to manifest a most delicate sensitiveness to the slightest appearance of so fatal a fault, and great solicitude to obviate misunderstanding.

Of that literature, consisting of the four great Epistles to the Galatian, Corinthian, and Roman Churches, we must next take a rapid survey. But, before doing this, it will be advantageous to form as definite a conception as possible of the nature and import of the writer's religious experience.

CHAPTER II

ST. PAUL'S RELIGIOUS HISTORY

A STUDY of St. Paul's conception of Christianity may very fitly begin with an inquiry into his religious history, for two reasons. First, because his theology is to an unusual extent the outgrowth of his experience. He is as remote as possible in his whole way of thinking from the scholastic theologian, being eminently subjective, psychological, autobiographical in spirit and method. In this he resembles Luther, and indeed all the chief actors in epochs of fresh religious intuition. Next, because acquaintance with the apostle's spiritual history helps us to assume a sympathetic appreciative attitude towards a theology which, though utterly non-scholastic in spirit, yet, owing its existence to controversy, deals to a considerable extent in forms of thought and expression belonging to the period, which, to modern readers, are apt to wear an aspect of foreignness. How many words occur in St. Paul's letters bearing apparently a peculiar technical meaning; words the signification of which cannot easily be ascertained, remaining still, after all the theological discussion they have provoked, of doubtful import. Law, righteousness, justification, adoption, flesh, spirit—words these eminently Pauline, and in a high degree original, therefore interesting, as used by him, yet at the same time presenting a somewhat artificial appearance, and withal belonging to the region of theology rather than to the region of religious intuition. Something is needed to help one to overcome the prejudice thence arising, and it may be found in the intense tragic moral struggle lying behind St. Paul's theology, and possessing the undying interest of all great spiritual crises. In the case of our Lord, we need no such aid to sympathetic study of His teaching. His mind moved in the region of pure spiritual intuition, and His words therefore possess perennial lucidity and value. They are indeed, in form as well as in substance, words of eternal life. We have no information as to His inner spiritual history, and we do not feel the want of it, for the lapse of time has no antiquating effect on His profound yet simple utterances.

The autobiographical hints contained in the Epistles which are to form the basis of our study, though comparatively few, are valuable. The passages which exhibit most conspicuously the autobiographical character occur in the first chapter of the Epistle to the Galatians, and in the seventh chapter of the Epistle to the Romans. From the former we learn that St. Paul, before he became a Christian, belonged to the class which in the Gospels appears in constant and irreconcilable antagonism to Jesus. His religion was *Judaism*; in the practice of that religion he was exceptionally strict; he was beyond most of his contemporaries a zealot for the legal traditions of the fathers.[1] In other words, he was a Pharisee, and

[1] *Gal.* i. 13, 14.

a virtuoso in Pharisaism. His great aim in life was to be legally righteous, and his ambition was to excel in that line. How much this implies! It means either that this man will never become a Christian, but remain through life the deadly foe of the new faith, or it means that the very intensity of his Pharisaism will cure him of Pharisaism, and make him a Christian of Christians, as he had been before a Pharisee of Pharisees, possessing exceptional insight into the genius of the new religion, and a wholly unexampled enthusiasm in its propagation.

Which of the two ways is it to be? The autobiographical hints in the seventh chapter of Romans enable us partly to foresee. As St. Paul advanced in Judaism,[1] he made one day a great discovery. He noticed for the first time that one of the commandments in the Decalogue, the tenth, forbade *coveting*;[2] that is to say, that a mere feeling, a state of the heart not falling under the observation of others, was condemned as sin. This was a revelation to the Pharisaic zealot as instructive for us as it was momentous for him. Two things that revelation shows us. One is how completely the Pharisaic system had deadened the conscience to any moral evil not on the surface. For the average Pharisee there was unrighteousness within in countless forms—evil appetites, desires, passions, yet totally unobserved as states of feeling requiring to be corrected, giving him no trouble or distress, because, forsooth, all was clean and fair without. Jesus often declared this to be the case, and that His judgment was just, nothing can more convincingly prove than the fact that for Saul of Tarsus, a

[1] *Gal.* i. 14, προκόπτον ἐν τῷ Ἰουδαϊσμῷ.   [2] *Rom.* vii. 7.

disciple of the Rabbis, insight into so commonplace a truth as that coveting is sinful, was an important discovery. The other thought suggested by the great revelation is that Saul, even while a Pharisee, was an extraordinary man. The ordinary man is a complete slave to the moral fashions of his time. He thinks that only evil which passes for evil in his social environment. If it be the fashion to disregard evil within, so long as external conduct is in accordance with rule, there is no chance of his discovering that covetousness or any other plague of the heart is morally wrong. He will go serenely on his way, unobservant of the inner world, as a stupid peasant might pass heedless through picturesque scenery. But Saul of Tarsus cannot permanently do that, for he has moral individuality; therefore, he discovers what others miss. He notes that while one precept says, Thou shalt not *kill*, another forbids what may lead to killing—desire to have what belongs to another. Not all at once, indeed, for the system under which he has been reared has great power over him. But, eventually, insight into the searching character of God's law must come to such a man. For his conscience is not conventional; it has sharp eyes, and can see what to dimmer vision is unobservable, and new moral truth once seen it will not be able to take lightly, merely because for other men the truth it has discovered is of no account.

The momentousness of the discovery for St. Paul himself it is impossible to exaggerate. It is very easy to under-estimate its importance. That to covet is sin is so axiomatic to the Christian mind, that it is very difficult to imagine a state of conscience for which it could be a great moral revelation. And familiarity deadens the power to realise the significance of the new truth for one to whom it was a revelation. We can trace the effect of this influence in the recent literature of Paulinism. Interpreters forget that what is commonplace now was once very uncommon, and that truth, when first revealed, produces very different results from those which accompany traditional belief. In the instance before us the new revelation may be said to have been the beginning of the end. From the day that the eye of Saul's conscience lighted on the words, "Thou shalt not covet," his Judaism was doomed. It might last a while, so far as outward habit and even fanatical zeal were concerned, but the heart was taken out of it. That is the import of the other autobiographical hint in Rom. vii.: "When the commandment came, sin revived and I died."[1] Hope died, because the zealot saw that there was a whole world of sin within, of which he had not dreamed, with which it was hard to cope, and which made righteousness by conformity with the law appear unattainable. This was a great step onwards towards Christianity. All along the youthful enthusiast, according to his own testimony in after years,[2] had been outrunning his fellow-religionists in pious attainments. His advance hitherto had been within Judaism. But now, without being aware of it, he advances away from Judaism, the outward movement being the natural consequence of the previous rapid movement within. He had been trying to satisfy the innate hunger of his spirit

[1] *Rom.* vii. 9.   [2] *Gal.* i. 14.

for righteousness with the food that came first to his hand—legal ordinances. It took him some time to discover that what he had been eating was not wheat but chaff. That discovery once made, the imperious appetite of the soul will compel him to go elsewhere in quest of true nourishment. It will not surprise us if he forsake the school of the Rabbis and go to the school of Jesus.

This we know was what eventually happened. Saul of Tarsus became a convert to Christianity. The Pauline letters give no detailed account of the memorable event similar to the narratives contained in the book of *Acts*. But the main feature in the story, as there told, is referred to in the First Epistle to the Corinthians, at the place where the apostle enumerates the different appearances of the risen Christ. "Last of all He was seen of me also."[1] Modern students of sacred history approach this great turning-point in St. Paul's life with very diverse bias. Naturalistic theologians desire by all means to resolve the objective appearance into a subjective experience, and to see in the self-manifestation of Jesus to the persecutor not a real Christophany, but a vision due to the convert's excited state of mind. Others, dealing with the subject in an apologetic interest, make it their business to vindicate the objectivity of the Christophany, and its independence of subjective conditions.[2] Our

---

[1] 1 *Cor.* xv. 8. Vide *Acts* ix. 1-9; xxii. 6-11; xxvi. 12-18 for the detailed accounts.

[2] So Weiss, *Introduction to the New Testament*, vol. i. p. 152; also Stevens, *The Pauline Theology*, p. 15. Dr. Stevens' work is a valuable contribution to the study of Paulinism, though traces of a disciple's reverence towards Dr. Weiss are not wanting. In one very impor-

present concern is not to refute, and still less to advocate, naturalistic theories of the conversion, but to learn all we can as to the inner history which led up to it, that we may the better understand the event itself and what it involved.

If the comments above made on the autobiographical hint in Rom. vii. be correct, it follows that the conversion of St. Paul, however marvellous, was not so sudden and unprepared as it seems. There was that in the previous experience of the convert that pointed towards, though it did not necessarily insure, his becoming a Christian. Nothing is gained by denying or ignoring this fact. And there is more to be included under the head of preparation than has yet been pointed out. While the objective character of Christ's appearance to St. Paul is by all means to be maintained, it is legitimate to assume that there was a subjective state answering to the objective phenomenon. This may be laid down as a principle in reference to all such supernatural manifestations. Thus the visions and the voices seen and heard by Jesus at His baptism, and at the transfiguration, corresponded to and interpreted His own thoughts at the moment. Applied to the case of St. Paul, the principle means that before Christ appeared *to him* on the way to Damascus, He had been revealed *in him*,[1] not yet as an object of faith, but as an object of earnest thought. The Christ who appeared to him was not an utterly unknown personality. He had heard of Him

tant point, however, as will appear, he dissents from his master's teaching.

[1] Vide *Gal.* i. 16.

before, he knew that His followers believed Him to have risen again from the dead, and he had had serious reflections as to what such an event implied. As to the precise character of these reflections we have no information, but it is not difficult to make probable conjectures. He who was said to have risen from the dead had been crucified, mainly by the instrumentality of the Pharisaic party to which Saul belonged. By the resurrection, if it occurred, the stigma of crucifixion had been removed, and the claims of the crucified one to be the Christ vindicated. But if Jesus was the Christ, what view was to be taken of His death? Men thought that He had suffered for His own offences. What if He had really suffered for the sins of others, like the servant of Jehovah of whom it was written in ancient prophecy: "He was wounded for our transgressions, He was bruised for our iniquities"? And what if the crucified and risen one were a new way of salvation for men who like himself had begun to despair of reaching salvation by the old time-honoured way of legalism?

That such thoughts had passed through St. Paul's mind is rendered probable by the fact, vouched for by his own confession, that before his conversion he persecuted the disciples of Jesus with passionate zeal.[1] His ardour in this bad work was partly due to the energy of a man who put his soul into everything. But it was due also to what he knew about the object of his fanatical animosity. The new religion interested him very much. It seems to have fascinated him. He hated it, yet he

[1] *Gal.* i. 13: "Beyond measure I persecuted the church."

was drawn towards it, and could not let it alone. He was under a spell which compelled him to inquire into its nature, and strive to penetrate into the secret of its growing power. In consequence, he understood it as well as was possible for an unfriendly outsider. He evidently regarded it as a rival to Judaism, antagonistic thereto in its whole spirit and tendency, as otherwise it is difficult to comprehend his fiercely hostile attitude towards it. If he did not get this view of the new religion from Stephen, as the accounts in *Acts* would lead us to infer, it must have come to him from his own keenly penetrating insight. A man like Saul of Tarsus sees below the surface of things, and can detect there what is completely hidden to the ordinary eye. In this respect he may have divined the genius of the new faith better than its own adherents, who for the most part very imperfectly comprehended what was to grow out of the apparently insignificant seed contained in the confession that Jesus was the Christ. He perceived that that confession was by no means insignificant. What, a crucified man the Messiah, shown to be such by resurrection! That, if true, meant shame and confusion to the Pharisees who had put him to death; yea, and something more serious, death to Pharisaism, condemnation of legalism. How, might not be immediately apparent, but the fact must be so. It cannot be that a crucified risen *Christ* should remain an isolated barren portent. It must have been God's purpose from the first, though men knew it not, and it must bear consequences proportioned to its own astounding character.

Only on the assumption that some such thoughts had

been working in Saul's mind does his furious *hyperbolical* [1] hostility to Christians become intelligible. These thoughts combined with those ever-deepening doubts as to the attainability of righteousness on the basis of legalism fully account for his mad behaviour. They also prepare us for what is coming.[2] A man in whose soul such perilous stuff is at work cannot be far from a spiritual crisis. By the time the Damascus expedition was undertaken the crisis was due. Is it asked, " How could one on the eve of a religious revolution undertake such a task ? " The answer must be that men of heroic temper and resolute will do not easily abandon cherished ideals, and never are less like surrendering than just before the crisis comes. In the expressive phrase put into Christ's mouth by the historian of *Acts* they " kick against the pricks." [3]

"Who lights the faggot?
Not the full faith; no, but the lurking doubt."

When a spiritual crisis does come to a man of this type, it possesses deep, inexhaustible significance. Such was the fact certainly in the case of Saul. In the view,

---

[1] *Gal.* i. 13, καθ᾽ ὑπερβολὴν ἐδίωκον.

[2] The above account of the preparation for the conversion is, not in intention, but in result, a combination to a certain extent of the views of Beyschlag on the one hand and of Pfleiderer on the other. Beyschlag lays the emphasis exclusively on the fruitless struggle after righteousness; Pfleiderer insists with equal onesidedness on the familiarity with the Christian beliefs about Jesus and the processes of thoughts these originated in Saul's mind. It seems perfectly feasible to take both into account. For the views of Beyschlag, vide *Neutestamentliche Theologie* (1892), vol. ii. p. 14 ; for Pfleiderer's, his *Paulinismus*: Einleitung.

[3] *Acts* xxvi. 14.

of some writers the spiritual development of this remarkable man took place mainly in the period subsequent to his conversion to the Christian faith. They find in the period antecedent to the conversion little or no struggle, and in the conversion itself they see nothing more than the case of one who, previously an unbeliever in the Messiahship of Jesus, had at length been brought to acknowledge that Jesus was the Christ, through a miraculous demonstration that He was still alive.[1] It would, however, be nearer the truth to say that, on the day Saul of Tarsus was converted, his spiritual development to a large extent lay behind him. For him to become a Christian meant everything. It meant becoming a *Paulinist* Christian in the sense which the famous controversial Epistles enable us to put upon that expression. The preparation for the great change had been so thorough, that the convert leaped at a bound into a large cosmopolitan idea of Christianity, its nature and destination. The universalism, *e.g.*, which we associate with the name of the Apostle Paul, dates from his conversion. It was not, as some imagine, a late growth of after years, due to the accident of some persons of Gentile birth showing a readiness to receive the gospel.[2] Such a view is contrary at once to the apostle's own statements,[3] and to intrinsic probability.

---

[1] So Dr. Matheson in his very suggestive and ingenious work on *The Spiritual Development of St. Paul*, pp. 39, 65. In his treatment of the subject the alleged development has reference rather to St. Paul's views of the Christian ethical ideal than to his theological conceptions.

[2] So Weiss, *Introduction*, vol. i. pp. 154, 164; also Stevens, *The Pauline Theology*, p. 21.

[3] *Gal.* i. 15.

The truth is, that a whole group of religious intuitions, the universal destination of Christianity being one of them, flashed simultaneously into the convert's mind, like a constellation of stars, on the day of his conversion. As soon as he had recovered from the stunning effect of the strange things that befell him on the way to Damascus, and emerged into clear, tranquil, Christian consciousness, he saw that it was all over with Judaism and its legal righteousness, all over with the law itself as a way to salvation; that salvation must come to man through the grace of God, and that it might come through that channel to all men alike, to Gentiles not less than to Jews, and on equal terms, and that therefore Jewish prerogative was at an end. The eye of his soul was opened to the light of this constellation of spiritual truths almost as soon, I believe, as the eye of his body had recovered its power of vision. For thought is quick at such creative epochs, and feeling is quicker still, and we can faintly imagine with what tremendous force reaction would set in, away from all that belonged to a past now for ever dead: from Pharisaic formalism, pride and pretension, and from Judaistic narrowness, and from intolerance, fanaticism, and wicked, persecuting tempers, towards all that was opposed to these in religion and morals.

The foregoing view of St. Paul's conversion, as ushering him at once into a new world of anti-Judaistic thought, is borne out by the autobiographical notices of that eventful period contained in the first chapter of Galatians. Four points deserve attention here.

1. The term employed by the apostle to describe his

old way of life invites remark. He calls it *Judaism*.[1] He was not shut up to the use of that term; he might have employed instead, Pharisaism or Rabbinism. He obviously has present controversies in view, and wishes to make his references to past experiences tell against those whose great aim was to get Gentile Christians to Judaise.[2] It is as if he had said: "I know all about Judaising and Judaism. It was my very life element in long bygone years. There never was such a zealot as I was for national customs on grounds at once of patriotism and of conscience. I was a perfect devotee to the Jewish way of serving God. It is a miracle that I ever escaped from its thrall. It was certainly by no ordinary means that I was set free; not by the method of catechetical instruction, whether through apostles or any others. God alone could deliver me. But He could and He did, effectually and once for all. To His sovereign grace I owe my conversion to Christianity, which meant breaking away completely and for ever from Judaism and all that belonged to it." If this be indeed a true interpretation of what was in the apostle's mind, we can see with what perfect truth he could protest that he did not get his Christianity from men in general, or from any of the apostles in particular. Which of the apostles could have taught him a Christianity like that, radically and at all points opposed to Judaism?

2. The apostle virtually asserts the identity of his gospel throughout the whole period during which he had been a Christian. It is the same gospel which he

---

[1] *Vide* vers. 13 and 14. [2] *Gal.* ii. 14: 'Ἰουδαΐζειν.

received "by revelation"[1] at his conversion, which he had preached to the Galatians,[2] and which he is obliged now to defend against men who call it in question, and seek to frustrate it by every means, as, *e.g.*, by denying the independent apostolic standing of him who preaches it. It is a gospel which from the first has addressed itself to Gentiles not less than to Jews, and which has treated circumcision and the Jewish law, as a whole, as possessing no religious value for Christianity. It may indeed appear as if the assertion that St. Paul preached such a gospel to the Galatians at the time of his first visit were irreconcilable with what has been stated in the first chapter concerning the apostle's mode of presenting Christian truth to infant churches. But the contrariety is only on the surface. Paulinism was implicitly involved in St. Paul's mission-gospel, though the implications were not explicitly stated and commented on. Universalism and denial of the religious significance of the Jewish law were latent in it. Universalism was involved in the simple fact that the preacher addressed himself to a Gentile audience, and the abrogation of the Jewish law was quietly taken for granted by the simple fact that the rite of circumcision was never mentioned. The preacher held up a crucified and risen Christ broadly sketched[3] to the eye of faith as the all-sufficient means of salvation, and left it to work its own effect. Unfortunately it soon appeared that his Galatian hearers did not understand the drift of his gospel as he understood it himself. They saw no inconsistency in be-

---

[1] *Gal.* i. 12.   [2] *Ibid.* i. 8.
[3] *Ibid.* iii. 1 : προεγράφη.

ginning with faith in a crucified Jesus and ending with Jewish legalism; but for him these two things then and always appeared utterly incompatible. The position he laid down in his interview with Peter at Antioch, "If by the law righteousness, then Christ died in vain,"[1] had appeared to him self-evident from the time of his conversion onwards. Becoming a believer in Christ meant for him renouncing legal righteousness.

3. The apostle connects his conversion with his call to be an apostle to the Gentiles, representing the one as a means to the other as an end. "When it pleased God to reveal His Son in me, that I might preach Him among the Gentiles."[2] According to Weiss he is simply reading the divine purpose of his conversion in the light of long subsequent events, which for the first time made him conscious that he was being called in God's providence to a specifically Gentile mission.[3] Now it need not be denied that such a procedure would be quite in keeping with St. Paul's habits of religious thought, but it may gravely be doubted whether it suited the position in which he was placed when he wrote the Epistle to the Galatians. What the circumstances required was, that he should make it clear beyond all dispute that he was an apostle, and an apostle to the Gentiles, by immediate divine authority and equipment; that both his gospel and his call came to him direct from the hand of God.

---

[1] *Gal.* ii. 21. [2] *Ibid.* i. 15.
[3] *Vide* his *Introduction to the New Testament*, vol i. pp 154, 164. Here also Dr. Stevens follows Weiss, *vide The Pauline Theology*, pp. 21, 22.

In presence of men lying in wait for his halting, and even ready to charge him with falsehood, if they got the chance, could he have so spoken of a call which came to him late in the day, from the fact of Gentiles giving an unexpected welcome to a gospel, which, so far as the preacher's intention was concerned, had not really been meant for them? If that was how the call came, why should he regard himself as an apostle to the Gentiles more than any of the eleven apostles, who in like manner saw in events God's will that Gentiles should be admitted to the fellowship of the Christian faith? Would his opponents have recognised him as the Gentile apostle had they known the facts to be as supposed? Would he have dared to state the case as he does in his letter to the Galatians, with solemn protestations that he was not lying,[1] had his heathen mission been a tardy afterthought? What could give him the courage to make the statement but a distinct recollection that the change which made him a Christian gave him also the presentiment that the destiny of the converted Pharisee was to be Christ's missionary to the pagan world? It is scarcely necessary to add that the view advocated by Weiss totally fails to do justice to the strength of St. Paul's feeling as the Gentile apostle, to the way in which he habitually magnified his office, to his fervent devotion to the grand programme, Christianity for the world. Such an enthusiasm could not be the product of external circumstances. It must have been the birth of a great religious crisis. Just here lay the difference between St. Paul and the Eleven. Their

[1] *Gal.* i. 20.

universalism, if it may be so-called, consisted in bowing to God's will revealed in events; his was a profound conviction rooted in a never-to-be-forgotten personal experience. He was born, and born *again*, to be the Gentile apostle, gifted both by nature and by regeneration for his high calling; and only one of whom this could be said could have undertaken its arduous tasks, and endured its severe trials.

4. Finally, not without bearing on the question at issue are the particulars mentioned by the apostle as to his first visit to Jerusalem after his conversion. The precise purpose of this visit is probably not fully indicated. The apostle deems it sufficient to say that he went up to make the acquaintance of Peter, one of the leading apostles.[1] But two points are noteworthy: the careful specification of the date and duration of the visit, and the not less careful exclusion of the other apostles from participation in it. St. Paul wishes it to be understood that it was a private friendly visit to Peter alone, in which the other apostles had no concern. To be strictly accurate, he admits that he did see James, the Lord's brother, but he alludes to the fact in such a manner as to suggest that the meeting was accidental and of no significance. There could thus be no question

---

[1] *Gal.* i. 18, ἱστορῆσαι Κηφᾶν. The verb is used in connection with going to see important places, great cities, etc. Bengel remarks: *grave verbum, ut de re magna.* St. Paul wishes to suggest that he went to visit the great man of the Christian community; not sneeringly, but possibly not without a slight touch of humour. His opponents laid great stress upon important personalities. He too recognised Peter's importance, but only as an equal, after he had kept three years aloof, and he now went to see him as a man who sought neither patronage nor advice.

of apostolic authority brought to bear on him on this occasion, as at the conference held in the same city fourteen years later. Then, as to the date and duration of the visit: it took place, says the apostle in effect, three years after my conversion, and it lasted just fifteen days. Very suggestive specifications, and meant to be reflected on in relation to each other. Three years passed before he saw any of the apostles, or had any opportunity of learning from them. And what eventful years in his life, those immediately succeeding his conversion; how much of his spiritual experience he lived through in that time, in the solitude of the Arabian desert! Not till those memorable years of intense meditation are over does he go up to Jerusalem to see Peter; and he goes then, not as a man still at sea and needing counsel, but as one whose mind is clear and whose purpose is fixed. He remains with Peter *fifteen days.* After so long a period he still remembers the exact number of days, for it was a happy time, and one remarkable man does not readily forget the time he has spent in another remarkable man's company. And what passed between them? Much talk on both sides doubtless, Paul relating to Peter his personal history and present views, Peter communicating in turn copious reminiscences of his beloved Master. The writer of the Epistle to the Galatians can have no desire to under-estimate the value of these communications, otherwise he would not have stated how long he was with Peter, but would rather have indicated that his stay lasted only for a short while. Very much could be said in a fortnight, and it is quite likely that in the course of that time, Peter told Paul all he remembered of Jesus.[1] Yet fifteen days are a short period compared with three years; quite sufficient for a full rehearsal of the Evangelic memorabilia, but hardly enough for a vital process of spiritual development. Paul might learn then the contents of our Gospels, such facts as we read of in the Gospel of Mark, but it was not then that he learned, or could possibly learn, his own gospel. That he had got by heart before he made his visit to Peter.

All this the apostle means to hint, by his brief, rapid jottings relating to this early period. He would say, "After my conversion I took no counsel with men in the church who might be supposed able to advise me, in particular I did not put myself in communication with any of the apostles. I retired into the desert for a lengthened period, that there I might be alone with God At length, when thought and prayer had borne their fruit in an enlightened mind and a firm purpose, and the time for action had come, after three full years,[2] I felt a craving to meet one of the men who had been with Jesus, that one who had ever been the foremost man and spokesman of the Twelve, that I might hear him talk of the earthly life of the Lord to whose service I had consecrated my life. I went to see Peter in Jerusalem, desiring from him neither recognition nor counsel, but

[1] Though the apostle quotes very few of our Lord's sayings, yet it is not to be doubted that he took pains to make himself acquainted with the Evangelic tradition. This may be inferred from the fact that he recognised Christ's word as *authoritative*, as can be gathered from 1 Cor. vii. 10, 12, 25; ix. 14. *Vide* on this Weizsäcker, *Das apostolische Zeitalter*, p. 595.

[2] The expression $\mu\epsilon\tau\grave{\alpha}\ \dot{\epsilon}\tau\eta\ \tau\rho\acute{\iota}\alpha$ does not necessarily mean three full years, but the purpose of the apostle in making the statement justifies the assumption that he is speaking exactly.

simply to enjoy friendly intercourse on perfectly equal terms with one for whom I entertained sincere respect. It was a time of delightful fellowship which I can never forget. I remember still the very number of the days, and the topics of our conversation each day. The memory of it is unmarred by any lingering recollections of discord. I opened my heart to Peter and told him all my past experiences and my present thoughts and purposes. He showed no sign of dissent, and as for the other apostles, not even excepting James, whom I did see for a few moments, they had no part in our intercourse. Yet, what I thought and said then, was just what I think and say now."[1]

From the foregoing interpretation of the apostle's statement regarding his first visit to Jerusalem, it follows that his universalistic antinomian gospel goes back, if not to the very hour of his conversion, at least to the years immediately following that event and preceding the visit.[2] This period might be included within the

---

[1] *Vide* on this visit to Peter, Weizsäcker, *The Apostolic Age*, pp. 95–98. Weizsäcker thinks that St. Paul avoided Jerusalem after his conversion, because he knew that the spirit prevailing there was alien to his own, and that he went up at the end of three years because he felt he could now afford to do so, that is, because he had established his independence, adopted a definite attitude, and opened his apostolic career. From the fact that the visit lasted fifteen days, he infers that Peter and he did not quarrel but came to an understanding.

[2] Such is the view of Holsten : *vide* his *Evangelium des Paulus*, p. 9 ; also of Beyschlag in his *Neutestamentliche Theologie* : " The main lines of his (Paul's) system " (remarks the latter writer), "as sketched in his interview with Peter at Antioch before any of his Epistles were written, go back, without doubt, to his retirement in Arabia." Vol. ii. p. 8.

conversion, as the time during which the convert attained to a full conception of the significance of the great event.

The view advocated in the foregoing pages does not imply that St. Paul's system of Christian thought underwent no expansion in any direction after the initial period. We must carefully distinguish here between his *religious intuitions* and his *theological formulations*. The former fall within the early years or even days of his Christian career, the latter may have been the slow growth of time; though even they may to a large extent have been worked out during the period of retirement in Arabia. The distinction may be illustrated by a single instance. Among the "intuitions" may be reckoned the perception that righteousness and salvation are not attainable by legal performances, but only by the grace of God as exhibited in a crucified Christ. This we are to conceive St. Paul as seeing from the first. But he may have had to go through a lengthened process of reflection before he reached a compact theoretic statement of the truth such as we find in the words: "Him who knew not sin, He made sin on our behalf, that we might become the righteousness of God in Him." That pithy, pregnant sentence has all the appearance of being the ripe fruit of much thought.

Another distinction has to be taken into account in discussing the question as to the development of Paulinism. We must distinguish between the positive doctrines of the Pauline system and its *apologetic elements*. At certain points, St. Paul's conception of Christianity appears weak and open to attack, or, to say the least, as standing in need of further explanation. He teaches that righteousness comes not by the law, but by faith in Christ, and that it comes on equal terms to all, without distinction between Jew and Gentile. Three questions are immediately raised by this threefold doctrine. First, if righteousness come not by the law, what end does the law serve? Next, what guarantee is there for ethical interests, for real personal goodness, under the religious programme of righteousness by faith? Lastly, if the benefits of Christ are open to all men on absolutely equal terms, what comes of the Jewish election and prerogative? The answers to these questions constitute the Pauline apologetic. It is probable that the apologetic ideas of his system came to the apostle latest of all; first the intuitions, next the positive dogmatic formulæ, lastly the apologetic buttresses. It need not be supposed that he never thought of the defences till some antagonistic critics arose to point out the weak side of his theory. We may be sure that he was his own severest critic, and that answers to the three questions were imperiously demanded by his own reason and conscience. But even on that view the apologetic would naturally come last. In logical order, a theory must be formed before objections can be taken to it. It must first be affirmed that righteousness comes by faith in Christ before the question can be raised, But what about personal righteousness on that hypothesis? The apostle's solution of the difficulty is his doctrine of the mystic solidarity between the believer and Christ. It was probably one of the latest, as it is certainly one of the most beautiful developments in his system of Christian thinking.

CHAPTER III

THE EPISTLE TO THE GALATIANS

LIKE most of the great agents of divine providence, St. Paul had large experience of waiting. He had to wait a considerable time before an opportunity occurred for entering on the mission to the Gentiles to which from the first he had felt himself called. He got the "wink of opportunity," when, according to the narrative in *Acts*, Barnabas went down to Tarsus to seek Saul, and brought him to Antioch, to take part in the movement that had begun there.[1] He had to wait still longer before he could utter his deepest thoughts concerning the Christian faith. The Gentile mission did not of itself bring the fitting occasion, for, as we have seen, he did not judge it needful or desirable to say all that was in his mind to infant churches, whether of Jewish or of Gentile origin. He gave them the benefit of his Christian intuitions, in which all was involved for himself though not for them, and kept in reserve the deeper ideas of his

---

[1] *Acts* xi. 25. *Galatians* i. 21-23 shows that St. Paul had not been altogether idle up till this time. His first mission was in the regions of Syria and Cilicia, and there is no reason to suppose that his efforts were confined to Jews, at least on principle. But those were the days of small things. Weiss thinks that St. Paul simply passed through Syria and Cilicia on his way home.

theology, content to find in these rest for his own heart, conscience, and reason. At length controversy brought the hour for speaking. His success as a Gentile apostle raised the inevitable question, Must heathen converts submit to Jewish rites in order to obtain the benefits of salvation and of fellowship with Christians of Hebrew extraction? St. Paul became the earnest champion of Gentile liberties, but, as was to be expected, many took the opposite view; hence came bitter conflict, and the need for unfolding the latent implications of the common faith in Jesus. Of this conflict, on the issue of which it was to depend whether Christianity was to have a future, the four great Epistles to the Galatian, Corinthian, and Roman Churches are the literary monument.

The trouble began at the conference at Jerusalem, when the question was debated: Must Gentile Christians be circumcised? The settlement then arrived at was not radical nor final. It seems to have been tacitly assumed that in the case of Jewish Christians circumcision remained as obligatory as ever, and, while it was agreed that the rite was not to be imposed on heathen converts, the delicate question connected with the social relations between the two sections of the Church appears to have been left in a vague indeterminate state. There was room for misunderstandings and the development of opposite tendencies, in the direction either of reducing the agreement to a minimum by attaching disabilities to the position of an uncircumcised Christian, on the one hand, or, on the other hand, of treating the exemption of Gentile converts from subjection to Jewish rites as involving the principle that circumcision was no longer of any religious importance either for Jewish or for Gentile Christians.[1] The collision between the two leading apostles at Antioch revealed the existence of the two tendencies.[2] The cause of that collision was Peter's refusal, at the instance of men from Jerusalem, to eat with Gentile Christians, after having previously done so without scruple. The position taken up by these men seems to have been: Gentiles may become *Christians* without being circumcised, but they may not eat with us Jews so long as they are uncircumcised; they must pay the penalty of their freedom by being treated by us as unclean. This was in effect to adhere to the Jerusalem compact in the letter, and to set it aside in the spirit. St. Paul felt this, and took occasion to state very plainly to his brother apostle his view of the situation in a speech in which Paulinism was for the first time definitely formulated. The speech was delivered in public, "before all," and produced momentous consequences. The conservatives became a party bitterly opposed to St. Paul, and bent on counteracting his influence, apparently organising for that purpose a regular anti-Pauline propagandism, following in the

---

[1] Holsten too strongly characterises the Jerusalem compact as a separation-union (*Sonderungs-einigung*), based on an inner contradiction of views. Vide *Das Evangelium des Paulus*, p. 24.

[2] Some writers place this collision between the second and third missionary journeys, during the visit of St. Paul to Antioch, referred to in *Acts* xviii. 22, two or three years after the Jerusalem Conference. But if the agreement come to was diversely understood as above indicated, the misunderstanding would not take years to show itself. It would appear on the earliest opportunity. Men like the false brethren referred to in *Galatians* ii. 4 would be on the outlook for a chance of making the compact null and void.

apostle's footsteps wherever he went, not to convert pagans to Christianity, but to pervert converts to their own Judaistic views of the Christian faith.

Though the controversy between St. Paul and the Judaists originally and immediately referred to the rite of circumcision, it involved wide issues and raised more than one question of grave import. As the conflict went on, three topics assumed in succession the place of greatest prominence: the perpetual obligation of the law, the qualifications for apostleship, and the prerogatives of Israel as an elect people. To set aside circumcision was virtually to annul the whole law, argued St. Paul's opponents, and he admitted the accuracy of their logic, and drew the seemingly impious inference that the gospel of salvation through faith in Christ involved the entire abrogation of the law as a way to acceptance with God. Thereupon the Judaists raised a new question: Who is the man who dares to teach so blasphemous a doctrine against the divinely-given law of Moses? By what authority does he take it upon him to interpret Christianity in this revolutionary sense? He calls himself an apostle: what right has he to the name? He is not one of the Twelve who had been with Jesus, and none but they can authoritatively bear witness to, or interpret, the mind of the Lord, nor can anyone be a true teacher, not to say an apostle, whose doctrine is not in accordance with their testimony. It is easy to see how the logic of their position led the Judaists to make such an assault upon St. Paul's claim to be an apostle, and how he in turn could not shirk the question thus raised, but was equally bound by the logic of his position to show that in calling himself the apostle of the Gentiles he was not guilty of usurpation, though he was neither one of the Twelve nor acting under their authority. But that question disposed of, still another remained: On St. Paul's view of Christianity in relation to the law, what about the election of Israel? She had long been God's chosen people, enjoying valuable privileges—could that be a true conception of Christianity which involved the virtual denial or cancelling of Israel's election? Here again the apostle of the Gentiles was put upon his defence, and summoned to the solution of a hard problem —the reconciliation of his gospel with the past history of the Jewish nation.

These three questions respecting the law, the apostolate, and the election, were all essentially involved in the great controversy, and they were probably all from the outset present, more or less distinctly, to the thoughts of both parties. Yet one may be said to have been more prominent at one time and another at another, so that the three topics may be regarded as denoting distinct stages in the controversy. The three stages are easily recognisable in the relative literature. For while one or other of the four Epistles may contain passages bearing on all the three topics, more or less clearly, yet they may be classified according as this or that topic is the one chiefly discussed. The Epistle to the Galatians is occupied predominantly with the first of the three themes, the two Epistles to the Corinthians (to be regarded in this connection as one) with the second, and the Epistle to the Romans, in the matter peculiar to it, with the third. In *Galatians* St. Paul defends the independence of Christianity against those who would make Christendom subject to Jewish law and custom; in 1 and 2 *Corinthians* he defends his own independence and authority as a God-commissioned apostle of the Gentiles against those who asserted the exclusive authority of the Eleven; in *Romans*, while giving a comprehensive statement of his views on the gospel, he addresses himself very specially to the solution of the problem how to reconcile his idea of Christianity with the admitted truth that Israel had for many centuries been God's elect people.

In all our references to the four Epistles, it has been assumed that their proper order is that in which they have been named in the foregoing paragraph. That they were actually written in this order is the opinion of the majority of commentators. Some English scholars, however, favour a different order, placing the Epistles to the Corinthians first, and *Galatians* between them and *Romans*. In his valuable commentary on *Galatians*, Bishop Lightfoot has carefully discussed the question, and given weighty reasons in support of this arrangement.[1] His two main arguments are based on the great similarity in thought and expression between *Galatians* and *Romans*, and on the manner in which the apostle speaks in these two Epistles and 2 *Corinthians* respectively concerning his tribulations: with copious details in the last-mentioned Epistle, with one pointed reference in *Galatians*,[2] very mildly and but seldom in *Romans*. In both cases the facts are as stated; the only point open to dispute is whether the inference be irresistible. The

[1] *Vide* the Introduction, pp. 36-56.   [2] *Gal.* vi. 17.

similarity between *Galatians* and *Romans* is explained by the supposition that the latter Epistle was written shortly after the former, while the echoes of its utterances still lingered in the writer's mind. But this is not the only possible explanation of the phenomenon. It may be accounted for by the hypothesis that the apostle in both Epistles was drawing upon a stock of Christian thought which in its essential positions, in the arguments on which these rested, and even in verbal expression, was to a large extent stereotyped, and thoroughly familiar to himself, though new to his readers. In that case letters touching on the same topics, no matter what interval of time separated them, would exhibit such resemblances as have been shown to exist in the two Epistles in question. The other set of facts also admits of another explanation besides that given by Bishop Lightfoot. His theory is that the Epistle which says most about apostolic tribulations must have been nearest them in the date of its composition. But the truth is that the prominence given to that topic in 2 *Corinthians* is not due to the recentness of the experiences, but to their appositeness to the purpose on hand. As will hereafter appear, the trials he endured formed an important part of St. Paul's argument in support of his apostleship.[1]

---

[1] In a recent article in the *Expositor* (April 1894), the Rev. F. Rendall, M.A., discussing the two topics as to the locality of the Galatian Churches, and the date of the Epistle to them, comes to the conclusion that this Epistle is not only earlier than the other three of the same group, but "the earliest now extant of St. Paul's Epistles," dealing with the agitation created in Galatia, by what he calls "a last effort of the Judaising party in 51." On Bishop Light-

I adhere therefore to the order previously indicated, which, apart from all historical questions as to dates of composition, best suits the logic of the controversy, and proceed to take a rapid survey of the Epistle to the Galatians.

The very first sentence shows that something has occurred to disturb the spirit of the writer. In his letters to the Thessalonians St. Paul gives himself no title; here, on the other hand, he not only calls himself an apostle, but takes pains to indicate that for his apostolic standing he is indebted neither primarily nor subordinately to any man or body of men, but to God alone.[1] The same thing may be said of every true apostle and prophet, but why so peremptory an assertion of independence? Because there are those who assail his independence, and desire to make out that he is either no apostle at all, or one subordinate to the Eleven, and therefore bound to conform in opinion and action to their authority; and all this in order to undermine his influence as a teacher of views which the assailants regard with aversion. Fully aware how closely belief in his authority as a teacher is connected with continued adherence to his doctrine, the apostle commences with this topic, and sets himself in a very thorough, earnest way to demonstrate the originality of his gospel, and his entire freedom as the apostle of the Gentiles from all

---

foot's argument from similarity of style he remarks: "A man may well repeat the same thoughts and the same expressions at considerable intervals if the intervening tenor of his life and his environment continue constant."

[1] οὐκ ἀπ' ἀνθρώπων, οὐδὲ δι' ἀνθρώπου; not from men (*e.g.* the Eleven), as ultimate source, nor by any man as instrument.

dependence on the other apostles. This, however, is not the leading aim of the Epistle, though it forms the topic of the first two chapters. The main purpose is revealed in the sentence following the salutation and doxology, in which the apostle suddenly and indignantly exclaims: "I am surprised that ye have so soon turned away from him who called you in the grace of Christ unto another gospel."[1] The unhappy change alluded to is from a gospel of salvation by grace to a gospel of salvation by circumcision, and the leading aim of the apostle is to check the perverse movement, and to bring back the Galatians to their first faith. The section bearing on the apostleship from chap. i. 11 to the end of chap. ii. may be viewed as a long parenthesis, after which the main theme is resumed, and the Galatians are again directly addressed and remonstrated with for allowing themselves to be led away.

This section, though parenthetical, is very important in its bearing on the main design of the Epistle. It consists of three parts, of which the first is intended to show that St. Paul was not indebted to the other apostles for his knowledge of Christ and of the gospel (i. 11–24); the second, that he was in no wise controlled by them in regard to his preaching of the gospel (ii. 1–10); the third, that so far from any of the apostles prescribing to him what he should preach, the fact was that he, on the contrary, had occasion to remonstrate with one of the

---

[1] *Gal.* i. 6. The expression οὕτως ταχέως is founded on by most interpreters as proving that *Galatians* must have been written before 1 and 2 *Corinthians*, shortly after St. Paul's second visit to Galatia, at the beginning of his three years' residence in Ephesus.

pillar-apostles, St. Peter, in regard to unstable, inconsistent conduct, fitted to compromise the great principles of the gospel (ii. 11–21). What he says on the first head amounts to this, that he had neither the inclination nor the opportunity to learn much about Christianity from the apostles. In the second part, he gives an extremely interesting account of important occurrences in connection with the Jerusalem Conference, which unfortunately has given rise to much diversity of opinion among critics and interpreters. But amid much that is doubtful one thing is clear. The apostle most distinctly states that the pillar-apostles with whom he held conference, "added nothing to him,"[1] that is, gave him no additional instructions as to what he should preach, found no fault with his gospel as frankly explained to them, were content that he should continue preaching as he had preached. They reverently recognised the hand of God in the whole career of this man: in his conversion, in his conception of the nature and destination of Christianity, in his success as a missionary to the Gentiles. They acquiesced in his gospel of uncircumcision as at least suitable for heathen converts, and wished him all success in preaching it in heathen parts, while they confined their own ministry to the Jewish world, being humbly conscious of unfitness for work in any other sphere. Such being the attitude of the

[1] *Gal.* ii. 6. οὐδὲν προσανέθεντο. The verb in classic Greek means to lay on an additional burden. In later Greek it means to impart to, either to give or to get advice, instruction, or injunction. Here it means that the apostles gave no additional instructions. In chap. i. 16 the same word is employed in the other sense: οὐ προσανεθέμην. "I did not consult in order to *get* advice."

Eleven, their authority could not truthfully be appealed to in support of a reactionary movement which strove to reduce the Jerusalem compact to a minimum, or even to make it a nullity by endeavouring to induce Gentile Christians to submit to circumcision, as the Judaist sectaries seem to have done in Galatia.

The third division of the long parenthesis respecting the apostleship is the most important of all. It exhibits St. Paul as teaching one of the pillar-apostles, instead of being taught by them, the true nature of the gospel; yet not teaching a new gospel, as if his gospel were different from that of the other apostles, but rather showing to St. Peter the true import of his own gospel; the scope, tendency, and logical consequence of his own professed principles. The doctrinal statement it contains is an epitome of Paulinism, given in a few rapid, impassioned sentences, charged at once with the thoroughgoing logic of a powerful intellect, and the intense emotion of a great manly heart. There is nothing more stirring in the whole range of the Pauline literature, nothing more convincing, than this swift, eloquent sketch of the gospel of uncircumcision, brought in incidentally, in the course of a historical narrative intended to vindicate the apostle's independence, but serving a far higher purpose also, viz., to vindicate the independence of the gospel itself as a gospel of free grace, meant for the salvation of all sinners alike, and able to save all in the most efficient manner without the aid of legal ordinances. As against Peter the memorable utterance makes good three serious charges: that he has been guilty (1) of virtually excommunicating the Gentile Christians by insisting on their complying with Jewish custom as a condition of fellowship,[1] (2) of self-stultification in building again the things he had destroyed, (3) of frustrating the grace of God by in effect declaring that it is insufficient for man's salvation, and needs to be supplemented by legal performances. Viewed not polemically but didactically, the passage briefly indicates all the leading ideas of the Pauline theology in much the same order as in the Epistle to the Romans. Jews by birth and Gentile "sinners" on a level, as unable to save themselves by their works, Jews being sinners not less than Gentiles, though proudly applying the epithet to the latter as if it had no reference to themselves; faith the sole way to justification for both, faith in Jesus Christ crucified; justification by faith and justification by the law mutually exclusive; by faith, therefore, the law abolished, so that the believer in Jesus is no longer bound by it; finally, the Christian life a life of mystic union and communion with Christ, and of devoted love to Christ in response to the love wherewith He loved us, in giving Himself to death for our salvation. It is obviously not solely for historic reasons that the apostle repeats here this remarkable confession of his faith. He has in view the present instruction of the Church to which he writes, and means, though he does not put it down on paper, "this is what I said to Peter then, and this I say to you now."

We come now to the main part of the Epistle (chaps. iii.–v). The contents of this part may be summed up

[1] *Gal.* ii. 14: πῶς τὰ ἔθνη ἀναγκάζεις Ἰουδαΐζειν. The compulsion lay in Peter's example.

by three phrases: 1. *Legalism condemned*, chap. iii.; 2. *Christian liberty asserted*, chap. iv.–v. 1–6; 3. *Abuse of liberty censured*, chap. v. 13–26.

1. Full of enthusiasm for the creed which he has just expounded, the apostle passes on to its defence with a natural feeling of surprise and vexation that so unwelcome a duty should be necessary. He cannot understand how a church to which a crucified Christ had been broadly proclaimed[1] should lapse into legalism. A crucified Christ meant everything to him, why should He not be everything to them? Who could have bewitched them? for it seemed as if the result could be accounted for only by the fascinating spell of some malign power. Alas! the unhappy change is not so difficult to understand as St. Paul seems to have imagined. There is nothing so natural as this lapse in the case of the average Christian, nothing so common; Christian life habitually maintained up in the pure Alpine region of the Pauline faith is the exception rather than the rule. For few are so consistent in their logic as St. Paul, so thorough in the application of first principles, so possessed by the love of Christ, and therefore so jealous of every other servitude. St. Paul's doctrine is, after all, a heroic doctrine, and it needs spiritual heroes to appreciate it and do it justice. Besides, it has to be remembered that while the apostle had his experience of legalism before his conversion, for most men it comes after. Few escape taking the spiritual disease at some time or other.

The Galatian Church caught the evil infection from the Judaist propagandists, and so their first teacher must

[1] *Gal.* iii. 1, προεγράφη; well rendered by Lightfoot, "placarded."

argue the matter with them. The heads of his argument lie before us. How it told on the Galatians we do not know; to ourselves it may appear of varying value, and occasionally such as to remind us that the writer was once a disciple of the Rabbis. The first proof is not the least convincing, being a direct appeal to experience. "How," asks the apostle, "did ye receive the Spirit who wrought in you and through you so mightily; by doing legal works, or by believing the good tidings ye heard from my lips? And if in this way your Christian life began, why forsake it now? If faith was so powerful at first, why should it not be equally powerful all through? Listen not to the men who would enslave you to the law; listen rather to God, who gave you His Spirit and wrought miracles among you, before ever you heard a word of circumcision or the Jewish law, thereby showing that these things are no wise necessary or conducive to salvation."

To be noted in this first line of reasoning is the pointed way in which law is opposed to faith, and flesh to spirit. "Received ye the Spirit from the works of the law, or from the hearing of faith?" "Having begun in the Spirit, are ye now being perfected in the flesh?" We have here two of the great Pauline antitheses.

The apostle's next appeal is to the history of Abraham,[1] obviously an important topic in an argument with men enamoured of Judaism. If he could make it appear that history was on his side, a great point would be gained. To what extent is he successful? To this extent, at least, that in the patriarch's

[1] *Gal.* iii. 6–9.

history acceptableness to God is associated with faith, and the promise embraces in its scope the Gentiles. The story makes the broad impression that men please God not by doing this or that, but by believing in Him, and that whoever believes in God, whether Jew or Gentile, may hope to share in His grace. This length a modern student of Scripture may go, without pretending to find St. Paul's doctrine of justification by faith, in the technical theological sense, in the Book of Genesis.

The next point the apostle makes is this: while by faith you share the blessing of Abraham, what you get from the law is not blessing but *cursing*.[1] Is it not written, "Cursed is every one that continueth not in all things which are written in the book of the law to do them"? The most notable thing in this section of the argument is the saying concerning the function of Christ in relation to the law's curse. "*Christ hath redeemed us from the curse of the law, being made a curse for us;*" the proof that He was made a curse being that He suffered death in the form of crucifixion.[2] This is doubtless one of the great Pauline *logia*; a new utterance but an old thought, dating even in its expression from early years. It is more than the simple statement of a religious faith, it contains the germ of a theological theory; for latent in it is the principle that the Redeemer of men must share their lot in order that they may share His privilege, a principle of which we shall find other exemplifications in the Pauline Epistles.

The apostle proceeds to base an argument on the mere date of the Sinaitic legislation.[3] Given above four

[1] *Gal.* iii. 10-14.   [2] *Ibid.* iii. 13.   [3] *Ibid.* iii. 15-18.

hundred years after the promise, and of course not for the purpose of setting it aside, the law must have been intended to perform some function in subordination to the promise. This at once raises the question, What was that function? "What then the law?"[1] St. Paul's full answer to the question is not given here; we must wait for it till we come to his Epistle to the Romans. What he does say in the present Epistle is a little obscure, owing to the rapid movement of his thought, which rushes on like a mountain torrent. Had we no other information as to his doctrine concerning the law, we might readily take his meaning to be that it was added to *restrain* transgression. It would be nearer the truth to say that he means to suggest that the law was given *in favour* of transgression,[2] to provoke resistance to its behests. This is certainly a very bold idea, but it is none the less likely to be Pauline. The apostle's whole doctrine of the law is one of the most startlingly original features in his apologetic system of thought, which we might be tempted to regard as an extravagance into which he was driven by the exigencies of controversy. This, however, would be a very mistaken idea. It is, we may be sure, no hastily extemporised theory, but the carefully thought-out solution of a problem which pressed heavily on the apostle's mind, from the day he arrived at the conclusion that the law, whatever it might be good for, was certainly not the way to the attainment of righteousness.

[1] *Gal.* iii. 19.
[2] So Lipsius, *Die Paulinische Rechtfertigungslehre*, p. 75 (1853), Ménégoz, and many others.

While failing to give a full statement of the solution in this Epistle, the apostle makes some very instructive suggestions respecting the law's function. For this purpose he employs three comparisons, likening the law first to a gaoler, who, after provoking men to transgression, throws them into prison, and keeps them there under lock and key;[1] next to a *pædagogus*, entrusted with the moral supervision of a child;[2] lastly to the guardians and stewards who have charge of the person and property of the heir to an estate during the time of his minority.[3] All three comparisons have one general object in view, to show how the law might have a real function, yet only a *temporary* one issuing in release from its power. The gaoler's function is real and necessary, but the time comes when the prisoner must be set free. The *pædagogus* in a Greek or Roman family served a useful if humble purpose in the moral nurture of a child of tender years, but in due course the child outgrew his influence. The care of guardians and stewards is most necessary to the well-being of an heir and the preservation of his inheritance, but it ceases, as a matter of course, when he comes of age. The figures all serve further to convey a hint as to the comparatively ungenial nature of the law's function; to exhibit it as such, that the subject of it will be glad to escape from it when the time of release arrives. It appears at its worst under the figure of a gaoler; less repulsive under

---

[1] *Gal.* iii. 23.

[2] *Ibid.* iii. 24. παιδαγωγός is untranslatable because the function is unknown among us.

[3] *Ibid.* iv. 2. ἐπιτρόπους, having charge of the person; οἰκονόμους, having charge of the property.

the guise of the *pædagogus*, because the subject is now conceived not as a criminal but as a child, though even his mode of treatment is harsh compared with that of a parent;[1] least irksome under the final figure, for now the child is grown to be a youth, and the guardians and stewards do not forget what he will be ere long, yet becoming increasingly unwelcome as the future heir advances towards maturity, and longs with growing eagerness for escape from authority into self-control. Under all three aspects, even the mildest, the reign of law is bearable only for a time, creating in the subject an irrepressible desire for *liberty*.

2. Liberty came with Jesus Christ. Of this congenial theme the apostle goes on to speak. He introduces the subject in connection with the last of the above-mentioned comparisons, which he regards as the most important of the three, as appears from the formal manner in which he brings it in: "Now I say," etc.[2] He has hinted already at the truth that with Christ the era of liberty or true sonship began,[3] but he is able now to make a more adequate statement of the fact, in connection with the figure of the heir in a state of pupilage, which gives it an effective setting, *and brings out the epoch-making significance of the advent of Jesus in the general religious history of the world*. In terms of that figure he represents the advent as marking

---

[1] This is the point emphasised by Lipsius, *Die Paulinische Rechtfertigungslehre*, p. 80. The *pædagogus* acts with rigour, not with love. On the other hand, Ménégoz thinks that the temporariness of the office is the one thing to be insisted on, *Le Péché et la Redemption*, p. 115. But there is a reference to both aspects.

[2] *Gal.* iv. 1 : λέγω δὲ [3] *Ibid.* iii. 26.

the point at which mankind, the son of God, arrived at its majority. Then commenced the era of grace, of liberty, of sonship, of the new humanity in which is neither Jew nor Greek, slave nor free, male nor female, but all are one in Christ.¹ It is a truly magnificent thought, one of the greatest in the whole range of Paulinism. And one cannot but feel with what powerful effect Christ's agency in bringing about the great change is spoken of in association with this grand philosophic idea. "*But when the fulness of the time came, God sent forth His Son, made of a woman, made under the law, that He might redeem them that were under the law, that we might receive the adoption of sons.*" ² Here is another great Pauline *logion*, a fresh contribution to the theology of the cross, applying the principle of solidarity between Redeemer and redeemed in a new direction. The subject of redemption being under law, the Redeemer also came under law, that by this act of grace He might put an end for ever to the state of legal bondage. It is noteworthy that the apostle refers not only to Christ's subjection to law, but to His birth. Why is this? Perhaps we should avoid too recondite explanations, and adopt the simple suggestion that the form of subjection to law which he has in his mind is *circumcision*, the bone of contention between himself and the Judaists. In that case his thought may thus be paraphrased: Jesus came to be born of a woman, and then, being a Jew, to be cir-

---

¹ *Gal.* iii. 28.
² *Ibid.* iv. 4, 5. The idea of adoption will come up for discussion at a later stage.

cumcised, and so to deliver us from bondage to that rite and all that goes along with it. Thus viewed, this great text ascribes redemptive power, not merely to Christ's death, but *to His whole state of gracious humiliation.*

The objective ideal significance of Christ's coming being that it inaugurated the new era of filial freedom—prison doors opened, children grown to manhood, the heir no longer a minor, it is easy to see what duty is incumbent on the Christian. It is to understand the nature of the new era in which he lives, to enter sympathetically into its spirit, and subjectively to realise its lofty ideal. Obligation lies on him to be free indeed, as a son of God arrived at his majority. That accorddingly is what the apostle next proceeds to insist on. Appealing once more to the experience of his readers in confirmation of the view of Christianity he has just presented, " Did you not," he asks in effect, " find something in your own hearts which told you that Jesus came to introduce the era of sonship ? Was there not a spirit in you which made you call God Father ? It was God sending the Spirit of His own well-beloved Son into your breasts, that you might be sons in feeling as well as in legal standing. Be faithful, then, to that spirit whose promptings ye once obeyed. Return not again to bondage to the weak and beggarly elements, whether of Jewish legalism or of Pagan superstition, from which it was the very purpose of Christ's coming to redeem you."[1] Such is the drift of chapter iv. 6–20, omitting points of minor importance.

[1] The words τὰ ἀσθενῆ καὶ πτωχὰ στοιχεῖα are generally interpreted as having this double reference. Στοιχεῖα means literally the

With this pathetic appeal the apostle might well have concluded his argument. But his active mind is full of ideas, and he has yet another train of thought in reserve by which he hopes to commend his doctrine of Christian freedom from the law to the acceptance of his readers. Abraham having done service in establishing the doctrine, his family is now made to perform its part by the allegory of Sarah and Hagar and their sons.[1] Here again the Christian apostle and prophet may appear to be clad in the robe of a Rabbi, but let not that be to his prejudice. Take the allegory for what it is worth; as poetry rather than logic, meant not so much to convince the reason as to captivate the imagination. If it served that purpose at a great crisis in the world's religious history, was it not worth while, even if it should be of little value to us? At the very least, it has autobiographical interest, for the prose poem obviously bears a date upon it. It comes to us from the period of the retirement in Arabia, and we scent the keen air of the desert as we read it. Let us read and silently enjoy, abstaining from the stupidity of a prosaic detailed interpretation.

One can understand the passionate earnestness with which this man of prophetic, poetic soul, true son of the Jerusalem above, once more appeals to the Galatians to

letters of the alphabet ranged in rows, and the idea suggested is that the Jewish and Pagan religions were fit only for the childhood of the world, when men were, as it were, only learning their letters.

[1] Chap. iv. 21-31. *Vide* on this Professor Findlay's most felicitous commentary on the Epistle (*Expositor's Bible*). He hits off the spirit of the passage by the remark: "He will tell his 'children' a story."

stand fast in their Christ-bought liberty, and not to become re-entangled in a yoke of bondage, and warns them that that must be the inevitable effect of their submitting to the rite of circumcision.[1] And how welcome, after the subtle argumentation of the previous chapter, the brief sententious statement of the healthy normal Christian attitude on all such questions as were in debate. " *We* (Christians who know where they are) *in the Spirit from faith wait for the hope of righteousness. For in Christ neither circumcision availeth anything nor uncircumcision, but faith energetic through love.*" This is another of the great Pauline words, having for its import: circumcision *et hoc genus omne*, good for nothing, faith good for everything; good to begin with, and not less good to end with; good to sanctify as well as to justify, because it is a powerful practical force operating through the highest motive, love.[2]

3. On the apostle's warning against the abuse of liberty (chap. v. 13–26) little need be said, beyond remarking that on this score he exhibits here, as always, a most becoming sensitiveness. He traces the source of abuse to the *flesh*, and finds the antidote in walking by the Spirit.[3] He makes no attempt here, as in *Romans*, to show how moral licence is excluded by a right view of the relation subsisting between the Christian and Christ, but he compensates for that lack by drawing up two lists of the works of the flesh and of the Spirit respectively, that the one may repel by its hideousness,

---

[1] Chap. v. 1–4.
[2] More will be said on this text in a future chapter.
[3] Chap. v. 16.

and the other draw by its winsomeness. How strange that the facts of human life should supply material for so tremendous a contrast! Stranger still that it should be possible to find materials for the contrast within the religious world! For the fruit of the Spirit: love, joy, peace, etc., is set over against the spiritual vices connected with the "carnality of religious contention," not less than against the coarser vices of the irreligious sensualist. It is easy to be a religious partisan, regeneration is not necessary for that; the difficulty is to be a true Christian.

The postscript[1] must not be passed over in silence. After the speech to Peter, it is the most characteristic thing in the Epistle. The letter has been written at white heat, dictated more rapidly than the amanuensis can write it down. The author reads it over, finds he has still something to say, writes it down himself, in large, bold, inelegant characters, unmistakable by anyone who has seen his handwriting before. The sentiments are as unmistakably Pauline as the penmanship. Here is no elaborate reasoning, whether of the ex-rabbi or of the theological doctor, but abrupt, impassioned, prophetic utterances of deepest convictions: the zealots for Judaism, hollow hypocrites; the cross of Christ the sole worthy ground of glorying; circumcision nothing, the new Christian creation in the individual and in the community everything; the men who adopt this for their motto, the true Israel of God, on whom may God's peace ever rest.

[1] Chap. vi. 11-17.

CHAPTER IV

THE EPISTLES TO THE CORINTHIANS

In these Epistles the controversy between St. Paul and his opponents takes the form of an attack and a defence of his apostolic standing, and of his personal character in connection therewith. The advocates of a Judaistic Christianity do not seem to have made, in Corinth, any direct attempt to induce the members of the Church to submit to the rite of circumcision, or any other part of the Jewish law, probably for the simple reason that such an attempt in that centre of Greek life would have been futile. They appear to have confined their efforts in fostering a legal temper to questions of detail, such as the eating of meats offered to idols. Amid the Greeks of Corinth, with their liberal instincts, the anti-Paulinists would be obliged to pursue their end, the destruction of a free independent Christianity, by a circuitous course. They could not, with hope of success, teach their own doctrines, but they might assail the man who taught doctrines of an opposite nature, might blacken his character, and plausibly deny, or cunningly undermine, his apostolic standing. The spirit of the people gave them a good chance of success in this bad line of action, for the Greeks in general, and the Corinthians in particular, were volatile, opinionative, addicted to party spirit, and to the faithlessness and heartlessness which that spirit usually engenders.

There is very little bearing on the great controversy to be found in the First Epistle, which treats mainly of the multifarious disorders and irregularities of the Corinthian Church, the various questions of casuistry therein debated, relating to sacrificial meats, marriage, the dress and deportment of women, etc., and an eccentric opinion entertained by some concerning the resurrection. Only a few slight hints occur here and there of the presence of a hostile element bent on undermining the apostle's influence and authority, such as the reference to the parties into which the Church was divided,[1] the allusion to some who were puffed up because they thought the apostle was frightened to visit Corinth,[2] and the abrupt manner in which, in the ninth chapter, the writer, in interrogative form, asserts his apostolic dignity and privileges.[3] Were it not for the prominence given to the element of self-defence in the Second Epistle, one might even legitimately doubt whether these stray hints did really imply the existence in the Corinthian Church of a mischief-making Judaistic section; but in view of the peculiar contents of the later Epistle, it seems proper to attach more significance to them than we should otherwise have done. It is, of course, quite conceivable that between the writing of the First Epistle and the date of the Second a new situation had emerged, that a party of legalists had in the interval arrived on the scene and created other

[1] 1 *Cor.* i. 11, 12.   [2] *Ibid.* iv. 18.   [3] *Ibid.* ix. 1-6.

work for the apostle than that of correcting Corinthian abuses. Thus we might explain why there is so little in the First Epistle of that which constitutes the peculiarity of the Second. But the fact might be otherwise accounted for. It may be due in part to the circumstance that in his First Epistle the apostle had so many urgent matters to write about, that the personal question was crowded out; in part to his adversaries not having as yet found their opportunity, so that their presence in the Church might meantime be disregarded, or alluded to only in a distant manner.

However it is to be explained, the fact certainly is, that the allusions to a hostile party in the First Epistle are very slight and vague. What is said concerning the divisions in the Church is far from clear. How many parties were there, and what were their respective characteristics? Baur reduces them to two, a Petrine and a Pauline, the other two being varieties of these, or the same party under a different name; the Petrine party, *e.g.*, calling itself now after Peter, the chief of the original apostles, now after Christ, to imply that in their view companionship with Jesus was an indispensable qualification for apostleship.[1] According to Holsten, those who called themselves after Christ were a distinct party, consisting of strangers who had come into the Church, men who had personally followed Jesus, belonging indeed to the Seventy, therefore claiming the title of apostles.[2] It is assumed .by both these

[1] Vide *Paulus der Apostel*, i. 291-8.
[2] Vide *Das Evangelium des Paulus*, pp. 196-232, where there is a very able discussion of the question, Who were the Christ party?

writers that the divisions rested on a doctrinal basis, which, however, is denied by others, who think that they amounted to little more than personal preferences.[1] The whole subject is enveloped in obscurity, but the probability is that there was a Judaistic leaven in the Corinthian Church even when the First Epistle was written, as it is certain there must have been at the date of the Second.

On this view we can best understand 1 *Cor.* ix. 1–6, though that the apostle is on his defence is far from self-evident even in this passage, especially as it stands in the correct text, according to which the question, "Am I not free?" comes before the question, "Am I not an apostle?" According to this reading, the reference to the apostleship and its rights comes in simply as an illustration of the maxim previously laid down, that a Christian must sometimes deny himself the use of an undoubted liberty. The only thing that makes us suspect that the apostle has something more in his mind is the abruptness with which the reference to the apostleship comes in, and the strange emphasis with which the theme, once introduced, is insisted on. While ostensibly only illustrating a general doctrine concerning Christian liberty, he drags the apostleship into the discussion as if desirous to speak of it for its own sake, and he makes statements regarding it which seem irrelevant to the previous connection of thought, in a tone that nothing going before accounts for. "Have I

Holsten finds the proof of his view above stated, in 2 *Cor.* x.–xiii., the whole of which he regards as a polemic against this party.

[1] So Sabatier.

not seen the Lord Jesus? Are not ye my work in the Lord? If I be not an apostle to others, yet at least I am to you, for the seal of my apostleship are ye in the Lord." Why such questions and assertions, unless some were calling in question his claim to be an apostle?

Statements introduced in this indirect, passing manner could not satisfactorily dispose of the subject to which they referred. Nevertheless, in the light of the ampler treatment in the Second Epistle, one can discover in the ninth chapter of the First the leading points of St. Paul's apology for his assailed apostolic standing. "I am an apostle," he says in effect, "because (1) I have seen the Lord,[1] (2) I have been signally successful in my preaching,[2] (3) I have endured hardship in the cause." The hardship he has in view is the obligation imposed on him by the state of feeling in the Church to refuse support, and to work for his own livelihood.[3] Now, when we pass to the Second Epistle, we find that what St. Paul there says on the same topic amounts simply to an expansion of these three arguments.

In proceeding to consider the eloquent and triumphant apologetic of that Epistle, I begin by remarking that the whole defence rests on the general axiom that the qualifications for the Christian apostleship are spiritual, not technical. In this respect there is a close resemblance between St. Paul's argument in defence of his apostolic standing and the argument of the author of the Epistle to the Hebrews, in defence of the priesthood of Christ. In both cases the presumption from a legal point of view was against the position defended. Christ

[1] 1 Cor. ix. 1.   [2] Ibid. ix. 2.   [3] Ibid. ix. 7–12.

possessed none of the legal qualifications for the priesthood. In like manner St. Paul's qualification for the apostleship might well appear questionable. He had not been one of the companions of Jesus. On a *primâ facie* view, that was a grave defect in his title; for not to Judaistic prejudice alone, but to right reason, it could not but appear important that the authoritative teachers of Christianity should be able to say from their own knowledge: "Thus spake and acted the Lord Jesus." It is indeed obvious that, as eye-witnesses of Christ's personal ministry, the Eleven were authorities in a sense in which St. Paul could not pretend to be authoritative. But how then does he vindicate his claim to rank with the Eleven as an apostle? Let us see.

1. His first line of defence is that *he has seen the Lord.* "Have I not seen Jesus our Lord?" asks he in the First Epistle, alluding primarily to the vision on the way to Damascus, but not to that alone, or perhaps even chiefly, as we can gather from various texts in the Second Epistle. He lays chief stress, in reality, on the vision of Jesus with the eye of the spirit, the insight he has gained into the true meaning of Christ's whole earthly history. Sufficient vouchers for this statement may be found in 2 *Corinthians* iii. 18 and iv. 6, which tell of the writer's unveiled view of the glory of the Lord, and of an inward illumination granted to him worthy to be compared to the illumination of the world when God uttered the creative fiat: "Let there be light." His contention, virtually, is that the vision of the spirit is more important than the vision of the bodily eye; that indeed the latter without the former possesses no value.

His tacit assumption is, that the vision of the spirit is possible without the vision of the eye, and that there may be a vision of the eye unaccompanied by the vision of the spirit. If these positions be admitted, then there is no reason why a Paul should be behind the chiefest of the apostles. In matters of fact pertaining to the life of Jesus, their testimony, of course, possessed unique authority. But were they necessarily entitled to speak with exclusive or even superior authority as to the religious significance of the facts? Their claim to be heard there would depend on the measure of their spiritual illumination. But the question between St. Paul and his opponents was precisely this: Who is the most authoritative and reliable interpreter of Christ's mind? It was not, Who is most likely to know the facts? but, Who best understands the facts? And St. Paul's claim was that he possessed an understanding of the facts at least equal to that of the Eleven. And to that claim it would have been an utter irrelevance to have objected: " Ah, but you never were a companion of the Lord like Cephas." It would have been an irrelevance of the same kind as it would be to say to a man of genius: " It is impossible you can be a great poet, for your father was not a man of wealth or of rank." It would have been to lay stress on what was at best a matter of prestige, in a spirit of vulgar worldliness; in St. Paul's own words, to make knowledge of Jesus *after the flesh* [1] the one thing needful. It would have been, in short, to make the definition of apostleship turn upon something outward, in which case St. Paul could only make his opponents welcome to the name,

[1] 2 *Cor.* v. 16.

and claim for himself the substance—the right, viz., to come before the world as an independent interpreter of the Christian religion.

But does St. Paul's argument not prove too much? On naturalistic principles it certainly does. The scope of his argument, interpreted by naturalism is: "Every man an apostle who has spiritual insight, a Luther not less than a Paul. No man an absolute authority in matters of faith, not Paul any more than Luther, but each man authoritative according to the measure of his light." St. Paul did not mean to go this length. He regarded the apostles as exceptional characters, not merely in view of the measure of their inspiration, but because they were eye-witnesses of the resurrection. Hence the stress which he lays on the fact of having himself seen Jesus, not only in 1 *Corinthians* ix. but also in the fifteenth chapter of the same Epistle, where he enumerates the appearances of the risen Christ. He was not wrong in attaching importance to that fact in connection with the vindication of his apostleship. For no one who believed that the alleged appearance of Jesus to the persecutor on the way to Damascus was a reality, would be disposed to deny that its final cause was to convert a bitter enemy of the faith into a divinely commissioned preacher of it. Of course it was open to his opponents to deny the reality of his vision; probably they did deny it, resolving the event into a purely subjective impression, as was done in later days in writings of intensely anti-Pauline bias like the Clementines. But they could not well admit the objectivity of the Christophany, and deny the inference to apostolic vocation.

2. The second line of defence is *success in the work of the apostleship*. St. Paul says much of his success as an apostle to the Gentiles, and that not merely by way of stating facts, still less in a spirit of idle boasting, but consciously and seriously in the way of argument and self-defence; as if to say, "Providence has set its seal upon my ministry." He hints at this part of his apology in the First Epistle, as when he says to the Corinthians: "If to others I am not an apostle, yet at least I am to you, for the seal of mine apostleship are ye in the Lord"; and again, when he writes: "By the grace of God I am what I am; and His grace which was bestowed upon me was not found vain, but I laboured more abundantly than they all."[1] But it is in the Second Epistle that he develops the argument so as to do it full justice. It is the main theme of the remarkable passage beginning at chapter ii. verse 14, and extending to the end of the third chapter.[2] The argument worthily opens with the words: "Now thanks be to God who causeth us ever to triumph in Christ, and maketh manifest by us the savour of His knowledge in every place."[3] They are in the

---

[1] 1 *Cor.* ix. 2; xv. 10.
[2] We might even include in this section chap. iv. 1–6.
[3] 2 *Cor.* ii. 14. The word θριαμβεύοντι has caused much trouble to interpreters. I retain the rendering of the A.V. as best suited to the connection of thought, though recent writers, while admitting its suitableness, reject it as contrary to usage. *Vide*, however, Schmiedel in *Hand-Commentar*, who also adheres to the old view. That similar verbs are sometimes used in a *factitive* sense is not denied (*e.g.* βασιλεύειν, 1 *Sam.* viii. 22, and μαθητεύσατε in *Matt.* xxviii. 19, the neuter form occurs in *Matt.* xxvii. 57); but it is contended that θριαμβεύειν is never used in this sense, but only in the sense of triumphing over one, as in *Col.* ii. 15, the only other instance of its use in the New Testament. But the basis of induction is narrow,

heroic style, and suggest the idea of a great victorious general receiving a triumphal entry into the city, in honour of his victories, followed by a train of captives marching towards their fate, some to deliverance and some to death. It looks like boasting, but it is boasting in self-defence; therefore, though conscious, and frankly owning that he is using language of self-commendation, he yet boldly employs it; and to make the argument from success more telling he gives it a personal turn by appealing to the effect of his work among the Corinthians themselves. "Are we beginning again to commend ourselves, or need we, as do certain persons, epistles of commendation to you or from you? Ye are our epistle, written in our hearts, known and read by all men."[1] The certain persons referred to are of course legalist opponents, whose manner of action St. Paul loses no opportunity of contrasting with his own. They brought letters of introduction from influential men, coming not to preach the gospel, but to neutralise his influence. He needed no such letters, at least among the Corinthians; the success of his labours, as evidenced

and the question is just whether the connection does not justify us in finding an instance of the factitive use here. In any case we must think of St. Paul as sharing the triumph of God, not as triumphed over, as at least an incense-bearer, not as a captive (*vide* the translation of the passage in *The Scripture for Young Readers*, 1892). I cannot close this note without referring to Professor Findlay's article on the word in *The Expositor* for December 1879, in which he ably contends for the Greek sense as distinct from the Roman, according to which the reference is not to a military triumph, but to a sacred procession of enthusiastic worshippers led by the inspiring god. The stress, on this view, lies on the apostle's *enthusiasm*, not on his success.

[1] 2 *Cor.* iii. 1, 2.

by their renewed hearts, was all the commendation he required.

The apostle would have the Corinthians carefully consider what this success meant, and takes pains in the sequel to make them understand its significance. It was, he tells them, a proof of sufficiency or fitness for the work. For when he asked, "Who is sufficient or fit for such a ministry?"[1] he did not mean to suggest that no one was. He himself claimed to possess the necessary aptitude. He disclaimed only a sufficiency self-originated. He devoutly ascribed his sufficiency to God; and just on that account he assigned to it very great significance, as revealing a divine purpose. When God fits a man for a work He calls him to the work, such is his argument. Drawn out in full his logic is to this effect: It is not an accident that a man succeeds in the work I have on hand. Success proves fitness, and fitness in turn proves divine vocation.

One would like to know how St. Paul defined sufficiency. He has anticipated our wish and given a full satisfactory answer to our question. The gist of his answer is, that sufficiency or fitness for Christian apostleship consists in insight into, and thorough sympathy with, the genius of the Christian religion. Thus the second line of defence runs up into the first; brilliant success springing out of clear vision. The sentences in which the apostle gives practical proof of his insight and appreciation form one of the golden utterances of this Epistle.[2] It is the one passage in the two Epistles to the Corinthian Church kindred in its doctrinal drift to

[1] 2 *Cor.* ii. 16.   [2] *Ibid.* iii. 6-11.

the teaching of the Epistles to the Galatian and Roman Churches concerning the law. It is a two-edged sword, which may be used either for defence of St. Paul's apostleship, or in defence of his conception of Christianity. If his apostleship be admitted, then we have here an authoritative exposition of the nature of Christianity. If the correctness of the exposition be conceded, then it makes for St. Paul's apostleship, for he certainly possessed qualities fitting him in a peculiar degree to be the propagator of such a religion. The apostle's own mind seems to oscillate between the two lines of inference. At first the apologetic interest seems to be in the ascendant; but when he has once entered on a description of the economy whereof he claims to be a fit minister, he forgets himself, and launches out into an enthusiastic eulogium of New Testament religion, as the religion of the *spirit*, of *life*, and of *righteousness*, as opposed to legalism, the religion of the letter, of death, and of condemnation, so giving us an utterance not merely serving a temporary apologetic purpose, but of permanent didactic value. Whatever impression it made on the Corinthian Church, it leaves no doubt in our minds as to St. Paul's peculiar fitness to be an apostle of the Christian faith. Who so fit to propagate the religion of the spirit, of life, and of justification by faith, as the man who had by bitter experience proved legalism to be indeed a religion of condemnation and death, and to whom Christianity had come as a veritable year of jubilee, proclaiming liberty to the captives and the opening of prison doors to them that are bound? Of this experience, however, the apostle *says* nothing here, though doubtless he thinks of it as he writes. It suits his purpose rather to refer to another element of sufficiency, *straightforward sincerity*, standing in contrast as it does to the double dealing of his opponents. His argument now takes this turn : " The religion of spirit and life, eternal because perfect,[1] has nothing to hide ; the better it is known the more acceptable it will be ; it is only the religion of written rules, and legal bondage, and fear, that needs a veil to cover its inherent defects. I therefore am congenially outspoken, as becomes the servant of a religion, not of mystery, but of light, bright and glorious as the sun. I am not one of your huckstering merchants who adulterate their wares.[2] I convey the truth in Jesus, in its simplicity and purity, from land to land ; in this differing from my opponents, who mix gospel and law to the injury of their customers. Not only am I sincere, speaking nothing but the truth, but I am frank, speaking the whole truth, herein differing even from Moses, who put a veil on his face." At this point the apostle may appear to lapse into a rabbinical way of thinking, but the thought wrapped up in his allegory of the veil is clear, and as precious as it is clear. The law did not announce its own transitoriness ; it could not afford to do so. It had to practise reserve to uphold its authority. If it had said plainly, " I am for a time, I am but a means to an end," it would have encouraged disrespect for its requirements. Therefore, just because it was a defective religion it had to be a religion of mystery. Christianity, on the other hand,

---

[1] 2 *Cor.* iii. 11.
[2] *Ibid.* ii. 17 ; καπηλεύοντες, another of St. Paul's strong graphic words in this context, found here only in the New Testament.

needs no such veil; the more plainly its ministers speak the better. The frank man is the fit man, the most successful, the God-appointed.[1]

3. But the treasure is in a fragile earthen vessel, and that may seem to detract from the fitness. Far from admitting that it does, however, St. Paul rather insists on the fact as a third argument in support of his claim to be an apostle. "I have," he says in effect, "earned the right to be regarded as the apostle of the Gentiles by manifold sufferings, endured in connection with my work." He has already used this argument in his Epistle to the Galatians, expressing it in these pathetic terms: "Henceforth let no man trouble me, for I bear branded on my body the marks of Jesus."[2] The words, as Hausrath finely remarks, suggest the picture of an old general, who bares his breast before his rebellious legions, and shows them the wound-prints which prove that he is not unworthy to be called their commander.[3] The apostle resumes the plea and urges it with great force and with much iteration, in the Epistle now under consideration, the passages in which it recurs rising to the dignity and grandeur of the greatest utterances to be found within the whole range of tragic poetry, and constituting together what might not unfitly be called the "Pauline Iliad." The first of these impassioned outbursts begins at chap. iv. ver. 7, and, running through a series of bold paradoxes, ends by comparing the life of the writer to a slow, cruel crucifixion, or to a continual

---

[1] 2 *Cor.* iv. 7. [2] *Gal.* vi. 17.
[3] *Neutestamentliche Zeitgeschichte*, vol. ii. p. 584.

descent from the cross.¹ The apostle returns to the theme again in the sixth chapter, this time entering much more into detail. Appealing to the Corinthians to see to it that they receive not in vain the message of reconciliation so earnestly delivered by his lips, he backs up the appeal by a reference to those manifold sufferings which at once gave him a claim on their consideration, and commended him as a true apostle.² In a third passage of similar character, in the eleventh chapter,³ he reaches the climax of his argument from tribulation, taking occasion there to mention some particulars in his history not elsewhere alluded to, one being that five times he had received from the Jews forty stripes save one.⁴ He is not ashamed to mention such ignominious facts; he rather glories in them, because they all tend to vindicate his claim to be the divinely-commissioned apostle of the Gentiles. It is even possible that in enduring such evil treatment at the hands of the Jews, he was glad to have an opportunity of bearing for Christ's sake what he had made others bear, as a sort of atonement for past sin.

The chapter from which the last citation is made is one of four (chaps. x.–xiii.), which are distinguished from the rest of the Epistle by a bitterly controversial tone. The difference is so marked as to have suggested the idea that they originally formed a distinct letter, the very letter indeed referred to in 2 *Cor.* vii. 8, which is there

---

¹ So Stanley (*St. Paul's Epistle to the Corinthians*), who takes νέκρωσιν to mean, not "dying" nor "death," but "deadness." "It is as if he had said, We are living corpses. It is a continual 'Descent from the Cross.'"

² 2 *Cor.* vi. 5-10.   ³ *Ibid.* xi. 23-33.   ⁴ *Ibid.* xi. 24.

spoken of as having by its severity deeply wounded the feelings of the Corinthian Church. The suggestion, though not without plausibility, is not hastily to be adopted. The diversity between the two parts of the Epistle can easily be reconciled with its unity by the supposition that in the earlier part the apostle had in his view mainly the faithful majority in the Corinthian Church who had supported his authority in the case of discipline, and were generally friendly to him, and that after he had written what he had to say to them in a tone of gentleness, he turned his thoughts to the minority and the men by whose malign influence they had been misled, and dealt with them as they deserved, with a rod rather than in a spirit of meekness.[1]

These four chapters contain copious materials bearing on all the three branches of St. Paul's argument in defence of his apostleship. To the first head, the argument from insight, belongs chap. xii. 1–6, where he boasts of the visions and revelations he had enjoyed more than fourteen years previous to the date of the Epistle, that is about the time of his conversion. To the second head, the argument from success, belongs chapter x. 12–18, where the apostle refers to the wide area over which his missionary labours had extended. It is noticeable that he emphasises the *pioneering* character of his work not less than its extent; here again, as in so many

---

[1] Henrici (*Das zweite Sendschreiben des Apostel Paulus an die Korinthier*, 1887) points out that if the Epistle had ended with the details about the collection for the poor in chap. ix., it would have been a fragment, and that chaps. x.–xiii. were necessary to explain and justify the hard judgments incidentally pronounced in the earlier chapters on the character of the Judaists.

other connections, with an eye to the contrasted conduct of his opponents. They could point to no Churches founded by their efforts, but only to Churches already established which they had sought to disturb and corrupt by their sectarian animosities and legalist doctrines. He, on the other hand, had never entered on another man's province, taking up work already begun, either to further or to mar it, but had always broken new ground. Which of the two modes of action was most worthy of an apostle he would leave them to judge. To the third head, the argument from suffering, belong, over and above the passages already cited containing the long catalogues of woes, all the places in which Paul alludes to his refusal to receive from the Church of Corinth any contributions towards his maintenance. His adversaries appear to have put a sinister construction on this refusal, suggesting that it sprang from his not feeling quite sure of his ground. "He calls himself an apostle," so they seem to have argued; "why then does he not use his privilege as an apostle, and claim maintenance from his converts like the other apostles? Evidently it is because he is afraid lest his pretensions should not be recognised." Thoroughly selfish themselves, these base-minded men could not so much as imagine the generous motives by which the apostle was really actuated. They took for granted that he would be glad to get money from all the Churches if he could. They even seem to have gone the length of insinuating that he did get it in a roundabout way; that in fact that collection for the poor in Palestine, which he was always making such a fuss about, was merely a scheme for getting money into his own pocket while pretending to be very independent. Such seems to be the plain sense of chap. xii. 16–18, the first sentence giving the substance of what St. Paul's enemies said of him, and some members of the Corinthian Church were base enough to believe. "He does not burden us with his maintenance: no, not directly; but he is crafty, catches us with guile, in connection with that collection." Feeling keenly the humiliation of being obliged to answer such a charge, the apostle replies: "Did I make gain of you by any of them whom I sent unto you? I asked Titus to go, and I sent with him the brother. Did Titus overreach you? Walked we not in the same spirit, in the same steps?" The apostle's true motive in the whole matter of his support was a noble spirit of self-sacrifice, which, itself divine, was a sure mark that his mission was from God. The suggestion of his enemies, that if he were sure of his apostolic standing he would demand a maintenance, resembled Satan's suggestion to Jesus: "If thou be the Son of God, command that these stones be made bread." "If thou be an apostle," said these children of Satan, "command the Churches to support thee." But the reasoning was as inconclusive in the one case as in the other. Jesus showed Himself to be the Son of God just by refusing to turn his Sonship to His own advantage. Paul showed himself to be an apostle of God by refusing with equal steadfastness to set his personal interests above the public interests of the divine kingdom. Though he was an apostle he was willing to suffer in every way, and by that will to suffer for God's glory and man's good, he gave the most convincing evidence that he was a true apostle; not one who arrogated the dignity to himself, but called of God thereunto.

In the foregoing statement we have been occupied exclusively with those parts of the two Epistles which bear on the question of the apostleship, and have met with little that throws light on St. Paul's conception of Christianity. The doctrinal element is indeed not abundant, even for one who is in quest of it. It is, however, not altogether wanting. Besides the important passage already referred to, exhibiting a contrast between the legal and the Christian dispensations, the Second Epistle contains two striking *logia* bearing on the significance of Christ's death. These are, "If one died for all, then all died,"[1] and, "Him who knew not sin, He made sin on our behalf, that we might become the righteousness of God in Him."[2] These great Pauline words show two complementary aspects of the apostle's doctrine of the atonement. The First Epistle contains, in the eighth and fifteenth chapters, important contributions to the doctrine of Christ's Person.

[1] *2 Cor.* v. 14.   [2] *Ibid.* v. 21.

CHAPTER V

THE EPISTLE TO THE ROMANS—ITS AIM

THIS Epistle is distinguished from those already considered belonging to the same group by broadly marked characteristics. In the first place, it is more placid in tone. If it be indeed a contribution to the vindication of Paul's Gentile gospel against Judaism, it contains few traces of the controversial spirit. Polemic passes into calm didactic statement. Then, secondly, while the present Epistle contains much in common with the Epistle to the Galatians, we find that the same truths are set forth here in a more expanded and elaborate form. In the third place, to the old materials amplified, the Epistle adds a new phase of Pauline thought, in the important section in which an endeavour is made to reconcile the apostle's views of Christianity with the prerogatives of Israel as an elect people. This section, consisting of chapters ix.–xi., if not the most important, is at least the most distinctive part of the Epistle, presenting what has not inappropriately been called St. Paul's philosophy of history.

It is natural to assume that these characteristics are due to the circumstances amidst which the Epistle was written. The historical spirit of modern exegesis does not readily acquiesce in the view which, up till the time of Baur, had been almost universally accepted, that the Epistle to the Romans, unlike the Epistles to the Galatian and Corinthian Churches, is a purely didactic treatise on Christian theology, for which no other occasion need be sought than the desire of the writer to give a full connected statement of the faith as he conceived it. More and more it has been felt that such a production is hardly what we expect from an apostle, and that, however didactic or systematic it may appear, the Epistle in question must have been, not less than its companion Epistles, an occasional writing.

There are indeed still those who lean to the old traditional opinion, and seek the initiative, not in any outward circumstances, whether of the Church at Rome, or of the Church generally, but solely in the apostle's mind, and in his wish to draw up an adequate statement of the Christian faith. Among these is Godet, certainly a most worthy representative of the class, in all whose commentaries one discovers that faculty of psychological divination which is the sure mark of exegetical genius, and whose exposition of Romans cannot be charged with the "oppressive monotony"[1] that has been complained of as characterising expository treatises on this Epistle written in the interest of dogmatic theology. Godet's idea is, that St. Paul was in the habit of giving such developed teaching as we find in Romans to all the Churches he had founded, and that he wrote an Epistle

---

[1] Mangold speaks of the *drückende Monotonie* of the dogmatic commentaries. *Vide* his *Der Römerbrief und die Anfänge der Römischen Gemeinde*, p. 20 (1866).

to the Church in Rome simply in order to give, in a written form, to an important body of Christians with which he had not come into personal contact, the instruction which he had given *vivâ voce* to the churches in Ephesus, Thessalonica, Corinth, etc.¹ This is an assumption which readily suggests itself to minds familiar with theological systems, and accustomed to regard all the doctrines of an elaborate creed as essential elements of the faith. But the position is one which it is easier to assume than to prove. Godet offers no proof, but contents himself with referring to a work by Thiersch, published nearly fifty years ago, which, by mistake, he represents as having very solidly demonstrated the apostle's practice to have been as alleged.² The assertion that the Epistle to the Romans is only a sample of the writer's ordinary teaching stands very much in need of proof. The presumption is all the other way. The two Epistles to the Thessalonians, we have seen, supply evidence to the contrary, and the occasional character of the Epistles to the Galatians and the Corinthians, which contain more advanced teaching, justifies the inference that the Epistle to the Romans also is an occasional writing containing special instruction called for by exceptional and urgent circumstances. To this it must be added, that the whole notion of Godet and those who agree with him is not easily reconcilable with a just

¹ *Commentaire sur l'épitre aux Romains*, vol. i. pp. 122, 123.
² *Commentaire*, vol. i. p. 120. The work of Thiersch referred to is *Versuch zur Herstellung des historischen Standpunkts für die Kritik der neutestamentlichen Schriften* (1845). Thiersch distinctly states that the Epistle to the Romans was called forth by the controversy with the Judaists. *Vide* p. 235 of the above-named work.

conception of the apostolic vocation and temper. An apostle is in spirit and mental habit a very different man from a systematic theologian. He deals in inspirations rather than in laborious theological reflection. He has neither the time nor the patience for system building. He may have in his mind many deep thoughts, but he keeps them till they are wanted. He utters his thoughts under constraint of urgent need. He speaks rather than writes, because speaking is more spontaneous than writing; and when he writes it is *currente calamo*, and under pressure of emergent demands.

What the precise situation, in all its details, was, which the apostle had in view, when he wrote this Epistle, it may be difficult, or even impossible, to determine. But of one thing it does seem possible to be assured, viz., that the Epistle belongs to the literature, and deals with a phase, of the Judaistic controversy. One could even tell *à priori* what phase it must be with which the last of the controversial group of Epistles is occupied. Already, the apostle has discussed two aspects of the great quarrel, those relating to the perpetual obligation of the Jewish law, and the qualifications for the apostleship. The one topic remaining to be taken up is the prerogative or primacy of Israel. Without doubt it must have its turn. It had its own proper place in the dialectics of the debate, and it may be taken for granted that a dispute so keen about matters so vital will not stop till it has run its natural course. The fire will burn till the fuel is exhausted. The rapid development of Gentile Christianity made it inevitable that the question should arise, What does the existing state of matters mean? Gentiles are pouring in increasing numbers into the Church. Jews, with comparatively few exceptions, are holding aloof in sullen unbelief: are these facts to be construed as a cancelling of Israel's election; or, if the election stands, does it not necessarily involve the illegitimacy of Gentile Christianity? The question may have suggested itself to some of the more reflecting at the very commencement of the Gentile movement, and to St. Paul especially it may have been all along clear that it must come to the front ere long, but it could not become a burning question till conversions from heathendom had taken place on a great scale. The first effort of the Judaist would naturally be to nip the new departure in the bud, by compelling Gentile converts to comply with Jewish customs. The next would be to cripple a movement which could not be crushed, by disputing the apostolic standing and assailing the character of its leader. When both attempts had been rendered futile, by the triumphant progress of the movement in spite of all opposition, the only course open would be to enter a protest in the name of the elect people, and pronounce the evangelisation of the Gentiles a wrong done to Israel.

It is to the temper which would enter such a protest, or to any extent sympathise with it, that the apostle addresses himself in the ninth, tenth, and eleventh chapters of the Epistle to the Romans. That this part of the Epistle at least has to do with the final phase of the Judaistic opposition to a free independent Christianity I take to be self-evident. The only thing that may seem open to doubt is, whether it was worth while taking any notice of the sullen mood of the men who were disaffected, and out of sympathy with the cause St. Paul had so much at heart. Could he not have afforded to treat it with contempt as utterly impotent? For what could the protesters do; what would they be at? They had no practicable programme to propose. Could they seriously wish the work of Gentile evangelisation to be stopped till the bulk of the Jewish people had been converted to the faith, insisting on the principle *the Jew first*, not merely in the sense that the Jew should get the first offer, but in the sense that all the world must wait till the Jews *en masse* accepted the offer? If they had not the hardihood to make so absurd a demand, there was no course open to them but to accept the situation and reconcile themselves with the best grace possible to accomplished facts.

Had St. Paul been a man of the world, he might have adopted the attitude of silent contempt. But being a man of truly Christlike spirit, he could not so treat any class of men bearing however unworthily the Christian name. He knew well that a disaffected party was none the less formidable that it was conscious of defeat, and had no outlook for the future; that in such a case chronic alienation and ultimate separation were to be apprehended. He would do his utmost to prevent such a disaster. And it is obvious in what spirit such a delicate task must be gone about to have any chance of success. An irenical generous tone was indispensable. No bitter irritating words must be indulged in, but only such thoughts and language employed as tended to enlighten, soothe, and conciliate. The Epistle to the

Romans fully meets these requirements by an entire absence of the controversial style. It has been customary to explain this feature of the Epistle by the fact of its having been written to a Church with which Paul had no personal relations, and this may count for something. But there is a deeper and a worthier reason for the contrast in tone between this Epistle and those written to the Galatian and Corinthian Churches. The whole situation is changed. Then Paul was fighting for existence with his back to the wall, now he writes as one conscious that the cause of Gentile Christianity is safe Therefore, while careful to do justice to his convictions, he expresses himself throughout as one who can afford to be generous. Thus in chapters ix.–xi., while maintaining that God had the right to disinherit Israel (ix.), and that she had fully deserved such a doom (x.), he declares the disinheritance to be only temporary and remedial, and anticipates a time when Jew and Gentile shall be united by a common faith in Christ (xi.). Then he not only abstains personally from a tone of triumph in speaking of unbelieving Israel, but he earnestly warns the Gentile members of the Roman Church from indulging in a boastful spirit.[1] And the irenical tone, conspicuous in these three chapters, pervades the whole Epistle. In the first eight chapters stern things are said about Jewish moral shortcomings, and Judaism judged by its results is pronounced not less a failure than heathenism.[2] At the same time it is admitted that the Jewish people possessed eminent and valuable religious distinctions.[3] Similar is the treatment of the

[1] *Rom.* xi. 16-21.   [2] *Ibid.* ii.   [3] *Ibid.* iii. 1, 2.

Jewish law. While it is declared to be of no value for the attainment of righteousness, not less peremptorily than in the Epistle to the Galatians, its ethical worth is recognised with a frankness which we miss in the earlier Epistle.[1]

The situation as above described explains not only the calm, irenical, didactic tone of the Epistle, but also its broad comprehensive method. At first sight it seems as if it were top-heavy. If the writer's aim be to deal with a new Judaistic objection to Gentile Christianity, based on the prerogative of Israel, why not content himself with making the statement in chapters ix.-xi. ? To what purpose that elaborate argumentative exposition of the gospel as he understood it in the first eight chapters ?

Baur's answer to this question was in effect that these eight chapters are an introduction to the next three, which form the proper kernel of the Epistle.[2] I do not accept this statement as altogether satisfactory, though I frankly own that I would rather regard the three chapters as the *kernel*, than relegate them to the subordinate position assigned them by the dogmatic school of interpreters, that of a mere *appendix*. But the truth is, that these famous chapters are neither kernel nor appendix, but an integral part of one great whole. They deal with a question of national privilege. But there is a previous question involved, that as to the claims of Christianity. For the position taken up by opponents virtually is, the rights of Israel *versus* the rights of universal Christianity. The proper antithesis

[1] *Rom.* vii. 12.   [2] *Paulus der Apostel,* i. 351.

to that is, the rights of Christianity first, and Israel's rights only in the second place, and as far as compatible with the supreme interests of the true religion. The Epistle to the Romans is devoted to the advocacy of this position, the first eight chapters dealing with the larger, more general claims of Christianity, the next three dealing with the less important narrower question as to the real value of Israel's claim. Obviously both sections of the Epistle are essential to the purpose in hand. And that purpose guides the course of the apostle's thought throughout. In brief what he says is this: " Christianity is in its nature a universal religion. It is needed by the world at large, by Gentiles and by Jews alike. For both heathenism and Judaism, judged by their practical results, are failures. Christianity is not a failure. It solves the problem aimed at by all religion ; brings men into blessed relations with God, and makes them really righteous. Christianity, therefore, must have free course; no prescriptive rights can be allowed to stand in its way. As for the Jewish people I am heartily sorry for them. They are my countrymen, they are also God's people. But their right is not absolute, and they deserve to forfeit it. Yet I do not believe they are permanently doomed to forfeiture. God will continue to love them, and in the course of His beneficent providence will give effect to their claims in a way compatible with Christian universalism and with Gentile interests."

Thus by a train of thought of which the foregoing is the gist, does the apostle storm the last stronghold of Judaists without ever mentioning their name. The absence of any allusion to Judaistic opponents in the

Epistle has been adduced as a reason for calling in question its connection with the Judaistic controversy. The writer, we are told, betrays preoccupation in the treatment of his subject, but it is not relative to Judeo-Christians, or to Judaisers, but to the Jews and to Jewish incredulity.[1] As if the one reference excluded the other! The only effective way to meet Judaistic antagonism to Gentile Christianity in its final phase, was to form a just estimate of the true value of the pretensions of the Jewish people based on their national religion and their covenanted relation to God. It is in harmony with the irenical spirit of our Epistle that this is done without making the controversial reference manifest.

But if Judaistic tendencies were the real though hidden foe, where were they to be found? Within the Church of Rome; or without, and threatening to invade that Church, and work mischief there as elsewhere; or merely in St. Paul's own mind, prompt to conceive new possible forms of antagonism, and restless till it had seen its way to intellectual victory over these, and found solutions of all religious problems arising out of the Pauline conception of Christianity? All three views have found influential advocates, and it is by no means easy to decide confidently between them. As to the last of the three, which has been adopted by Weiss,[2] there is no objection to be taken to it on theoretical or à priori grounds. As I have already stated in the second chapter, I believe that St. Paul was his own

---

[1] So Oltramare, *Commentaire sur l'épitre aux Romains* (1881), vol. i. p. 48.
[2] *Vide* his *Introduction to the New Testament*, vol. i. p. 306.

severest critic, and that he did not need external antagonism to indicate to him the weak points of his religious theory, or to suggest the relative apologetic problems, and that when once these presented themselves, both his reason and his conscience would imperiously demand solutions. Of these problems the last to suggest itself might well be that relating to Jewish prerogative, as it naturally arose out of the extensive development of Gentile Christianity. And it is not inconceivable that, when the apostle had thought himself clear on this final apologetic topic, he might feel an impulse to reduce his thoughts to writing, and in doing so to work out in literary form his whole religious philosophy from that point of view, and so " bring as it were the spiritual product of the last years to his own consciousness."[1] Nor does it seem incredible that he might send such a writing in epistolary form to the Roman Church without any urgent external occasion, simply because he deemed it fitting that a church presumably Gentile for the most part in its membership, and situated in the metropolis of the world, should be the recipient of a work containing a statement and defence of Christianity as a universal religion from the pen of its apostle.

While recognising the legitimacy of the theory propounded by Weiss, I can hardly regard it as probable, or as justified by any supposed impossibility of giving any other account of the matter. I doubt, in the first place, if the question discussed in chapters ix.–xi. was so new to the apostle's mind as the theory implies. I

[1] Weiss, *Introduction*, vol. i. p. 306.

rather incline to think that all the possible issues involved in the Judaistic controversy were clear to his view from an early period, and also the answers to all possible objections to his conception of Christianity. Then, on the other hand, I think that he would keep these answers to himself, till a need arose for communicating them to others. One fails to see why he should trouble others with his thoughts on the comparatively speculative topic of the prerogatives of Israel, if nobody was stirring the question. Why deal with a difficult problem like that, not vital to faith, before it had arisen? At the very least St. Paul must have regarded it as possible that the question would be raised ere long in the Church to which he sent the letter treating it. That this would happen was not only possible but probable. Assuming with Weiss, and the majority of recent writers on the Epistle, that the membership of the Roman Church was mainly of Gentile extraction, how natural that men connected with the Judaistic propagandism should regard with envy and chagrin a flourishing Christian community in the capital of the empire! How unwelcome to their mind these increasing signs that the stream of spiritual life was cutting out for itself a new channel, and leaving Palestine, formerly the centre of religious influence, high and dry! What more likely than that the impulse should arise in their hearts to make a last effort to recover lost power, and if possible win over to their side a church which, though Gentile, might not yet be decidedly Pauline? An attempt of this kind, however desperate, was by no means improbable. It might even have been in contemplation when the apostle wrote his Epistle, and as Weizsäcker suggests, the fact coming to his knowledge may have been what determined him to take that step as a means of frustrating by anticipation the sinister scheme.[1]

If the membership of the Roman Church was mainly of *Jewish* birth, the mischief would not need to be imported. What the actual fact was in the matter of nationality has since the days of Dr. Baur been a *quæstio vexata* for theologians. Baur himself was a strenuous advocate of the Jewish hypothesis, and through his influence, reinforced by that of Mangold, it became for a time the prevailing view. But the weighty interposition of Weizsäcker on behalf of the opposite hypothesis changed the current of opinion, and now it may be said to be the generally accepted theory that the Church of Rome, at the time our Epistle was written, was predominantly Gentile. In absence of information from other sources as to the origin and composition of the Church, disputants are obliged to rely on the general impression which the Epistle makes on their minds, and on individual texts and phrases. The advocates of either hypothesis are able to explain away to their own satisfaction the passages founded on by the champions of the opposite hypothesis. Thus, "all the nations among whom are ye,"[2] seems beyond dispute to make for a Gentile constituency. But the supporter of the rival opinion contends that it suited the apostle's purpose in the connection of thought to include the Jews among the peoples to which his commission extended. In like

[1] Vide *Das apostolische Zeitalter*, p. 441.   [2] Rom. i. 5, 6.

manner the expression, "I speak to you that are Gentiles,"[1] is disposed of by the remark that, if the membership of the Church had been mainly Gentile, it would not have been necessary to state that he addressed himself to such. On the other hand, the pro-Jewish allusions are disposed of by patrons of the Gentile hypothesis with at least equal facility. "Abraham our father"[2] finds its parallel in the phrase "our fathers" occurring in the First Epistle to the Corinthians,[3] and "ye are become dead to the law through the body of Christ,"[4] might be said to Gentile believers in Rome with as much propriety as that God sent His Son "to redeem them that were under the law" to Gentile Christians in Galatia.[5] I do not mean to suggest, however, that the balance is even between the two parties. The weight of argument inclines to the Gentile side. While I say this I must acknowledge that my own mind is influenced not so much by particular texts, but rather by the general consideration that the hypothesis of a Gentile constituency best fits in to the situation required by the Epistle. In that case the Roman Church becomes the proof and symbol of that triumph of Gentile Christianity which *ex hypothesi* is the occasion of the complaint wherewith the apostle feels called on to deal.

It is important to observe that the determination of the question as to the nationality of Roman Christians is in no way necessary to the understanding of the Epistle to the Roman Church. The one thing indispensable is to grasp firmly the fact that the Epistle was meant to

---

[1] *Rom.* xi. 13. [2] *Ibid.* iv. 1. [3] 1 *Cor.* x. 1.
[4] *Rom.* vii. 4. [5] *Gal.* iv. 4, 5.

deal with the final manifestation of Judaistic sentiment, the jealousy awakened by the progress of Gentile evangelisation. That is far more certain than either of the views as to the composition of the Church, as is shown by the fact that the advocates of both are at one as to the aim of the Epistle. Who the Roman Christians were may for ever remain doubtful; but that jealousy for the prerogative of Israel existed when St. Paul wrote his Epistle to the Romans may be regarded as beyond doubt, and that the Roman Church was somehow connected with it may be inferred from the simple fact of the Epistle which handles the topic being addressed to it.

Besides his chief aim in writing the Epistle the apostle might have other subordinate ends in view, and among these one arising out of his new mission plans doubtless had a place. To these plans he refers in chap. xv. 22-33. He had wound up one chapter of his mission history by the settlement of the Corinthian troubles. He was about to visit Jerusalem, carrying the gifts of the Gentile Churches founded by himself to the poor saints of the holy city. That done, he will be ready and eager to break new ground, and to visit the regions of Western Europe, bearing to the nations the gospel of peace. For this new campaign Rome will form the natural base of operations. He must make the acquaintance of the Church there, and get her goodwill and cordial support in his new enterprise. In view of this great missionary project, our Epistle may be regarded as a pioneer, or preparer of the way; a first step towards the execution of the contemplated operations. In the circumstances it was almost a matter of course that the apostle should write a letter of some sort to the Church in Rome. But something more than mission-schemes is needed to account for the actual character and contents of the letter he did write. Possibilities of misunderstanding due to sinister influences, threatening to appear or actually at work, must have been in his view.

It is not an altogether idle fancy that in composing this remarkable letter the apostle's mind was influenced by the thought that he was writing to a church having its seat in *Rome*. His religious inspiration came from above, but it is permissible to suppose that his theological genius was stimulated by the image of the imperial city presenting itself to his susceptible imagination. The Epistle is truly imperial in style. It deals in large comprehensive categories: Jew and Gentile, Greeks and barbarians, wise and unwise. It draws within the scope of its survey the whole human race, throughout the entire range of its religious history. It breathes the spirit of a truly imperial ambition. The writer aspires to the conquest of the world, and holds himself bound to preach the gospel to all nations for the obedience of faith, that Christ may become in the spiritual sphere what Cæsar was in the political. And he is animated by a magnanimity becoming the ambassador of One whom he regards as by divine right and destiny the universal Lord. He believes in no unconquerable enmities or final alienations. He will have all men be saved, all peoples reconciled to God and to one another; Jew and Gentile, united in a common brotherhood, and living peaceably together under the benign rule of King Jesus. The leading aim of the Epistle, as we have seen, required the apostle so to write, and apart altogether from the exigencies of the situation, the grand style of thinking came natural to him. But the consciousness that his letter was going to Rome made it all the easier for a man of his kingly temper. Before the majesty of the greatest city in the world meaner natures might feel abashed. But St. Paul was not ashamed or afraid either to preach there or to send a letter thither. He could rise to the occasion, witness this magnificent Epistle!

CHAPTER VI

THE EPISTLE TO THE ROMANS—THE TRAIN OF THOUGHT

THE theme of the first eight chapters is "the gospel of God," for the whole world, needed by all men, available for all who will receive it in the obedience of faith, and thoroughly efficient in the case of all who so receive it; a gospel which the apostle is not ashamed to preach anywhere, because he believes it to be the power of God unto salvation.

The writer enters at once on the explanation of the nature of this gospel. "Therein is revealed a righteousness of God from faith to faith."[1] These words contain only a preliminary hint of St. Paul's doctrine concerning the gospel. He does not expect his readers to understand at once what he means by δικαιοσύνη θεοῦ. He simply introduces the topic to provoke curiosity, and create a desire for a further unfolding, to be given in due season. Therefore it is better, with the Revised Version, to translate "*a* righteousness of God," than with the Authorised Version, "*the* righteousness of God"; for the idea the words are intended to express is by no means, for the first readers, a familiar theological commonplace, but a peculiar Pauline conception standing

[1] *Rom.* i. 17.

in need of careful explanation. Two things, however, are clearly indicated in this preliminary announcement: that the gospel, as St. Paul understands it, is saving through *faith*, and that it is a *universal* gospel; "a power of God unto salvation to every one that believeth, to the Jew first, and also to the Greek."

Having thus proclaimed the cardinal truth that salvation is through faith, the apostle proceeds to shut all men up to faith by demonstrating the universality of sin.[1] The section of the Epistle devoted to this purpose presents a grim, repulsive picture of human depravity, and on this account it may appear a most unwelcome and uncongenial feature in a writing having for its express theme the praise of divine grace. But this dark unpleasant excursus is relevant and necessary to the argument in hand. What more directly fitted to commend the Pauline doctrine both as to the gracious nature and the universal destination of the gospel than a proof of the universal prevalence of sin? If sin be universal, then God's grace seems the only open way to salvation, and no ground can be found in man why the way should not be equally open to all. There is no moral difference worth mentioning, all distinctions disappear in presence of the one all-embracing category, *sinners*. However disagreeable, therefore, it may be to have it elaborately proved that that category does embrace all, however unpleasant reading the proof may be, however hideous and humiliating the picture held up to our view, we cannot quarrel with the apostle's logic, but must be content to take the bitter with the sweet, the dark with the bright.

[1] *Rom.* i. 18 ; ii. 24.

Far from being a blot on the Epistle, this *sin-section*, as we may call it, is one of its merits, when regarded as an attempt at a fuller statement of St. Paul's conception of the gospel than any supplied in previous Epistles. We miss such a section in the Epistle to the Galatians. Hints of a doctrine of sin are indeed not wanting in that Epistle,[1] but in comparison with the elaborate statement in the Epistle to the Romans they are very scanty, and give hardly an idea of what might be said on the subject. For what we have here is not vague gentle allusions, but a tremendous exhaustive indictment which overwhelms us with shame, and crushes our pride into the dust, the one effect being produced by the description of Gentile sinfulness in chap. i. vers. 18–32, the other by the description of Jewish sinfulness in the two following chapters.

Remarkable in the former of these two delineations is the exact knowledge displayed by the apostle of the hideous depravity of Pagan morals, and also the unshrinking way in which he speaks of it, not hesitating out of false delicacy to allude to the most abominable of Gentile vices, and to call them by their true names. All who know the Greek and Roman literature of the period are aware that the picture here given of contemporary Paganism, in respect both of religion and morals, is absolutely faithful to fact. Never perhaps in the history of the world did mankind sink so low in superstition and immorality as in the apostolic age; and it was fitting that the apostle of the Gentiles should say what he thought of it in an Epistle to the

[1] *Gal.* ii. 15, 16; iii. 10, 19.

Romans, for in the city of Rome, the folly and wickedness of mankind reached their maximum. "The first age," writes Renan, "of our era has an infernal stamp which belongs to it alone; the age of Borgia alone can be compared to it in point of wickedness."[1] Surely it could not be difficult for men immersed in such a foul pit of senile superstition and unblushing profligacy to attain such a sense of guilt as should make them feel that their only hope of salvation lay in the mercy of God! But, alas, men get accustomed to evil, and are apt to regard all as right that is in fashion. A moral tonic is needed to invigorate conscience, and produce a healthy reaction of the moral sense against prevalent evil. This the apostle understood well, hence the abrupt reference to the wrath of God immediately after the initial statement of the nature of the gospel.[2] Here, as in reference to the whole sin-section, one's first impression is apt to be: how ungenial, what a lack of tact in thrusting in such unwelcome thoughts in connection with the good tidings of salvation! But the writer knows what he is about, and his usual tact is not likely to have deserted him at the very outset of so carefully considered a writing. He knows that his gospel will be welcomed only by those to whom the prevalent life of the age appears utterly black and abominable. The first thing therefore to be done is, to call forth the slumbering conscience into vigorous action. For this purpose he prefaces his description of Pagan

---

[1] *Melanges*, p. 167.
[2] *Rom.* i. 18. The idea of a revelation of wrath will be discussed at a later stage.

manners by a blunt downright expression of his own moral judgment upon them, pronouncing them to be the legitimate object of divine wrath.

In his indictment against the Gentile world, St. Paul has no difficulty in making out a case, his only difficulty is in making the picture black enough. But when he passes from Gentiles to Jews, his task becomes more delicate. He has now to deal with a people accustomed to speak of Gentiles as "sinners," and to think of themselves by comparison as righteous, and who could read such a description of Pagan morals as he has just given with self-complacent satisfaction. Therefore he makes this very state of mind his starting-point in addressing himself to his countrymen, and begins his demonstration of Jewish sinfulness by a statement amounting to a charge of hypocrisy. In effect he says: "I know what you are thinking, O ye Jews, as ye read these damning sentences about Pagans. 'Oh,' think ye, 'these wicked Gentiles! thank God, we are not like them.' But, I tell you, you *are* like them, in the essentials of conduct if not in special details, and to all this you add the sin of hypocritical censoriousness, judging others while you ought rather to be judging yourselves." It is noticeable that, though plainly alluded to, the Jew is not named. The reason may be that the apostle wishes absolutely to deny the right of any man to judge others; as if he would say: "The heathen are bad, but where is the man who has a right to cast stones at his brother man?" He knows very well where the men who claim such a right are to be found. He does not at first say where, but it goes without being said, every Jew reading the Epistle would know, for he would be conscious that he had just been doing the thing condemned. Having denounced the Jewish vice of judging, Paul goes on by a series of interrogations to charge Jews with the same sins previously laid to the charge of the Gentiles.[1] These implied assertions may seem a libel on a people proud of their God-given law; but doubtless the apostle was well informed as to the state of Jewish morality, and spoke as one conscious that he had no reason to fear contradiction.

It is important to notice that St. Paul's purpose in this sin-section is not simply to prove that both Pagans and Jews are great sinners, but to show that they are such sinners in spite of all in their respective religions that tended to keep them in the right way. He pronounces a verdict not merely on men but on systems, and means to suggest that both Paganism and Judaism are failures. He holds that even Paganism contained some elements of truth making for right conduct. He credits the Gentiles with some natural knowledge of God and of duty.[2] His charge against them is, that they held or held down [3] the truth in unrighteousness, and were unwilling to retain God in their knowledge. It may be thought that this judgment of the Pagan world is too pessimistic, and that there was a brighter side to the picture which is not sufficiently taken into account. But in any case it is to be observed that the pessimism of the author does not take the form of

---

[1] *Rom.* ii. 21-23.   [2] *Ibid.* i. 19-21; ii. 14, 15.
[3] *Ibid.* i. 18, κατεχόντων.

denying that the Pagans had any light, but rather that of accusing them of not being faithful to the light they had.

To the Jew the apostle concedes a still higher measure of light, representing him as having the great advantage over the Pagan of being in possession of the oracles of God.[1] But he is far from thinking that in this fact the Jew has any ground for assuming airs of superiority as compared with the Gentile. He alludes to the privilege with no intention of playing the part of a special pleader for his race.[2] On the contrary, he holds that the people who were in possession of the law and the promises and the Scriptures were just on that account the more to be blamed for their misconduct. For the benefit of such as made these privileges a ground of self-complacency, he points out that the very Scriptures of which they were so proud brought against the favoured race charges not less severe than he had just brought against the Pagan world.[3]

The apostle concludes his sombre survey of the moral condition of the world with a solemn statement, declaring justification by works of law impossible.[4] It is the negative side of his doctrine of justification based on his doctrine of sin. It applies in the first place and directly to Jews, but by implication and à fortiori to Gentiles.

---

[1] *Rom.* iii. 1, 2.

[2] *Ibid.* iii. 9. Such seems to be the meaning of προεχόμεθα, "are we making excuses for ourselves?" that is, for the people who had the λόγια τοῦ θεοῦ. *Vide* the elaborate discussion on this word in Morison's monograph on *Romans* iii.

[3] *Ibid.* iii. 10-18.   [4] *Ibid.* iii. 20.

Having reached the negative conclusion, the apostle proceeds to state his positive doctrine of salvation in one of the great passages of the Epistle, chap. iii. 21–26, which must occupy our attention hereafter. Here let it be remarked, that we get from this great Pauline text more light on the expression we met with at the commencement—" a righteousness of God." We now begin to understand what this righteousness is, which the apostle regards as the burthen of his gospel. He evidently feels that the expression in itself does not necessarily convey the meaning he attaches to it, for no sooner has he used it than he hastens to add words explanatory of his meaning. " By a righteousness of God," he says in effect, " I mean a righteousness through faith of Christ, unto all believers in Christ." God's righteousness, in St. Paul's sense, does not appear to signify God's personal righteousness, or our personal righteousness conceived of as well pleasing to God, but a righteousness which God gives to those who believe in Jesus; an *objective* righteousness we may call it, not in us, but as it were hovering over us. It seems to be something original the apostle has in mind, for he labours to express his thought about it by a variety of phrases: saying, *e.g.*, that it is a righteousness apart from law, and yet a righteousness witnessed to both by law and by prophets, how or where, he does not here state. Further, he represents it as given to faith. Faith is its sole condition, therefore it is given to *all* who believe, Jew and Gentile alike. Again he speaks of men as made partakers of God's righteousness, δικαιού- μενοι, " justified," *freely,* by His *grace,* which is as much as to say that the righteousness in question is a gift of divine love offered freely to all who believe in Jesus.

Apart from law this righteousness of God is revealed, according to the apostle, who lays great stress on the doctrine, as he feels that otherwise God and salvation would be a monopoly of the Jews.[1] Yet one cannot but note that he is very careful in this Epistle to avoid creating the impression that he undervalues law. Significant in this connection is the twice-used expression "the obedience of faith,"[2] also the curious phrase "the law of faith,"[3] by which boasting is said to be excluded; also the earnestness with which the apostle protests that by his doctrine he does not make void the law through faith, but rather establishes the law.[4] The proof of the statement is held over for a more advanced stage of the argument, as is also the proof of the thesis that by the law is the knowledge of sin.[5] The point to be noticed is the apostle's anxiety to prevent the rise of any prejudicial misunderstanding. It is explained in part by the irenical policy demanded by the situation in view of the writer, in part possibly by his recollecting that he writes to men who as Romans had an inbred reverence for law.

What follows in chapters iv. and v. may be summarised under the general heading of support to the doctrine of justification by faith. The support is threefold, being

---

[1] *Rom.* iii. 29.   [2] *Ibid.* i. 5; xvi. 26.
[3] *Ibid.* iii. 27. Compare the expression νόμος τοῦ πνεύματος τῆς ζωῆς (chap. viii. 2). These various expressions seem to indicate a desire to dissociate the idea of law from legalism, and to invest it with evangelic associations.
[4] *Rom.* iii. 31.   [5] *Ibid.* iii. 20.

drawn (1) from the history of Abraham (chap. iv.); (2) from the experience of the justified (chap. v. 1–11); (3) from the history of the human race (chap. v. 12–21). The first two lines of thought are anticipated in *Galatians* (chap. iii. 6–9, 3–5); the third is new, though texts in 1 *Cor.* xv., concerning Adam and Christ, show that such sweeping generalisations do not occur here for the first time to the apostle's mind.

"What of Abraham our forefather?"[1] so begins abruptly the new section. Is he no exception to the rule, that no man is justified by works? The Jews thought he was, and the apostle seems willing to concede the point out of respect to the patriarch, but not in a sense incompatible with his thesis.[2] Abraham as compared with other men might have in his works a ground of boasting, but not before God, not so as to exclude need of divine grace, not in the sense of a full legal justification. He was justified before circumcision, and by faith; and so he was not merely the fleshly father of Israel, but the spiritual father of all who believe, circumcised and uncircumcised. In the discussion of these points, there comes out in a remarkable degree a feature of St. Paul's style on which critics have commented, viz., the tendency to repeat a word that has taken a strong hold of his mind. "A word," says Renan, "haunts him, he uses it again and again in the same page. It is not from

---

[1] *Rom.* iv. 1. εἰρηκέναι is omitted by Westcott and Hort.

[2] So Lipsius, *Die Paul. Rechtfertigungslehre*, p. 35, with which cf. the same author in *Hand-commentar*. According to Weber, *Die Lehre des Talmuds*, p. 224, the Jews of the Talmudic period thought that all the patriarchs passed through life without sin, also other great saints, such as Elijah.

sterility, it is from the eagerness of his spirit, and his complete indifference as to the correction of style." [1] The word which haunts his mind here is λογίζομαι, which in one form or another occurs eleven times. The repetition implies emphasis, implies that the word is the symbol of an important idea in the Pauline system of thought, that it denotes a certain feature of the righteousness of God given to faith. It is an *imputed* righteousness, though strictly speaking St. Paul's idea is that *faith is imputed for righteousness*. So it was in the case of Abraham, according to the Scriptures; so in like manner, the apostle teaches, shall it be in the case of all Abraham's spiritual children.[2] For he regards the patriarch's case as in all respects typical, even in respect of the nature and manifestations of the faith exercised, as when he believed in God's power to quicken the dead, even as we do when we believe in the resurrection of Jesus.[3] "*Who*," adds the apostle, in one of his pregnant sentences, "*Who was delivered up for our trespasses, and was raised again for our justification.*"[4]

The way of justification by faith exemplified in the history of Abraham is, the apostle goes on to show, still further commended by its results in a believing man's experience. The style at this point passes out of the didactic into the emotional. The writer expresses himself as one who has known what it is to enter into a state of peace, hope, and joy, from a miserable state of fear, doubt, uncertainty, and depression, the sad inherit-

---

[1] *St. Paul*, p. 233.   [2] *Rom.* iv. 24.   [3] *Ibid.* iv. 24.
[4] *Ibid.* iv. 25. This text will come under our notice in chapter viii.

ance of legalism. So in cheerful buoyant tone he begins: "Justification being by faith, let us have peace with God,"[1] insisting that it is now possible and easy as it never was or could be for the legalist. And he continues in triumphant strain to exhibit the mood of the believer in Jesus as one of constant many-sided exultation. The keynote of this noble outpouring of an emancipated heart is καυχῶμαι, occurring first in ver. 2, and recurring in vers. 3 and 11, and presenting in its growing intensity of meaning a veritable Jacob's ladder of joy reaching from earth to heaven. "We exult in hope of future glory; not only so, we exult in present tribulations; not only so, we exult in God. The future is ours, the present is ours, all is ours because God is ours; all this because we have abandoned the way of works and entered on the way of faith." Such is the skeleton of thought in this choice passage, well hidden by a massive body of superadded ideas crowding into the writer's mind and craving utterance.

The famous parallel between Adam and Christ comes in partly as an afterthought by way of an additional contribution to the doctrine of sin, and therefore to the argument in support of the doctrine of justification. But it may also be viewed as a continuation of the foregoing strain, in which Christian optimism finds for itself new pabulum in a larger field. "It is well not only for the individual believer that salvation comes through faith in Christ, but for the human race. Christ is the hope of all generations of mankind. Through one

---

[1] *Rom.* v. 1; ἔχωμεν suits the emotional character of the passage. In didactic meaning it comes to the same thing as ἔχομεν.

man at the commencement of history came sin and death, and through this second Man came righteousness and life. The law did nothing to help sin and death-stricken humanity; it rather entered that sin might abound, so enhancing rather than mitigating its malign power. But that was merely a temporary evil, for the abounding of sin only called forth a superabundant manifestation of grace. Thus Adam and Moses, each in his own way, ministered to the glory of Christ as the Redeemer from sin." Such is the gist of the passage.

The apostle's thought is grand, bold, and true, but like all bold thought it brings its own risks of misunderstanding. What if this eulogium on the righteousness of God given to faith, or on the grace of God the more liberally bestowed the more it is needed, should be turned into an excuse for moral licence? Why then Christianity would prove to be a failure not less than Paganism and Judaism; nay, the greatest, most tragic failure of all. St. Paul has judged Paganism and Judaism by their practical fruits, and he cannot object to the same test being applied to the new religion he proposes to put in their place. Obviously it must be a matter of life and death for him to show that the gospel he preaches will stand the test. That, accordingly, is the task he next undertakes, with what success the contents of chapters vi.–viii. enable us to judge.

Chapters vi. and vii. deal successively with three questions naturally arising out of the previous train of thought. It is not necessary to suppose that they had ever been put by any actual objector—the dialectics are those of the writer's own eager intellect; but conceived as emanating from an unsympathetic reader they may be stated thus: The great matter, it seems, is that grace abound; had we not better then all play Adam's part that grace may have free scope?[1] The law too was given to make sin abound, and having rendered that questionable service retired from the stage and gave place to the genial reign of grace. Are we then at liberty now to do deeds contrary to the law?[2] Finally, if the function of the law was to increase sin, is not the natural inference that the law itself is sin?[3] The apostle's reply to the first of these questions is in effect this: "Continue in sin that grace may abound! the idea is abhorrent to the Christian mind; the case supposed absurd and impossible. Ideally viewed, a Christian is a man dead to sin and alive in and with Christ. That this is so, baptism signifies. The Christian life in its ideal is a repetition of Christ's life in its main crises; in its death for sin and to sin, and in its resurrection to eternal life. And the ideal becomes a law to all believers. They deem it their duty to strive to realise the ideal in their life." At this point in the development of St. Paul's thoughts we make the acquaintance of that "*faith-mysticism*" which is a not less conspicuous feature of Paulinism than the doctrine of objective righteousness, or justification by faith. We met it before for a moment in the Antioch remonstrance, in those stirring words, "I am crucified along with Christ";[4] and again, just for a passing moment, in the pregnant saying, "If one died for all, then all died along with Him."[5] But here

---

[1] *Rom.* vi. 1.   [2] *Ibid.* vi. 15.   [3] *Ibid.* vii. 7.
[4] *Gal.* ii. 20.   [5] *2 Cor.* v. 15.

we are brought face to face with it so that we cannot escape noting its features, and are compelled to recognise it as an organic and essential element in the Pauline conception of Christianity.

The second suggestion, that we may sin because we are not under law, the apostle boldly meets by the assertion, that just because we are not under law but under grace, therefore sin shall not have dominion over us. The announcement of this to a Jew startling, but to a Christian self-evident, truth conducts the apostle at length to his doctrine as to the function of the law which he has once and again hinted at in the course of his argument. He uses for his purpose the figure of a marriage. The law was once our husband, but he is dead and we are married to another, even Christ, through whom we bring forth fruit to God; very different fruit from that brought forth under the law's influence, which was simply fruit of sin unto death.[1] In so characterising the fruit of marriage to the law, the apostle is simply repeating his doctrine that the law entered that sin might abound. This doctrine, therefore, he must now explain and defend, which he does in one of the most remarkable passages in all his writings, wherein he describes the conflict between the flesh and the spirit and the function of the law in provoking sin, while holy in itself, through the flesh.[2] It is the *locus classicus* of St. Paul's doctrine of the flesh as also of his doctrine of the law, and as such must engage our attention hereafter. It is altogether a very sombre and depressing utterance,

[1] *Rom.* vii. 1-6.   [2] *Ibid.* vii. 7-24.

ending with the cry of despair: "Wretched man, who shall deliver me!"

The exposition of the gospel cannot so end. To let that be the last word were to confess failure. The exclamation: "Thanks to God through Jesus Christ" must be made the starting-point of a new strain, in which despair shall give place to hope, and struggle to victory. This is what happens in chapter viii. The apostle here returns to the happy mood of chapter v. 1–11. "There is now no condemnation" is an echo of "Being justified by faith, we have peace," and the subsequent series of reflections is an expansion of the three ideas, rejoicing in hope, rejoicing in tribulation, rejoicing in God. Yet along with similarity goes notable difference, due to the influence of the intervening train of thought. In the earlier place the ground of joy and hope is *objective*, the righteousness of God given to faith, faith imputed for righteousness. In the latter it is *subjective*, union to Christ by faith, being in Christ, *having Christ's Spirit dwelling in us*. The great Pauline doctrine of the Spirit immanent in believers as the source of a new Christlike life here finds adequate expression, after having been hinted in the Epistle to the Galatians,[1] and also in an earlier place of this present Epistle.[2] Here the indwelling Spirit is set forth as the source of several important spiritual benefits—(1) victory over sin, power to do the will of God, to fulfil the righteousness of the law[3] (the law is not to be made void after all, but established!); (2) filial confidence towards God;[4] (3) the sure hope of

[1] *Gal.* iv. 6; v. 5.
[2] *Rom.* v. 5.
[3] *Ibid.* viii. 4–10.
[4] *Ibid.* viii. 14–16.

future glory as God's sons and heirs;[1] (4) comfort under present tribulation, the Spirit helping us in our infirmities.[2] Along with this doctrine of the immanent Spirit goes a magnificent doctrine of Christian optimism, which proclaims the approach of an era of emancipation for the whole creation, and the present reign of a paternal Providence which makes all things work together for good.[3] Here St. Paul's spirit rises to the highest pitch of jubilant utterance, illustrating what he meant when he spoke of glorying in God (chap. v. 11): "If God be for us, who can be against us? . . . I am persuaded that neither death, nor life, nor angels, nor principalities, nor powers, nor things present, nor things to come, nor height, nor depth, nor any other creature, shall be able to separate us from the love of God which is in Jesus Christ our Lord."[4]

Thus, on eagle wing, does the apostle soar away towards heaven, whence he looks down with contempt on time and sense, and all the troubles of this life. But such lofty flights of faith and hope seldom last long in this world. Something ever occurs to bring the spirit down from heaven to earth, back from the glorious future to the sad present. Even such was St. Paul's experience in writing this letter. What brings his thoughts down to the earth, and back to the disenchanting realities of the present, is the prevailing unbelief

---

[1] *Rom.* viii. 17.   [2] *Ibid.* viii. 26.   [3] *Ibid.* viii. 18-25, 31-39.
[4] *Ibid.* viii. 31, 39. In this brief analysis of chapter viii. no reference has been made to a very important Pauline word in vers. 3, 4 : "God sending His own Son in the likeness of sinful flesh, and for sin, condemned sin in the flesh." Other opportunities will occur for discussing this passage.

of his countrymen. In the peace-giving faith and inspiring hope of Christians few of them had a share. The sad fact not only grieved his spirit, but raised an important apologetic problem. The nature of the problem has been indicated in a previous chapter, as also the gist of the apostle's solution as given in *Romans* ix.–xi., the further exposition of which is reserved for another place.

CHAPTER VII

THE DOCTRINE OF SIN

THE topical consideration of Paulinism on which we now enter may fitly begin with St. Paul's negative doctrine concerning justification, viz., that it is not attainable by the method of legalism. The proof of this position resolves itself practically into the Pauline doctrine of sin, which embraces four particulars. These are (1) the statement concerning the general prevalence of sin in the "sin section" of the Epistle to the Romans; (2) the statement respecting the effect of the first man's sin in *Romans* v. 12–21; (3) the statement concerning the sinful proclivity of the flesh in *Romans* vii.; (4) the statement concerning the action of the law on the sinful proclivity of the flesh in the same chapter. From all these taken together it follows that salvation by the works of the law is absolutely impossible.[1]

1. The apostle's first argument in support of his doctrine of justification on its negative side is that, as a matter of fact and observation, sin, even in intense

---

[1] Ménégoz truly remarks that to understand St. Paul's notion of sin we must remember that it is not his purpose to give a systematic course of instruction on sin, but simply to speak of it in its bearing on his doctrine of justification.—*Le Péché et la Rédemption*, p. 23.

virulence, is widely prevalent in the world, both among Pagans and among Jews. It may be called the popular argument, and its use is to produce a *primâ facie* impression or presumption in favour of the doctrine in connection with which the appeal to experience is made. It cannot be regarded as a strict proof that justification by works is impossible; at most it amounts to a proof that salvation by that method is very unlikely. To that it certainly does amount, very conspicuously in the case of the Jews. If, as is alleged, the people to whom had been given the law were as sinful as the rest of the world, the obvious inference is that the legal dispensation, viewed as a means of attaining unto righteousness, had proved a signal failure. And in view of the dark picture of the world generally, without distinction of Jew or Gentile, it is clear that, whatever might be possible for the exceptional few, the way of legal righteousness could never be the way of salvation for the million. But the empirical argument does not exclude the possibility of that way being open for the few; for though gross sin be very generally prevalent, it does not follow that such sin, or even sin in any degree, is absolutely universal. There may be some exceptionally good men capable of perfectly satisfying the law's requirements. The apostle makes it quite evident that he does not believe in any exceptions, for he winds up the account of the moral condition of the world in the early chapters of *Romans* with the unqualified statement: "Therefore by the works of the law shall no flesh be justified."[1] But that he does not rest the inference

---

[1] *Rom.* iii. 20.

solely on the foregoing statement concerning the extensive prevalence of sin appears from the appended remark, "For by the law is the knowledge of sin," which is a new reason for the assertion just made. It may be doubted whether the apostle rests his doctrine as to the absolute universality of sin even on the texts of Scripture he has previously cited,[1] which on the surface seem to teach the doctrine, though as they stand in the Old Testament they are not intended to state an abstract doctrine concerning human depravity, but simply characterise in strong terms the moral depravity of a particular generation of men. That he put on these texts a universal construction is not questioned, but he may have done so not so much as a mere interpreter of Scripture, but rather as one who believed in the universal diffusion of sin on other grounds. That the possibility of exceptions was present to his thoughts is evident from his reference to the case of Abraham.[2] We may expect, therefore, to find that he has in reserve some deeper, more cogent reasons for his thesis than either an appeal to observation or citations from the Hebrew Psalter.

2. The necessary supplement to the popular argument is to be found in the famous passage concerning Adam and Christ, and in the not less notable statement concerning the sinful proclivity of the flesh. As to the former, I remark that this section of *Romans* (v. 12–21) contains much more than a contribution to the Pauline doctrine of sin, or to the proof of the negative doctrine of justification. It serves the comprehensive purpose of

[1] *Rom.* iii. 10–18.   [2] *Ibid.* iv. 1.

vindicating the apostle's whole doctrine of justification, both on its negative and on its positive side, by fitting it into a grand philosophic generalisation respecting the religious history of the world. That history is there summed up under two representative men, the first man and the second, Adam and Christ. Between these two men St. Paul draws a parallel in so far as both by their action influenced their whole race. But beginning with a parallel, he forthwith glides into a contrast. Apology passes over into eulogy. For the writer, at the commencement of the chapter, has been extolling the benefits connected with the era of grace, and he is in the mood to continue in the same strain, and so having once suggested the thought: Adam and Christ like each other as both representative men to opposite effects, he introduces the new theme: "but not as the offence is the free gift; sin abounds, but grace superabounds."[1]

What we are now concerned with, however, is the bearing of this passage on the doctrine of sin, and so on the negative side of the doctrine of justification. That it was meant to have a bearing on these topics we need not doubt, though the direct purpose in view is more general and comprehensive. It may be said that the apostle here supplies a supplementary proof of the impossibility of attaining unto salvation by personal righteousness, a proof which converts his first statement concerning the general prevalence of sin into an absolutely universal doctrine as to the sinfulness of man.

And what then is the new proof? It starts from the universal prevalence of death. Indubitably *death*

[1] *Rom.* v. 15.

reigns over all. But death, it is assumed, is the wages of sin; there had been no death among men had there been no sin; therefore all must be in some sense and to some extent sinners simply because all die. Not improbably this was the original germ of the train of thought contained in the Adam-Christ section. But this germinal thought would inevitably suggest others. It would in the first place start a difficulty to be overcome, in grappling with which the apostle at last reached the magnificent generalisation contained in the antithesis between the two representative men. Death has swept away all the generations of mankind, therefore all men in all generations have sinned. But if so, men must have sinned before the giving of the law. But how could that be if where there is no law there is no transgression, and if by the law comes the knowledge of sin? This difficulty might be met by saying: there was a law before the lawgiving, a law written on the hearts or consciences of men, and sufficiently known to make them responsible. But this is not the way in which the apostle meets the difficulty, though, as we know from other places in his Epistles, such a line of thought was familiar to him. He is willing to make the concession that there was no law before the Sinaitic lawgiving, and that therefore men could not legally be treated as sinners, could not have sin imputed to them as a ground of condemnation and infliction of penalty, because he has in view another way of showing that in all the ages men were under the reign of sin, and therefore subject to death. That way he finds in the great principle of solidarity, or the moral unity of mankind. The first man sinned, and that is enough. By one man sin entered into the world, and death followed in its track legitimately, righteously, because when the one man sinned all sinned.

Such I take to be the meaning of the famous text *Romans* v. 12, and in particular of the last clause: ἐφ' ᾧ πάντες ἥμαρτον. The rendering of the Vulgate, *in quo omnes peccaverunt*, is grammatically wrong, for ἐφ' ᾧ does not mean "in whom," but "because," yet essentially right. It requires some courage to express this opinion, or indeed any opinion, when one thinks of the interminable controversies to which these four Greek words have given rise, and considers how much depends on the interpretation we adopt. The sense of responsibility would be altogether crushing if the matter in dispute, instead of being a statement connected with a theological theorem, were a vital article of the Christian faith. Of the possible meanings of the words in question, the one for which I, with something like fear and trembling, give my vote, is, it must be admitted, *à priori* the least likely. Who would ever think of saying himself, or expect another to say, that when Adam sinned all mankind sinned? But we know that St. Paul is in the habit of saying startling things, the sinless One made sin, *e.g.*, and therefore we cannot make it a rule of interpretation, in dealing with his writings, that the most obvious and ordinary meaning is to be preferred. Of course the most obvious meaning of the second half of *Romans* v. 12 is, that death passed upon all men because all men *personally* sinned, which accordingly is the interpretation favoured by an imposing array of modern expositors. Among the objections that might be stated to this view, not the least weighty is this, that it makes St. Paul say what is not true to the fact. If he really meant to say that all died because all personally sinned, he must have forgotten the very large number of human beings who die in infancy, an act of forgetfulness very unlikely in so humane a man and so considerate a theologian. The infants would not be left out of account if we adopted the interpretation which has on its side the great name of Calvin: all died, because all, even the infants, inherited a depraved nature, and so were tainted with the vice of original sin, if not guilty of actual transgression. But this is not exegesis, but rather reading into the word ἥμαρτον a theological hypothesis. We seem, therefore, to be thrown back, in spite of ourselves, on the thought, however strange it may seem, that when Adam sinned all mankind sinned, as that which the apostle really intended to utter. The aorist, ἥμαρτον, as pointing to a single act performed at a definite time, fits into, if it do not compel, this interpretation. Writing some years ago, one would have been able to cite in support of it the authority of Pfleiderer. In the first edition of his able work on Paulinism he remarks, that in *Romans* v. 12 two different reasons seem to be given for the entrance of death—Adam's sin and men's own sin, and it may seem strange that no attempt should be made to reconcile the two. But he goes on to say: "Just in this hard and completely unreconciled juxtaposition of the two reasons lies without doubt the hint that in the apostle's view they are not two, but one, that therefore the sinful deed of Adam is at the same time and as such the sinful deed of all." "This," he continues, "naturally must mean, that in the deed of Adam, as the representative head of the race, the race in virtue of a certain moral or mystic identity took part."[1] But in the second edition of this work, published in 1890, the author has, with an implicit faith which is almost pathetic, adopted as his guide in the interpretation of Paulinism Weber's account of the theology of the Talmud. In doing so he makes two great assumptions: that the theological opinions of the Jews in the time of St. Paul were the same as in the period, centuries later, when the Talmud was compiled, and that St. Paul's theology was to a large extent simply a reflection of that of the Jewish synagogue. Both assumptions seem to me very hazardous. It stands to reason that Jewish theological thought underwent development in the centuries that elapsed between the apostolic age and the Talmudic era. And it is by no means a matter of course that every theological theorem current in the synagogue, and as such familiar to Saul the Pharisee, was adopted into his system of Christian thought by Paul the apostle. That Rabbinism exercised a certain influence on his mind need not be questioned. The influence is traceable in his method of interpreting Scripture and in his style of argumentation, and it is not at all unlikely that it may here and there be discernible also in the thought-forms and phraseology of his Christian theology.[2] But of one

[1] *Der Paulinismus*, pp. 39, 40.
[2] Lipsius (*Hand-commentar on Rom.* v. 12) points out that the idea of death entering into the world through the sin of the first man was generally current among the Jews before and during Paul's time, citing in proof *Sirach* xxv. 24, *Wisdom of Solomon* ii. 23, and

THE DOCTRINE OF SIN

thing we may be sure, viz., that St. Paul was not the slave of Rabbinical theology, and that he would never allow it to dominate over his mind to the prejudice of his Christianity. He might use it as far as it served his purpose, but beyond that he would not suffer it to go. The view he expresses in *Romans* iv. 1–3 in reference to Abraham, as no exception to the thesis that men cannot be justified by works, illustrates the freedom of his attitude towards Jewish opinion.

The servile use of Talmudic theology as a key to the interpretation of Paulinism, which makes the new edition of Pfleiderer's work in some respects the reverse of an improvement on the first, suggests another reflection which may here find a place. It is a mistake to be constantly on the outlook for sources of Pauline thought in previous or contemporary literature. Pfleiderer is a great offender here. According to him one part of St. Paul's theology comes from Alexandria, and the other from the Jewish synagogue, and the original element, if it exist at all, is reduced to a minimum. He cannot even credit the apostle with the power to describe the vices of Paganism as he does in *Romans* i. without borrowing from the *Book of Wisdom*.[1] I may find another opportunity of expressing an opinion as to the alleged Hellenism; meantime I content myself with cordially endorsing a sentiment occurring in a book by a young German theologian, of whom Pfleiderer speaks in most appreciative terms. It is that "the theology of

iv. Esdras vii. 18–20. What St. Paul did was not to invent the idea, but to apply it in exposition and defence of the Christian faith.

[1] *Der Paulinismus*, 2te Aufl. pp. 83, 84.

the great apostle is the expression of his experience, not of his reading."[1] The remark applies even to the Old Testament, much more to the Apocrypha, or to the works of Philo, or to the dreary lucubrations of the scribes.

The doctrine of the Talmud on the connection between sin and death, as stated by Weber, is to this effect. Adam's sin is his own, not the sin of the race. Every man dies for his own sin. Yet the death of all men has its last ground in the sin of Adam, partly because the death sentence was pronounced on the race in connection with Adam's sin, partly because through Adam's sin the evil proclivity latent in the flesh not only first found expression, but was started on a sinister career of increasingly corrupt influence. Assuming that the apostle meant to echo the Talmudic theory in the text under consideration, the resulting interpretation would be something like a combination of two of the three interpretations which divide the suffrages of Christian commentators. Summarily these are: all die because of personal sin, all die because of inherited depravity, all die because involved in the personal sin of Adam the representative of the race. The Talmudic hypothesis is a combination of the first and second of these three views.

In the famous comparison between Adam and Christ, the terms ἁμαρτία and δικαιοσύνη appear both to be used *objectively*. Sin and righteousness are conceived of as two great antagonistic forces fighting against each other, not so much *in* man as *over* him, each striving for supremacy; the one manifesting its malign sway in

[1] Gunkel, *Die Wirkungen des heiligen Geistes*, p. 86 (1888).

death, the other in the life communicated to those who believe in Jesus. The one power began its reign with the sin of Adam. From the day that Adam sinned, ἁμαρτία had dominion over the human race, and showed the reality of its power by the death which overtook successive generations of mankind. The existence of this objective sin necessitated the coming into existence of an objective righteousness as the only means by which the reign of sin and death could be brought to an end. The existence of an Adam through whom the race was brought into a state of condemnation, made it necessary that there should appear a Second Adam in whom the race might make a new beginning, and in whose righteousness it might be righteous. As by the disobedience of the one man the many were constituted (κατεστάθησαν, v. 19) sinners, so also it was necessary that by the obedience of the One the many should be constituted righteous. Such seems to be the apostle's view. It may raise scruples in the modern mind on various grounds. Some may think that St. Paul has read far more theology into the story of the Fall than can be taken out of it by legitimate exegesis. The idea of objective sin may appear objectionable on ethical grounds; for what, it may be asked, can be more unjust or unreasonable than that one man should suffer for another man's sins? Yet modern science will teach even the freest theological thinker to be cautious in pressing this objection; for by its doctrine of heredity it has made it more manifest than ever that the solidarity of mankind is a great fact, and not merely a theological theory, and that the only question is as to the best way of stating it so as to conserve all moral interests. It may readily be admitted that a better statement is conceivable than that furnished by Augustinian theology. The question may very legitimately be raised: To what effect or extent does objective sin reign? in other words, What is meant by death in this connection? When St. Paul says, "so death passed upon all men," does he allude to the familiar fact of physical dissolution, or is death to be taken comprehensively as including at once temporal, spiritual, and eternal consequences? If my conjecture as to the genesis of the Adam-Christ train of thought be correct, we must understand θάνατος in the restricted sense.[1] In any case there is no ground for ascribing to St. Paul the dogma, that the *eternal* destiny of men depends on

[1] Lipsius in *Hand-commentar zum N. T.* maintains that θάνατος nowhere in St. Paul's writings means spiritual death, but physical death without hope of resurrection. *Vide* his notes on *Romans* v. 12 and vii. 10. Similarly Kabisch, *Die Eschatologie des Paulus* (1893). The views of Ménégoz will be stated in the next chapter. In referring to the work of Kabisch, I must acknowledge that the weight of his authority is much lessened by what I cannot but regard as the extravagant manner in which he fathers upon St. Paul all the grossly materialistic conceptions of the Apocalyptic writings and the Talmud. Nothing but perusal of the work will give one any idea of the extent to which this is carried. Take as a sample his account of the Fall in its origin, and its effects on human nature and on physical nature: "The Satanic substance through the medium of Eve (through sexual intercourse) entered into the flesh of the first man; there it blazed up, kindled by the divine command, and excited him to commit the first sin; as a poison it seized his body, not the ἔσω ἄνθρωπος which has nothing to do with these physical events, and changed him into a σῶμα τῆς ἁμαρτίας or a σῶμα τοῦ θανάτου, and as Φάρμακον ὀλέθρου has penetrated into all made of the same material as himself, into the whole κόσμος and made it a home of corruption and death," p. 168. The apostle is represented as regarding all sins, even "spiritual" sins, as purely

the sin of the race *apart from personal transgression*.¹
That through the sin of Adam eternal perdition overtakes children dying in infancy (unless averted by baptism!) formed no part of his theology. The idea is utterly irreconcilable with his optimistic doctrine of superabounding grace. It is excluded by his conception of objective sin and objective righteousness as forming two aspects of one system. He did not think of the former as reigning unconditionally. He thought rather of the Fall and its consequences as counterworked from the first by the reign of grace, Adam nowhere where Christ was not also in more or less potency; the curse therefore in all spheres, physical and ethical, to a large extent an unrealised ideal, because never operative unchecked by a redemptive economy. This covers infant salvation; for if infants perish, the common sin reigns unchecked and the common righteousness is convicted of impotence.²

3. Something more than the theorem of objective sin physical functions of the material body, p. 151. The influences of the Holy Spirit or of Christ are conceived of in the same materialistic manner. The book altogether is an extreme example of the "rigour and vigour" of German theorists.

¹ To understand Paulinism we must carefully note the distinction between ἁμαρτία and παράβασις. ἁμαρτία is objective and common; παράβασις is subjective and personal. ἁμαρτία entails some evil effects, but παράβασις is necessary to guilt and final condemnation.

² *Vide* on this *Christ in Modern Theology*, by Principal Fairbairn, pp. 460-2; also Godet, who on *Rom.* v. 12 remarks: "There is no question here about the eternal lot of individuals. Paul is speaking here above all of physical death. Nothing of all that passes in the domain in which we have Adam for our father can be decisive for our eternal lot. The solidarity of individuals with the head of the first humanity does not extend beyond the domain of natural life."

in the sense explained is needed to produce the conviction that sin is a universal reality. It must be shown that sin is a power at work in man as well as above him, influencing his character as well as his destiny. Till this is shown, men may remain unpersuaded that righteousness is unattainable by the way of legalism, deeming objective sin either an unreality or at most something external, affecting man's physical life, but not his moral being or his standing before God. To shut men up to the way of faith there is needed a demonstration of the inherent sinfulness of human nature. This demonstration the apostle supplies in his statement as to the sinful proclivity of the flesh. The relative section of the Epistle to the Romans is not indeed a formal contribution to the doctrine as to the universality of sin; it rather deals with the flesh as a hindrance to Christian holiness, under which aspect it will fall to be considered hereafter. It may seem unsatisfactory that so important a part of the doctrine of sin should be brought in as a sort of afterthought. But we must once for all reconcile ourselves to the fact that St. Paul is not a scholastic theologian, and be content to take his teaching as he chooses to give it.

The demonstration takes the form of a personal confession. In the first part of his doctrine of sin the apostle has described in dark colours the sins of other men; in this part he details his own experience in most graphic terms. "I am carnal, sold under sin, for what I do I know not; for not what I wish do I, but what I hate, this do I."[1] And he assumes that in this respect

[1] *Rom.* vii. 14, 15.

he is not exceptional. Personal in form, the confession is really the confession of humanity, of every man who is σάρκινος,[1] living in the flesh. The ego that speaks is not the individual ego of St. Paul, but the ego of the human race. It is idle therefore to inquire whether he refers to the period antecedent to his conversion or to the post-conversion period. The question proceeds upon a too literal and prosaic view of the passage, as if it were a piece of exact biography instead of being a highly idealised representation of human weakness in the moral sphere. In so far as the artist draws from his own experience the reference must be held to be chiefly to the pre-conversion period, for it is clear from the next chapter that the apostle is far from regarding the moral condition of the Christian as one of weakness and misery like that depicted in chap. vii.; though it need not therefore be denied that the conflict between flesh and spirit may reappear even in the life of one who walks in the Spirit. But we miss the didactic significance of this passage if we take it as merely biographical, instead of viewing it as typical and representative. That it is meant to be typical is manifest from the abstract manner in which the flesh is spoken of. It is not St. Paul's flesh that is at fault, it is *the* flesh, the flesh which all men wear, the flesh in which dwells sin.[2] What precisely the apostle means by σάρξ is a question for future consideration; meantime the point

---

[1] This is the approved reading. Adjectives terminating in νος indicate the material of which anything is made. *Vide* 2 Cor. iii. 3, καρδίαις σαρκίναις.

[2] *Rom.* vii. 25; viii. 3.

to be noted is, that the word does not denote something merely personal. It represents an abstract idea. The term may not signify the mere physical organisation, but we may safely assume that it has some reference thereto, and so find in this notable passage the doctrine that in man's material part resides a bias to sin which causes much trouble to the spirit, and prevents those who with their mind approve the law of God from actually complying with its behests. This doctrine St. Paul proclaims in the pathetic confession: "I know that in me (that is, in my flesh) dwelleth not good."[1] What dwells in the flesh is not good but sin.[2] "I know," says the apostle, expecting every man who has any sympathy with good to echo the acknowledgment. If he be right in this expectation, then it is all over with the hope of attaining to righteousness by personal effort. The appropriate sequel of such a confession is the groan of despair: "Wretched human being, who shall deliver me?"[3] If there be any hope for us, it must be in Another; our standing ground must be grace not law. "But," it may be said, "St. Paul may be wrong in his judgment; he may be taking too morbid a view of the moral disability of man." Well, it is a jury question; but, inspiration apart, I had rather take the testimony of St. Paul on this question than that of a morally commonplace, self-complacent person like the Pharisee of our Lord's parable. It is a fact that the noblest men in all ages have accepted his verdict, and this consensus of those most capable of judging must be held to settle the matter.

[1] *Rom.* vii. 18.   [2] *Ibid.* vii. 20.
[3] *Ibid.* vii. 24.   ταλαίπωρος ἐγὼ ἄνθρωπος.

THE DOCTRINE OF SIN 141

Granting the matter of fact to be as asserted, viz., that there is in the flesh a bias towards evil, what is its cause? Is the bias inherent in the flesh, inseparable from the nature of a material organism, or is it a vice which has been accidentally introduced into it, say by the sin of Adam? On this speculative problem St. Paul has nowhere in his Epistles pronounced a definite opinion. He declares the fact of an antagonism between flesh and spirit, but he gives no account of its origin. It may indeed seem possible to arrive at a solution of the problem which may reasonably be held to be Pauline by combining the statement in the Adam-Christ section with that of the section concerning the flesh, and drawing the inference that human nature, and in particular the bodily organism, underwent a change for the worse in consequence of the sin of the first man. This is the Church doctrine of original sin. A question has been raised as to the legitimacy of the combination on which this doctrine rests.[1] This question very naturally leads up to another: does the combination go to the root of the matter? From the sin of the first man came the corruption of human nature, but whence came his sin?

---

[1] In the first edition of *Der Paulinismus* Pfleiderer pronounced the combination inadmissible, and maintained that St. Paul gives two wholly different accounts of the origin of moral evil in *Rom.* v. and vii., that in the latter chapter being that sin has its origin in a flesh conceived to be inherently evil. *Vide* p. 62. In the second edition he regards it as possible that the Augustinian theory that the sinful bias of the flesh originated in Adam's fall was held by St. Paul, but thinks it more likely that he accepted the view of the Jewish schools, viz., that the evil bias was there from the first, and was only provoked and increased through the temptation to sin. *Vide* p. 71; and for the Jewish view, Weber, sects. 46, 48.

Was his flesh entirely free from evil bias, morally neutral, and containing no elements of danger to the spirit? Or had it too that in it—desire, passion—which might very readily tempt to transgression? If the Pauline literature contains any hints of an answer to this question, they are to be found in the terms in which in 1 *Cor.* xv. the first man is described as in contrast to the second, only a living soul, psychical as distinct from spiritual, and of the earth, earthy.[1] These expressions seem to point in the direction of a nature not very different from our own, and altogether suggest an idea of the primitive state of man not quite answering to the theological conception of original righteousness. The same remark applies to the account of that state in the Book of Genesis, wherein the first man appears in such a condition of unstable moral equilibrium as to fall before the slightest temptation, more like an innocent inexperienced child than a full-grown man, godlike in "righteousness and true holiness." Should a revision of the Church's doctrine concerning the initial moral condition of man be necessitated by the progress of modern science, it may be found that it is not the sacred historian or the Christian apostle that is at fault, but the dogmatically-biassed exegesis of the system-builders.[2]

---

[1] 1 *Cor.* xv. 46, 47.

[2] F. W. Robertson says that popular ideas of the paradise state are without the warrant of one syllable of Scripture. Vide *Lectures on the Epistles to the Corinthians*, apud 1 *Cor.* xv. 46, 47. Godet also on the same text remarks, that St. Paul does not share the traditional orthodox idea of the primitive state as one of moral and physical perfection.

4. The last particular in the Pauline doctrine of sin is the statement concerning the effect of the law's action on the sinful proclivity of the flesh. On this point the apostle teaches that in consequence of the evil bias of the flesh, the law, so far from being the way to righteousness, is rather simply a source of the knowledge of sin and an irritant to sin. The topic is handled chiefly in *Romans* vii. It is introduced at ver. 7 by the question: " What shall we say, then ? Is the law sin ? God forbid"; which is followed up by the explanatory statement that the law, though not sin, is the source of the knowledge of sin. This is explained in turn by the doctrine of the sinful bias of the flesh, in consequence of which it comes to pass that the law, in commanding the good, as it always does, being itself holy, simply comes into collision with contrary inclination, and so awakes the consciousness of a law in the members warring against the law in the mind. So by the law I simply know myself to be a sinner, to be morally impotent, to be a slave. To make one righteous is because of the flesh impossible for the law, a truth which the apostle states very forcibly in *Rom.* viii. 3, where he represents the fulfilment of the righteousness of the law in men as the impossible for the law in consequence of its weakness by reason of the flesh. Such being the fact, made known to him by bitter experience, he argued that the law could never have been intended to make men righteous. It could not have been instituted to accomplish the impossible. It must have been instituted with reference to an ulterior system which should be able to realise the legally impossible;

a means to an end destined to be superseded when it had served its ancillary purpose; a preparation for the advent of God's Son, who, coming in the likeness of sinful flesh, and with reference to sin, should condemn sin in the flesh, and help believers in Him to be indeed sons of God, walking not after the flesh but after the Spirit. We have seen with what fertile ingenuity the apostle describes the preparatory function of the law in the Epistle to the Galatians, and we shall have a future opportunity of considering his whole doctrine as to the legal economy from an apologetic point of view. Meantime what we have to note is the sombre aspect under which that doctrine presents the sinfulness of man. Human sinfulness is such as to make the question not an impertinence, whether the very law of God which reveals it and provokes it into activity be not itself sinful. Yet there is a bright side to the picture. The law does more than bring to consciousness human depravity. In doing that it at the same time makes man aware that there is more in him than sin: a mind in sympathy with the moral ideal embodied in the law, an inner man in a state of protest against the deeds of the outer man. The action of the law on the flesh on the one hand, and on the conscience on the other, makes me feel that I am two, not one, and this duality is at once my misery and my hope: my misery, for it is wretched to be drawn two ways; my hope, for I ever feel that my flesh and my sin, though mine, are not myself. This feeling all may share. On the bright hopeful side, as well as on the darker, St. Paul is the spokesman for the race. His ταλαίπωρος ἐγὼ ἄνθρωπος voices not only the universal need of, but the universal desire for, redemption. It is the *de profundis* of sin-oppressed humanity. The apostle's doctrine of sin is not flattering, but neither is it indiscriminate. It is not a doctrine of total unrelieved depravity. It recognises a good element in average human nature. As described, that element appears weak and ineffectual. But the important thing to note is that it is there.

CHAPTER VIII

THE RIGHTEOUSNESS OF GOD

THE idea expressed by the phrase "the righteousness of God" occupies the central place in St. Paul's theology, and contains his answer to the question, What was the great boon which came into the world by Jesus Christ? That the Christian *summum bonum* should assume this aspect to his mind was to be expected in the case of one who even in the pre-Christian period of his life had been animated by an intense though misguided passion for righteousness. Righteousness had always appeared the chief good to this man; he had sought it long in vain, and when at length he found it he gave to it a name expressive of its infinite worth to his heart: the righteousness of *God*. It is a name which he has deliberately chosen and to which he steadfastly adheres, using it in all his Epistles when opportunity occurs,[1] a fact all the more noteworthy that he is not, like the scholastic theologian, the slave of a phrase, or unable or unwilling to vary the mode of expression. He speaks now of the righteousness of faith,[2] anon of being justified by faith,[3] at another time of faith being imputed for

---

[1] *Rom.* i. 17; iii. 21, 22; x. 3; 2 *Cor.* v. 21; *Phil.* iii. 9.
[2] *Phil.* iii. 9.   [3] *Rom.* v. 1.

righteousness,[1] and in all these cases the idea he wishes to express is essentially the same.

The righteousness of God, as the apostle conceives it, is something which belongs to the Christian man, yet is not his personal righteousness. It is a thing revealed,[2] and to which a man submits.[3] It also belongs to God, yet is not His personal righteousness. It is a "gift"[4] from God to men. It is divine credit for being righteous bestowed on a man when he believes in, or trusts, God. God accounts one who believes in His grace righteous; He reckons his faith for righteousness. So the apostle puts the matter in *Romans* iv.

This is the Pauline doctrine in its simplest, most elementary, undeveloped form. It gives, it will be observed, great prominence and importance to *faith*. Why may appear on further inquiry, but meantime it may be worth while to lay to heart the fact, and to weigh the significance of St. Paul's doctrine in its most general and fundamental aspect.

1. The doctrine is in the first place the very antithesis of Judaism. The watchword of Judaistic righteousness was "works," individual acts of conformity to law; that of the new evangelistic righteousness is faith, trust in the living, loving God. "Do" said the one, "believe" says the other.

2. Obviously the change in the watchword implies *an altered idea of God*. For Saul the legalist, God was an exacting taskmaster; for Paul the Christian, God has become the God of Jesus, a benignant gracious giver. What a revolution! No wonder the term "grace," $\chi \acute{a} \rho \iota \varsigma$, is of frequent occurrence in St. Paul's pages, and also

[1] *Rom.* iv. 24. [2] *Ibid.* i. 17. [3] *Ibid.* x. 3. [4] *Ibid.* v. 17.

faith, πίστις, its counterpart; for to grace in God answers faith, recipiency, in man. And of what perennial value is the doctrine that man is justified by *faith* and not by works, and that God is such a being that justification by faith is possible and *alone* possible! It is the charter of Christian liberty for all time: of emancipation from legalism with its treadmill service, and fear and gloom and uncertainty; from laborious self-salvation, whether by religious ceremonial, or by orthodox opinions, or by the magic power of sacraments.[1]

3. We may be sure that for Paul the ex-legalist, the intense hungerer after righteousness, who had abandoned Judaism because he had discovered its righteousness to be a vanity and vexation of spirit, the new-found righteousness of God is a great reality. "Faith imputed for righteousness" may sound artificial, and provoke the reflection, What men need is not to be reckoned righteous, but to be made actually righteous; but we may be sure that something real and valuable lurks under the phrase. For one thing pardon of sin is covered by it. This appears from *Rom.* iv. 6, 7, where the non-imputation of sin is represented as the equivalent of the imputation of righteousness without works. It also appears from the notable text, 2 *Cor.* v. 21, where it is said that Christ was made sin for us, that we might become the righteousness of God in Him. This is one of a group of texts through which the principle runs, that sanctifier and sanctified are all of one; Christ becoming what we are and we becoming what He is. He comes under a curse, that

[1] On this *vide* J. Freeman's Clarke's *The Ideas of the Apostle Paul translated into their Modern Equivalents* (1884) chap. v.

we may become exempt from the curse; He comes under law, that we may be set free from law. On the same principle Christ the sinless becomes or is made sin, that we the sinful may become sinless. That is to say, "the righteousness of God" is equivalent to the pardon or non-imputation of sin. Surely a solid boon to all who know what an accusing conscience is.

4. It is not likely that for St. Paul the ex-legalist the imputation of faith for righteousness will bear a sense which implies any notion of merit in faith, or turn faith into a new form of work. On the contrary, he takes pains to inform us that he has no sympathy with such a thought. "Where then," he asks, "is the boasting? It is excluded. By what sort of a law? of works? Nay, but by the law of faith."[1] That is to say, the spirit of self-complacency and that on which it feeds, self-righteousness, are incompatible with the very nature of faith. This is sound wholesome teaching, but to maintain it, it is not necessary to hold that faith has no moral contents or value. The contrary is undoubtedly the fact. To believe in God, to trust in His grace, is emphatically a righteous act. It is to do justice to God, to His character, to His spirit; to think right thoughts about Him, and to cherish a becoming attitude and feeling towards Him. It is the fundamental act of true righteousness. It is the only form of righteousness possible for sinners; it is a form of righteousness possible for the greatest sinner; nay, which is not only possible for him, but which he of all men can best exhibit, for the greater the sinner the greater the honour done to God by trust in

[1] *Rom.* iii. 27.

His grace. He who having sinned much trusts in divine grace is "strong in faith giving glory to God."[1] But there is no ground for boasting in that fact. Boasting is excluded by the nature of the case. A great sinner trusting in God's grace is simply one who humbly yet trustfully confesses his deep need of forgiveness. Such an one may, as Jesus taught, be exalted by God, but he cannot possibly exalt himself. The denizens of the slums do not think themselves very virtuous in accepting the invitation to a free breakfast; they simply eat ravenously and thankfully.

The foregoing observations help us to see that the crude elementary form of the Pauline doctrine of Justification is by no means to be despised or neglected as unimportant. It is indeed as little to be despised as the foundation of a house. For it is the religious foundation, and all beyond is theological superstructure, though we in our familiarity with developed doctrines are very apt to forget the fact. On this foundation rested the salvation of many who lived before the Christian era, Abraham included. Abraham believed God, and it was accounted unto him for righteousness, but he knew nothing of St. Paul's developed doctrine of Justification. Similar was the case of devout souls even in the days of our Lord. The faith of the publican in the parable is still of the Old Testament type, expressing itself in a prayer which echoes the 130th Psalm: "God be merciful to me the sinner." Yet he went down to his house "justified."[2] Even now, in the Christian era, there are men who feel compelled to fall back on the ultimate

[1] *Rom.* iv. 20. [2] *Luke* xviii. 14, δεδικαιωμένος.

religious truth, that a sinner's hope is in the mercy and grace of God, as the only thing they are able to grasp. It is not for us to say that such men cannot go down to their house justified. The words of Jesus, "He that humbleth himself shall be exalted,"[1] express a universal law in the moral order of the world.

It will be noted that even when taken in its most general form, the Pauline conception of evangelic righteousness, while possessing important affinities with the doctrine of Christ concerning the righteousness of the kingdom in its religious presuppositions, yet is distinct from anything we find in the synoptical presentation of our Lord's teaching. There is a righteousness of God in the doctrine of the kingdom, but it is subjective and ethical, not objective and theological. The nearest approach to the righteousness of God in the Pauline sense in the teaching of Christ is the pardoning grace of God. To pardon in Pauline phraseology is to treat as righteous.[2]

Let us proceed now to consider the apostle's specific doctrine of justification. Insight into it may be gained by a careful study of his statements concerning the nature and functions of faith. We are justified by faith, he teaches; what then is the faith that justifies?

1. An important light is thrown on this question by *Rom.* iii. 21–26, which may in one aspect be viewed as a definition or description of justifying faith. There faith is in the first place defined with reference to its personal object as the *faith of Christ*, which means not the faith

[1] *Luke* xviii. 14.
[2] On Christ's positive doctrine of righteousness, vide *The Kingdom of God*, p. 207.

that Jesus is the Christ, but rather faith in Christ as the embodiment of divine grace. It is further indicated that that in Christ on which the eye of faith is chiefly fixed is the redemption achieved by His death, wherein the grace of God to the sinful manifests itself. According to this passage, therefore, the faith that justifies is not simply faith in God, or faith in God's grace, or faith in the truth that Jesus is the Christ, but faith in Jesus as one who gave Himself to death for man's redemption, and so became the channel through which God's grace flows to sinners. Following out this idea of faith, justification might be defined as a judicial act, *whereby God regards as righteous those who trust in His grace as manifested in the atoning death of Christ.* This account of the matter might serve all practical purposes, and even be preferable to more highly differentiated definitions, especially for the purpose of catechetical instruction in the elements of the Christian religion.

2. But St. Paul has more to say concerning faith. In certain texts he seems to conceive of faith as grasping and appropriating to itself the ideal righteousness as realised in the conduct of Christ. So for example in the words: "As by one man's disobedience many were made sinners, so by the obedience of one shall many be made righteous."[1] Sinful in Adam, righteous in Christ, such seems to be the apostle's thought. Faith is indeed not mentioned in this place, but it may be held to be implied as the condition of becoming righteous in Christ. What faith can appropriate, God may impute. Introducing this new idea of the imputation of Christ's

[1] *Rom.* v. 19.

righteousness we get a more developed definition of justification, such as that in the Westminster Assembly's Shorter Catechism, according to which it is "an act of God's free grace, wherein He pardoneth all our sins, and accepteth us as righteous in His sight, only for the righteousness of Christ imputed to us, and received by faith alone." This definition may be regarded as a fair inference from Pauline texts, such as that above cited,[1] though it must be admitted that it lacks support in express Pauline phraseology. The apostle nowhere speaks of the righteousness of Christ being imputed, nor does he anywhere identify the righteousness of God given to faith with the righteousness of Christ, even in places where he might have been expected to do so, assuming that his way of thinking on the subject was similar to that of the theologians who compiled the Shorter Catechism, *e.g.* in *Philippians* iii. 9.[2] On this ground so conservative a theologian as Weiss maintains that the idea that God imputes to men the righteousness of Christ does not belong to the Pauline system of thought.[3]

3. The apostle conceives of faith as performing yet another function in reference to Christ's righteousness,—

---

[1] To which may be added 1 *Cor.* i. 26 and 2 *Cor.* v. 21.

[2] Where instead of τὴν διὰ πίστεως χριστοῦ might have stood τὴν δικαιοσύνην χριστοῦ, more especially as faith is mentioned in the next clause.

[3] *Vide* his *Lehrbuch der Biblischen Theologie des N.T.*, sect. 82, *b*, note 2: Pfleiderer in his *Urchristenthum*, p. 250, and in the second edition of his *Paulinismus* (1890), p. 184, inclines to the same view. He remarks that the non-use by St. Paul of the expression "the imputation of Christ's righteousness" is the more remarkable, as the imputation of the merits of the fathers and of saints was a feature in the theology of the Jewish synagogue.

as not only appropriating it as a ground of pardon, but as establishing such a relation between Christ and a believer as guarantees that the ideal objective righteousness without shall eventually become a real righteousness within. So in these words, forming a part of the famous Antioch remonstrance: "I am crucified with Christ, yet I live; and yet no longer I, but Christ liveth in me, and the life which I now live in the flesh I live by faith in the Son of God who loved me, and gave Himself up for me."[1] Is this function of faith included *in the faith that justifies*? If so, then our formula will be: *God regards as righteous all whose faith in Christ not only lays claim to His righteousness as its own, but contains in itself the guarantee for the ultimate reproduction of a kindred righteousness in the character of the believer.* But here the theological ways part. There have always been two tendencies at work in the Church, one to restrict and minimise the function of faith in justification, the other to make it as comprehensive as possible. For those who follow the former tendency, faith is simply a hand laying hold of an external benefit, a garment of righteousness to cover spiritual nakedness; for the patrons of the latter, faith is the fruitful germ of all true righteousness, containing the promise and potency of a new Christlike life. Both parties are animated by a genuine religious interest, the one by a desire to exclude a new form of legalism coming in under the wing of faith, the other by a desire to make sure that the righteousness of God given to faith shall be something real and Godworthy, not something shadowy, formal and artificial.

[1] *Gal.* ii. 20.

Yet it is possible that in their antagonism to each other these two parties may both err in opposite directions.

As is well known, the Protestant theological tradition has very decidedly leant to the side of minimising faith's function. The great doctors of the Lutheran and Reformed Confessions emptied faith of all moral contents, that no pretext might remain for ascribing to it justifying virtue, and assigned to it simply the humble service of claiming an interest in the foreign righteousness of Christ. They even went the length of setting aside the scriptural idea of the imputation of faith, and substituting for it the idea of the imputation of Christ's righteousness, keeping themselves right with St. Paul by the ingenious device of taking faith, in the texts where it is said to be imputed, *objectively*, so bringing out the meaning that not the act of believing, but the object believed in, the righteousness of Christ, is imputed. This manner of handling the *locus* of justification is very open to criticism. In the first place, it is unfortunate that the Protestant doctors, in their laudable zeal against neo-legalism, should have found it necessary to become un-Pauline in their terminology, banishing from their theological vocabulary the imputation of faith as not only inexact but even heretical,[1] and employing exclusively a phrase which, however legitimate as an inference from Scripture texts, has no express scriptural warrant. This fact is an index that somehow they had got upon the wrong track, and had fallen into one-sided-

---

[1] This attitude is reflected in the *Westminster Confession*, chap xi., where among the false ways of justification that "by imputing faith itself" is specified.

ness in their way of thinking. Then, in the second place, the justifying faith of this very controversial, extremely anti-Romish, theology, is an abstraction. A faith which is no more than a mere hand to lay hold of an external righteousness has no existence except in the brain of a scholastic theologian. Faith, if it deserve the name, is always very much more than this. The more the better. Faith cannot have too much moral contents; the more it has, the better it will serve us from the beginning to the end of our Christian career. At the very least, true faith is always a humble trust in the grace of God, and that is a thing of real moral value. Then it lies in the very nature of true faith to open the soul to the influence of Christ, so that from the day we believe in Him He becomes a renovating power in our life. Lastly, the scrupulous anxiety to shut out legalism in the form of the imputation of faith, as the germ of a personal Christian righteousness, may readily defeat itself by introducing unawares legalism under another guise. We do not get rid of legalism by careful theological definitions designed to exclude it. We may introduce thereby a dogmatic legalism as blighting in its influence on the Christian life as the Judaism of the apostolic age or the Sacramentarianism of Rome. It cannot be good for the health of our piety that we should be constantly taking care that our faith in the God of all grace shall be as destitute as possible of moral contents, lest perchance we fall into the mistake of finding in an ethically rich faith a ground of boasting.

But on the other hand it may be well for the health of Christian piety that we should think of God as imputing faith for righteousness only in respect of its objective function. It is perfectly true that from the divine point of view the distinctions we make between the different stages in the process of salvation are evanescent. To the divine eye, contemplating all things *sub specie æternitatis*, the whole drama of salvation in its five acts—foreknowledge, foreordination, calling, justification, sanctification [1]—is one. Yet from the human point of view, it may be important to distinguish between the stages, especially between the two last named. It may be advantageous even in order to the consummation devoutly to be wished—conformity to the image of Christ—that we should conceive of God as justifying us on purely objective grounds, without reference to the work of grace He is to accomplish in us. It may give us a powerful initial impetus onwards towards the goal to be told that God pardons our sins, and accepts us as righteous, on account of the moral ideal realised in Christ, the object of our trust. It may start us on our way with a peace, joy, and hope impossible to one who is constantly thinking of the uncertainties of the future. So Jesus dealt with penitents. With cheerful, hope-inspiring tone He said unconditionally, "Thy faith hath saved thee, go into peace," while perfectly aware that there were risks ahead, and that peace could not last unless sin were finally forsaken.

Is it not thus that St. Paul also conceives God as dealing with men in the matter of justification? In answering this question in the affirmative, I do not lay much stress on the verbal interpretation of the Pauline

[1] *Rom.* viii. 29, 30.

words δικαιοῦν and δικαίωσις. The controversy as to the meaning of these words is now as good as ended. It is admitted on all hands by theologians of the most diverse schools, that in the apostle's use they bear a judicial or forensic sense. Dr. Newman in England, in 1838, taught that justification in the abstract, and as such, is an imputation and a counting righteous,[1] and Dr. Lipsius in Germany, in 1853, taught that δικαιοῦν never means *justum facere*, but always *justum habere*. But both strenuously opposed the purely forensic conception of justification. Dr. Newman held that while in the abstract it is a counting righteous, in the concrete it is a making righteous, and Dr. Lipsius maintained that in so far as it is a judicial sentence pronounced at the commencement of the Christian life, it is simply the pre-announcement of a real inward righteousness which God intends by His grace to make forthcoming.[2] In effect the position taken up by both is, that God justifies because He intends to sanctify.

Was that the apostle's position? I think not, though in saying so I do not for a moment doubt that what the apostle desired for himself and for all Christians, was a real personal inward righteousness, and that he would think nothing had been gained unless that were gained. Neither do I doubt that in his view God aimed at this result, even that believers should be conformed to the image of His Son. But two considerations lead me to believe that St. Paul did not conceive of future sanctification as the ground of initial justification. The first is

---

[1] *Vide* his *Lectures on Justification*, p. 70.
[2] Vide *Die Paul. Rechtfertigungslehre*, p. 17.

what he says in 2 *Cor.* v. 19 about "God in Christ reconciling the world unto Himself, not imputing their trespasses unto them." These words suggest the idea of a general justification of mankind, in the form of a non-imputation of sins, on the purely objective ground of God's satisfaction with the merits of Jesus Christ. Individual justification on that view will naturally mean entering by faith into the state of grace in which God for Christ's sake is pleased to place the world. Doubtless this is but the beginning of salvation, but it is a momentous beginning, which one who, like St. Paul, had tried to reach salvation by the legal method was not likely to undervalue. No wonder he appropriates to it the title, *the righteousness of God*, as if it were the principal thing or even everything. This does not mean that he undervalues what follows. It means that he has a due sense of the infinite importance of being at last *on the right road*. It indicates also, probably, his desire to give prominence to objective justification as a *great, public, world-wide fact*: God reconciling the world to Himself in Christ. Finally, it means giving the place of honour to that feature in the Pauline conception of Christianity, at which the antagonism between it and legalism is most conspicuous. The quest of personal righteousness was common to the two systems; in their attitude towards the righteousness of God, they were diametrically opposed.

The other consideration that weighs much with me is this: St. Paul in his Epistle to the Romans does not refer to the subjective aspect of faith as a renewing power till he has finished his exposition of the doctrine of justification. He takes up faith's function in establishing a vital union with Christ in the sixth chapter, continuing the theme to the end of chapter viii. But already he has said in exultant tone: "Being justified by faith, we have peace with God, and joy in hope of glory, in tribulation, and in God Himself." Does not this amount to the exclusion of faith's sanctifying function from the grounds of justification? To the end of chap. v. the apostle seems to be treating of an objective righteousness, and from that point onwards to the end of chap. viii. of a righteousness that is subjective. How the two aspects were related in his mind will be a subject of inquiry hereafter: meantime the important matter is to be satisfied in our own minds that there are two aspects to be frankly recognised.

4. There remain to be noticed two other statements in the Pauline Epistles respecting faith's functions which appear to have a bearing on the subject of justification. I refer to *Romans* iv. 25 and x. 9, in both of which faith seems to be viewed as having for its proper object the *resurrection* of Christ, and faith in Christ's resurrection seems to be regarded as the ground of justification. How are these texts to be understood? The suggestion that when St. Paul represents Christ as raised διὰ τὴν δικαίωσιν ἡμῶν he uses the term δικαίωσις in the sense of sanctification, is justly put aside on the ground that this interpretation is not in accordance with Pauline usage, or in keeping with the connection of thought in which the word here occurs. More acceptable is the explanation offered by the majority of commentators, that the apostle in these passages means to represent Christ's resurrection as the ground not of our

justification but of our *faith in the atoning character of His death*. "The resurrection of the sacrificed One was required to produce in men the faith through which alone the objective fact of the atoning offering of Jesus could have the effect of δικαίωσις subjectively."[1] But M. Ménégoz has propounded a new theory, which, because of the ability, freshness, and real value of his contribution to the elucidation of the Pauline system of thought, claims respectful consideration. Briefly it is this: that the resurrection of Christ was necessary in the first place for His own justification, and that through faith in that resurrection we become partakers of Christ's justification. The author of *Le Péché et la Rédemption* finds in *Phil.* iii. 8–10 the most precise statement of the Pauline doctrine of justification by faith, which he thinks no theologian has perfectly understood. "The key of the system," in his view, "is on the one hand the notion of the justification of Christ by death and resurrection, and on the other hand the notion of the identification of the individual with the person of Christ by faith."[2] "That which is peculiar to Paul is the mystic notion of the identification of man with Jesus Christ by faith, and the appropriation by that means of the justification of Christ."[3] The idea of Christ needing to be justified by resurrection may appear strange, but the author quoted is quite in earnest in broaching it. Its presuppositions in the Pauline system, as he understands it, are these:—Death is the punishment of sin; he that has paid the penalty of transgression has satisfied justice and is entitled to go free. The thief when his term of imprisonment is at an end must be

[1] Meyer *in loc.* [2] *Le Péché*, etc. p. 270.
[3] *Ibid.* etc. p. 271.

set at liberty. In like manner Christ, who died for our sins, had by death squared accounts with justice and was entitled to return to life. If it be asked, Would it not have sufficed that the crucified One should continue to live on in the spirit without a physical resurrection? our author replies that, according to the Pauline system, death is the destruction of life, and death in that sense, not the endurance of eternal pain, is the penalty of sin. Paul was a monist, a man for him was an animated body, and the destruction of the body by death was the destruction of life. Therefore it is not by accident that nowhere in his writings can we find a trace of a resurrection for the wicked. Hence also it follows that had Jesus not risen it would have meant that He had perished with the wicked.

Space will not admit of a detailed criticism of this theory on all sides, and especially in connection with its anthropological and eschatological presuppositions. A few remarks only can be offered here. It certainly has the merit of assigning a strong reason for the resurrection of Christ, in viewing it as what was due to One who had borne the full penalty of sin. Nor can we object to the theory that it leaves no room for an objective justification of sinners; inasmuch as, while the author certainly seems to lay chief stress on subjective justification by the mystic power of faith, he might quite legitimately regard the resurrection of Christ as a general justification of the world. But this novel and ingenious explanation of the apostle's doctrine is at fault in other directions. In the first place, under it justification bears two different senses, in reference to Christ on the one hand, and to believers on the other. In reference to us, it means either, according to one school, accounting those righteous who are not yet really righteous, or making them righteous by a gradual process, according to a different understanding of the apostle's meaning. In reference to Christ it means neither of these things, but acknowledging that the Just One had vicariously paid the full penalty of sin so that sin had no more right over him: He was *justified from sin*.[1] Then, secondly, a double meaning lurks under the word death also, as applied to Christ and to sinners. If death be the wages of sin, and Christ died in the capacity of a sinner, why should He rise any more than any other man who dies as a criminal? If one by death can be justified from sin so as to be entitled to rise again, why not all? Obviously in the case of Christ death is not taken in the sense of destruction, which it is held to bear in reference to the wicked, but simply in the sense of death's *pain*. The propounder of the theory now under consideration admits that this double sense of death is involved, but he charges it as a fault against the apostle's system of thought, not against his own interpretation of it. Finally, it is strange that this view, if really held by St. Paul, has left so little trace in his vocabulary. He is rich in words expressing co-partnership between the believer and Christ. There is a co-crucifixion, a co-dying, a co-burial, a co-rising, a co-living, a co-suffering, a co-glorification. The diapason would be complete if a co-justification found its place among these joint-experiences. But it is not forthcoming. If the apostle meant to teach the doctrine M. Ménégoz ascribes to him, he has not been happy in his language.[2]

[1] *Rom.* vi. 7.
[2] In the new edition of *Der Paulinismus*, Pfleiderer, while not adopt-

ing the theory of Ménégoz, speaks very favourably of it, as reasonable in itself and consistent with Pauline texts. *Vide* p. 160. I have read what my esteemed colleague Dr. Candlish says in the *Expositor* for December 1893, on the theory of Christ's justification by resurrection. He cites several authors as holding this view, and remarks that instead of being a novelty it might rather be regarded as a commonplace of theology. It is hardly that surely, but rather a curious opinion of certain theologians, concerning which Pfleiderer, Everett, and myself, might excusably be ignorant. In some respects, certainly, the view of Ménégoz is peculiar, *e.g.*, that the alternatives in the case of Christ were resurrection or annihilation; there being no life hereafter for the wicked.

CHAPTER IX

THE DEATH OF CHRIST

OF the four lessons which Jesus taught His disciples concerning the significance of His death, the first was that, in enduring a violent death at the hands of men, He should be suffering for righteousness' sake.[1] In this earliest lesson the Master presented His approaching end under a purely ethical aspect, and consistently therewith He spoke of it not as an isolated event, but as a fact falling under a general law, according to which all who are faithful to the divine interest in an evil world must endure suffering. From this point of view it is obvious that it is not for the death of Christ alone that a *rationale* is wanted. The question may legitimately be raised, What is the final cause of the sufferings of the righteous generally ? a question on which the thoughts of Old Testament prophets, psalmists, and sages had been much exercised. There is need of a theodicy along the whole line. Does the same theodicy suffice for the case of Jesus and for that of all His fellow-sufferers ? May we reason about the latter as St. Paul reasoned about the former, and say : If death be the

---

[1] Vide *The Kingdom of God*, chap. x.; *vide* also the supplementary note on the *Teaching of St. Paul compared with the Teaching of our Lord in the Synoptical Gospels*, at the end of this volume.

penalty of sin, there are only two alternatives: either all who suffer, suffer for their own sins—the theory of Job's friends; or some who suffer, suffer redemptively, for the sins of others—the theory hinted at in the fifty-third chapter of Isaiah interpreted historically as referring to the afflictions of God's faithful ones in Israel?

The ethical aspect of Christ's death is hardly touched on in the Pauline literature. What the apostle might have done had he written copiously and systematically on the subject one cannot guess, but it is certain that in the Epistles which form the basis of the present study he contemplates the death of Jesus by itself apart, and exclusively from a religious and theological view-point. His whole aim in all his statements regarding that event is, to point out the significance for faith of a unique experience befalling One believed to be personally sinless, who could not therefore be conceived of as in His passion suffering for His own sin. What we have to do now is, as far as possible, to ascertain the meaning and estimate the value of these statements.

In our rapid survey of the four principal Epistles we lighted on certain texts bearing all the appearance of being forms of language into which the brooding thought of the writer on the death of Jesus had finally crystallised. Among the great Pauline *logia* relating to that theme, fall to be classed those which speak of Christ being made a curse and sin for us that we might become curse-free and sinless.[1] To these, as not less important, must be added the word in Romans iii. 25, in which God is represented as publicly exhibiting Jesus in His death in a propitiatory

[1] *Gal.* iii. 13; 2 *Cor.* v. 21.

capacity. Having already used the passage in which that text occurs for the purpose of throwing light on the righteousness of God, and the faith which justifies, we may begin our study of St. Paul's teaching concerning the significance of Christ's death by returning to it to consider the instruction which it contains on the latter topic.

The word ἱλαστήριον has given almost as much trouble to commentators as θυμιατήριον in *Hebrews* ix. 4, though not for the same reason. In the latter case there would be little doubt as to the meaning were it not that the true rendering, "the altar of incense," *seems* to involve the writer in an inaccuracy as to the location of that piece of furniture in the tabernacle. In the case of the former, the difficulty arises from the paucity of material of kindred character in the Pauline literature to guide us in interpretation. On first thoughts one is inclined to assume that the term ἱλαστήριον is employed to represent Christ in His death as a propitiatory sacrifice or sin-offering. But then it is noticeable, and has indeed been insisted on by expositors of weight,[1] that St. Paul makes very little use elsewhere of the Levitical sacrificial system in the formulation of his doctrine of the cross, and there is force in the remark that that system would be far less congenial to his mind as a vehicle of thought than prophetic utterances concerning the suffering servant of Jehovah such as those contained in *Isaiah* liii. Then, further, it has to be considered that in the Septuagint the term in question is not employed to denote the sin offering. It is rather used as the Greek equivalent for the Kapporeth, the lid of the ark, or the mercy-seat. Accordingly, the older interpreters assumed

[1] So Weiss and Pfleiderer.

that the apostle followed the Septuagint usage, and found in the text the, in many respects attractive, idea that in Christ God had provided for a sinful world the mercy-seat of the new dispensation, a mercy-seat sprinkled with Christ's precious blood, like the lid of the ark with the blood of the victim on the great day of atonement. Those who, like most recent interpreters, reject this sense as fanciful, and not suitable in an Epistle written to Romans, have to choose between two other alternatives, either taking ἱλαστήριον as a noun signifying definitely a propitiatory victim, or as a neuter adjective signifying generally a means of propitiation.[1]

In our perplexity it may be well to see if we cannot to a greater extent than has been thought possible make St. Paul his own interpreter. For this purpose it is important to observe that in *Romans* iii. 21–26, he resumes the thought of *Romans* i. 17, 18. At least it is quite certain that *Romans* iii. 21 resumes the thought of *Romans* i. 17. In the latter text the apostle had spoken prelusively of a righteousness of God which he had not at that point the opportunity of further explaining, his mind going off immediately on the topic of the world's sin. The sin-section ended, he returns to the theme at *Romans* iii. 21, and tells his readers what the righteous-

[1] Wendt favours the old interpretation, *vide* his essay on "Die Lehre des Paulus verglichen mit der Lehre Jesu," in *Zeitschrift für Theologie und Kirche*, 1894. He says, p. 53 : " Indem Gott den Tod Christi zur Erweisung seiner den Sünder gnadenmässig gerechtsprechenden Gnade veranstaltet hat, ist Christus in seinem Blute, d. h. in seinem Kreuzestode, zu einer öffentlich dargestellten Kapporet, zu einer allgemein anschaulichen Offenbarung des Gnaden-willens Gottes geworden."

ness of God to which he had alluded really is. Now, this being the fact with regard to the topic of the *righteousness* of God, is it not every way likely that the same thing holds true regarding the other topic, mentioned in *Romans* i. 18, and that the apostle has in his mind the *wrath* of God when he speaks of God as publicly setting forth Christ as ἱλαστήριον in His blood? The suggestion needs only to be made to commend itself; but confirmation, if needful, may be found in *Romans* v. 9, where we find God's wrath and Christ's blood associated in the apostle's thought. But if at *Romans* iii. 25 the apostle reverts to what he had said in *Romans* i. 18, then it is natural to suppose that in the death of Jesus he sees two things: a *revelation* of divine wrath, and a *means of averting it*. Both point in the direction of a sacrificial victim; not necessarily after the analogy of Levitical sacrifices, for the apostle may have had in view the human sacrifices with which Greek and Roman story makes us familiar. That would be indeed a bold collocation; but boldness is what we expect from St. Paul, not to mention that what he says in *Romans* v. 7, about one man dying for another, tends to show that he would not have regarded the use of heathen instances in illustration of the gospel as improper or inadmissible. His appeal is to general human history.

The fact-basis of the idea that Christ suffered death as a sacrificial victim is that His blood was shed (ἐν τῷ ἑαυτοῦ αἵματι). His death was a violent one, and looking away from subordinate, human causality, the apostle sees in it only the hand of God; it was God that put Jesus to death as a lamb slain for the sin of the world. And by this act God in the first place, as St. Paul views the matter, demonstrated, revealed His wrath against sin. For this I take to be the revelation of wrath whereof the apostle speaks in *Romans* i. 18. Commentators have been at a loss to know what the revelation consisted in, or how it was made, and in their perplexity have taken refuge in the unnatural vices of the pagans as the divinely-appointed penalty of sin. It seems to me that we should find both the revelations spoken of, of righteousness and of wrath, in the death of Jesus. By that death, according to the apostle, God shows what He really thinks of sin. Apart from that death, men might be inclined to ask: If God be so angry at the wickedness of the world, why does He not make some signal display of His indignation? To judge from appearances, one would say He did not care. Men go on sinning, from bad to worse, and He makes no sign. St. Paul replies: Look to Calvary; there is the sign. God's wrath against sin is such that He inflicts that bloody, cruel death on His own Son, occupying the position of a propitiatory victim.

While assigning to Christ's death the double function of revealing and averting divine wrath, like the thunderstorm which at once reveals and heals electric trouble in the air, the apostle has in view chiefly the latter aspect. His aim is not to proclaim the fact that Christ was slain as a sacrifice, but rather to emphasise the gracious purpose for which He suffered. Therefore ἱλαστήριον is to be taken as an adjective rather than as a noun, because, so understood, the word makes the gracious purpose more prominent. The apostle leaves the revelation of wrath in the background, and brings to the front the revelation of love, providing a way of escape from wrath. He says here in effect what he says further on in express terms: "God commendeth His own love towards us, in that while we were yet sinners Christ died for us!"[1] He means to accentuate the love of God, not His wrath, or even His righteousness. He does indeed speak of God's righteousness— that is, of His regard for moral interests, but not dogmatically by way of teaching the necessity for the manifestation or "satisfaction" of divine justice in connection with human salvation, but rather apologetically by way of pointing out that the actual method of salvation is such that God cannot rightfully be charged with moral indifference; the death of Christ showing that, whatever facts in the world's history might seem to point in a contrary direction, sin is not really a trivial matter in God's sight.

By finding in the word ἱλαστήριον a real though tacit reference to the wrath of God, we bring this Pauline text into line with the two referred to on a previous page, and also with the *logion* in *Galatians* iv. 4. In these three passages one principle is involved, viz., that in His earthly experience Christ was subjected to all that is unblessed in man's unredeemed state, with the result of man being delivered from it. This is the principle of redemption. Christ's *whole state of humiliation* was the λύτρον, the resulting benefit for us is ἀπολύτρωσις. He was made under the law, by circum-

[1] *Rom.* v. 8.

cision and otherwise, and we are redeemed from subjection to law into sonship. He was made a curse, and we are redeemed from the law's curse. He was made sin, and we are made sinless. Adding to these three instances the fourth suggested in *Romans* iii. 25, Christ became in lot an object of divine wrath, with the effect that men guilty of sins provocative of God's indignation are shielded and saved from wrath. This principle, or law, well established by these examples, may be used as a clue to the meaning of a text which has given much trouble to commentators—*Romans* viii. 3. It has commonly been assumed that the condemnation of sin in the flesh referred to in the last clause took place in Christ's *death*, περὶ ἁμαρτίας being taken in the sense of a sin offering. God sending His Son in the likeness of sinful flesh, and as an offering for sin, in His sacrificial death condemned sin in the flesh—such is the traditional interpretation. Is it quite certain that this is the true meaning? Let us see. It may be assumed that St. Paul here points to an experience of Christ that meets a need of man which has been the subject of remark in the preceding context. But of what need has the apostle been speaking? Our need of help to resist and overcome the law of sin in the members, the preponderant and domineering influence of the flesh. But what is there in Christ's earthly experience that can give us help here? One would say, not His death, but rather His holy life in the flesh, demonstrating that bondage to the σάρξ is not inevitable, embodying in a successful experiment of resistance God's condemnation of sin in the flesh, as a thing that ought not to be and that need not be, Christ's life in the

Spirit being, not less than His death, a divine appointment for man's good. The application of the principle exemplified in the other four texts to this fifth one would lead to the same conclusion. That principle requires that the experience of Christ which is to benefit us in any given way must correspond to the nature of the benefit. The benefit in the present instance being emancipation from hopelessness as to the possibility of walking in the Spirit in spite of the flesh, the redemptive experience of Christ ought to be the proof supplied in His life that to walk in the Spirit is not impossible. It may indeed be asked, Where is the element of humiliation in that experience of Christ? The reply must be, In the fact that He was sent in the *likeness of sinful flesh*; in other words, that His life on earth was enacted, like ours, under conditions involving temptation to sin. God's whole aim in sending His Son into the world was with reference to sin ($\pi\epsilon\rho\grave{\iota}$ $\dot{a}\mu a\rho\tau\acute{\iota}a\varsigma$), that by every part of His earthly experience He might work in one way or another towards the destruction of sin. Christ's personal struggle with temptation arising out of the flesh was designed to make its contribution to this end; and it does so not merely by way of example, but by way of a divine proclamation that the malign dominion of the flesh is at an end, and that henceforth men shall be enabled to walk in the Spirit, even while living in the flesh. As the reign of law was doomed by the mere fact that Christ was made under the law, so the reign of the flesh is doomed by the mere fact that Christ was sent in the likeness of sinful flesh.[1]

[1] This is in substance the view of this text taken by Godet and

It is important to note that, in all these instances of the principle or law of redemption, the apostle gives us what he conceives to be the religious significance of the *obvious* facts of Christ's experience. When he says, *e.g.*, that Christ was made under law, he has in view mainly the fact that He was *circumcised*. In like manner he conceives of Christ as made sin by enduring *physical death*, the appointed and historic penalty of sin; as made a curse by enduring death *in the form of crucifixion*;[1] as made under God's wrath by enduring death *in a manner which involved blood-shedding*, as in the case of sacrificial victims; and as made in the likeness of sinful flesh, *because subject to temptation arising out of the affections of the flesh*, as in the case of the first temptation in the wilderness. To a dogmatically trained intellect, the fact-basis for the corresponding theological categories may appear slight, and the temptation is strong to supply for the doctrinal superstructure, either from the evangelic history or from imagination, a broader, more adequate foundation. The procedure may be very natural, but it is not exegesis. We must remember that St. Paul's problem was not the same as that of the scholastic theologian. When he became a believer, the imperative task for him was to read in a new light *the plain surface facts of Christ's earthly history*. The question he had to ask and answer as best he could was: What meaning am I to put upon the facts that One whom I now

Weiss. *Vide* Godet's *Commentary*, and Weiss's *Lehrbuch der Bibl. Theologie des N.T.*, p. 308.

[1] See note at the end of this chapter on Professor Everett's *The Gospel of Paul*.

believe to be the Messiah and the Holy One of God was circumcised, and endured death by crucifixion and by blood-shedding? On the other hand, the problem of the systematic theologian is to verify and justify the theological categories supplied to him in the apostle's answer to that question by an exhaustive statement of the relative facts. In doing this he is in danger of stepping out of the region of history into the realm of imagination, a danger which has been proved to be very real in connection with Christ's endurance of the wrath of God, and of death as the penalty of sin, representatives of Protestant scholastic orthodoxy not hesitating to say that Christ endured the essence of eternal death, and was the object of God's extreme hatred.[1] In so doing they might be very consistent and thoroughgoing as theorists, but the doctrine they thus taught is at once unscriptural and incredible. Let not St. Paul be made responsible for such extravagances.

Under the Pauline law of redemption, the benefit resulting to men from Christ's mediation is in the first place to be conceived objectively. Thus, Christ having been made under law, redemption from legalism *forthwith* ensues as the objective privilege of humanity. That, in the view of God and in the religious history of the world, is the significance of Christ's subjection to legal ordinances. The era of legalism therewith ended, and the era of liberty began. Very different was the construction the Judaist would be inclined to put on the fact. Christ was circumcised, therefore the

[1] For examples, *vide* my *Humiliation of Christ*, Lecture vii. Note B.

law must be perpetual, for has not the Lord of the Church given it the sanction of His example? so he would reason. On the contrary, replied St. Paul, the circumcision of Jesus was the death-knell of the law; He underwent the humiliation of subjection to law for the very purpose of putting an end to legal bondage; His experience in that respect was the ransom He paid for our emancipation. Similarly with all the other applications of the principle. Thus, because Christ was made sin for us by subjection to death, therefore, *ipso facto*, God was in Christ reconciling the world unto Himself, not imputing unto men their trespasses. So again, because Christ was made subject to temptation arising from the flesh, God condemned sin in the flesh, declared that the dominion of the flesh, as of the law must take end, and be replaced by the benign dispensation of the Spirit. In a word, at whatever point in our low estate Christ comes in contact with us, in life or in death, His touch exercises a magical emancipating influence, beneficently altering in relation to God the situation of the world.

But this is not the whole truth. The objective change takes place with a view to a corresponding subjective one, without which the former would remain an abstract ideal and a barren benefit. The objective privilege must be subjectively realised. The position of sonship must be accompanied with the spirit of sonship, otherwise I shall be a slave of legalism, though living in the era of grace. The general amnesty which ensued from Christ having been made sin must be realised individually as a divine forgiveness of personal sin. So the apostle views the matter, hence the stress which he everywhere lays on faith. For it is faith's function to transmute the objective state of privilege into a subjective experience; to turn an ideal redemption into an actual one all along the line. Thus it is to be noted that the apostle is careful to represent Christ's sacrificial death as propitiatory *through faith*. Codex A omits the words, but there can be no reasonable doubt as to their genuineness. The idea they express is so essential to the Pauline system of thought that even if they were not in the text they would have to be understood. It is through faith, and only for the believer, that Christ's death becomes effectively propitiatory, a real shield against the divine wrath. And so throughout the whole range of benefit. There must be appropriating faith if God's goodwill to men for Christ's sake is not to remain comparatively barren and inoperative.

But not even yet have we got to the bottom of St. Paul's mind. I have not hitherto attempted to translate the principle of redemption obtained inductively from Pauline texts into the technical terms of theology. It is not imperative on an interpreter to undertake the task of translation, and he might excusably feel some measure of perplexity in an endeavour to fit such non-scriptural terms as "substitute" and "representative" into his exegetical results. But perhaps it is not far off the mark to say, that while the idea of Christ as a substitute fits into the conception of His death as sacrificial, the idea of representation best accords with the whole group of texts from which I have gathered by induction the Pauline law of redemption. In these texts

Christ appears as a central person in whom the human race is collected into a moral-unity, having one responsibility and one interest, all things as far as possible common, even sin and righteousness, which one would think inseparable from personality, being treated as separable entities passing freely from one side to the other, sin to the sinless One, righteousness to the unrighteous. It is a case of *objective identity*. And the point I wish to make now is, that this objective identity does not content St. Paul, not to speak of substitution which expresses too external a relation to have any chance of satisfying his mind. He cannot rest content with anything short of *subjective identity* between Redeemer and redeemed, implying that Christ is not only by divine appointment and in outward lot, but in conscious sympathy, one with men, and on the other hand that they are one with Him in the same manner, making His experience their own. The former aspect of this subjective identity is not at all so prominent in the Epistles of St. Paul as in the Epistle to the Hebrews, in which the sympathy of Christ is one of the great outstanding ideas, the whole earthly career of the Captain of salvation, not excluding His passion, being regarded as a curriculum of trial and suffering designed to develop in Him the spirit of compassion essential to the priestly vocation. But there are significant hints of the truth, as when the apostle adduces as a motive for Christian consideration of others the fact that Christ pleased not Himself,[1] urges the duty of mutual burden-bearing as a

---

[1] *Rom.* xv. 3, which, however, is proved not by facts taken from Christ's history, but by a quotation from a psalm.

fulfilment of the law of Christ,[1] and represents the Lord Jesus as becoming poor for our sakes.[2] There can be no doubt that he would include in the self-impoverishment of Jesus the whole state of humiliation as voluntarily endured out of sympathy with men, though in mentioning the details of that state he presents the experience of Christ as something to which He was subjected rather than as something He voluntarily incurred.

The other aspect of the subjective identity, the sympathy of believers with Christ, is made very prominent in St. Paul's teaching. It is all due to the action of faith, which, as he conceives it, cannot be restricted to the act of appropriating a benefit, but, like ivy clinging to a wall, lays hold of everything in the experience of Christ that is capable of being turned into a source of spiritual life. As Christ in love made His own every detail in our unredeemed state, so faith in the exercise of its native clinging power makes its own every critical stage in Christ's redeeming experience, His death, burial, resurrection, and ascension, and compels the redeemed man to re-enact these crises in his own spiritual history. "I am crucified with Christ";[3] "if One died, then all died."[4] So St. Paul judged; so he viewed the matter; so judge all like-minded. To put it so may appear to be making it a matter of opinion, a mere affair of personal moral idiosyncrasy. And there can be no question that many who pass for believers do not so judge, at least with anything like the earnestness

[1] *Gal.* vi. 2. [2] 2 *Cor.* viii. 9.
[3] *Gal.* ii. 20. [4] 2 *Cor.* v. 14.

of St. Paul, and the fact gives urgency to the inquiry as to the guarantees for ethical interests in the Pauline system. This will come up for consideration hereafter; meantime our business is to understand the apostle's own way of conceiving the believing man's relation to the Redeemer. And the thing to be noted is, that in his view the function of faith is not merely to lay hold of a purchased benefit, but to impose a serious ethical task, that of dying to live. The fact suggests the query, whether after all he so entirely overlooked the ethical aspect of Christ's own death as I said, and as on the surface it seems. If for us being crucified with Christ is an ethical process, must not crucifixion for Him also have had an ethical motive and end? So it naturally appears to us, but it does not follow that that view of the matter was much or at all present to the apostle's mind. We must take his ideas as they stand, and the fact is that he does not present the death of Christ and the co-dying of Christians under the same categories of thought. Death in Christ's case is physical, in the case of the believer mystical. The reason for dying in the one case is a transcendent theological one, in the other it is moral. On this account the dying-to-live to which the Christian is summoned loses the impetus arising from its being presented as the ideal and universal law of all true life, and is based on the weaker though not lower ground of a believer's sense of congruity and honour.[1]

In St. Paul's own case the new life lost nothing on

---

[1] *Vide* the late Professor Green's "Witness of God," *Works*, vol. iii. p. 230, where a purely ethical view of Christ's death is presented.

that account, partly because the moral ideal was operative in his reason and conscience under disguise, but chiefly because the religious fervour and energy of his faith and the grateful devotion of his love were of themselves all-powerful motives to Christlike living. The love of Christ who died for him "constrained" him to die with Him and to live unto Him. Then his faith, with its power of vivid imaginative apprehension, laid Christ under contribution as a source of inspiration in every conceivable way. For it Christ was at once Vicar, Representative, and Brother blended together in indissoluble unity. There was therefore no risk in his case of justification taking place without sanctification, through faith laying hold of a certain benefit, objective righteousness, procured by Christ's death, and looking to nothing but its own private interest. His faith so contemplated Christ that He became at once and with equal certainty unto him believing, the ground of pardon and the source of a new life, Christ for him and Christ in him. And it was such faith as his own he had in view in all his discussions on justification. It was a yielding of the heart to the love of God and of Christ, and as such not merely the reception of the gift of salvation, but the entering into a mystic unity of life and of love with the source of salvation.

It will be well for the interests both of theology and of religion that we earnestly endeavour to make this Pauline conception of faith our own. The consequence of losing sight of it in theology is, that the living organism of Paulinism becomes resolved into a dead collection of scholastic dogmas standing side by side in a system, but having no vital affinities; and in religion that the unseemly spectacle is presented, in the case of many professed believers, of men looking to Christ for deliverance from guilt and wrath without devotion to Him as the Lord, or any trace of that all-pervading moral sensitiveness one expects to see in a Christian.

These dangers are by no means imaginary. They beset us both as Protestants and as Evangelic Christians. As Protestants, because our bias in that capacity is to empty faith of all moral contents on which a doctrine of merit might be based; and, as controversy with Romanist theology leads the Protestant dogmatist to give a very exceptional prominence to justification, it may readily come to pass that he shall hardly find leisure or opportunity, to say nothing of inclination, to regard faith under any other aspect. As Evangelic Christians, because in that character we naturally interest ourselves much in those whom Jesus pitied, the lost, and having them in view speak often and with emphasis of Christ as the Sin-bearer, inviting them to lay their sins on Him by faith that they may have peace with God, and probably endeavouring to make the act of faith as easy as possible by use of such phrases as, "Only believe that Jesus died on the cross in your stead and you are saved." A natural and yet a serious mistake. For it is a short-sighted evangelism which looks only to the beginning of Christian life and makes no provision for its continuance and progress; which thinks of justification and forgets sanctification; which cares not about the quality of faith, provided only faith of some kind of which Christ is the object be awakened, with as little delay as possible; which deems it the one thing needful to bring every sinner into a state of conscious peace, instead of aiming at rousing the conscience of the sinful into energetic activity and leaving them, as we so safely may, in God's hands. The true, healthy evangelism is that which offers Christ to men's faith as He is offered in the New Testament, in Christ's own teaching and life, and in the apostolic Epistles, in all the aspects of His character and work. That cannot be done in a day or in a single address, still less in a single sentence. But it can be done by giving prominence now to this side of truth, now to that, always aiming at exhibiting the many-sided wisdom of God in the gospel. The result will be a faith to which Christ is wisdom by being at once righteousness, sanctification, and redemption; a Prophet, a Priest, and a King; a Christ for us and a Christ in us; a Christ who died in our stead, and a Christ with whom we die daily; a faith which will work through fellowship with Christ in His sufferings to the effect of making us Christlike as surely as it will rest upon Christ as the Saviour from sin.[1]

---

[1] On the principle of learning from a foe, evangelical ministers would do well to read the last lecture in Newman's *Lectures on Justification,* on "Preaching the Gospel," which contains a very searching criticism of evangelical preaching. Newman brings against it a countercharge of legalism in the form of trust in states and feelings. He remarks: "The true preaching of the gospel is to preach Christ, but the fashion of the day has been instead of this to attempt to convert by insisting on conversion," p. 373.

NOTE ON PROFESSOR EVERETT'S
THE GOSPEL OF PAUL.

THE new work of Professor Everett on St. Paul's gospel is an entirely new reading of the apostle's doctrine as to the import and effect of Christ's passion. The author discards the received doctrine that Christ redeemed man from sin by enduring its penalty, as without support, either in the practice of sacrifice among the Pagans, in the Levitical ritual, or in the New Testament properly interpreted. Having made this position good to his own satisfaction, by a preliminary inquiry, he proceeds to expound his own theory, which is to the following effect. So far was Christ from suffering the penalty of sin that the primary reference of His death was not to sin at all. Its immediate aim and effect was to abrogate the law, and only in the second place, and as the result of the primary effect, to bring about remission of sins. But how did it abrogate the law? Thus: Christ died by *crucifixion*. But a crucified man, by the Jewish law, was "accursed"—that is, ceremonially unclean. And all who believed in the crucified Jesus as their Messiah become participators in his ceremonial uncleanness, and, as such, objects of abhorrence to orthodox Jews, deserving excommunication from synagogue and temple. They were "crucified" with their Christ, and, as such, freed from obligation to keep the law, for what claim had the law on outlawed, excommunicated men? And, of course, the law being cancelled for them, the pardon of sin followed, for sin is not imputed where there is no law. This theory rests mainly on two texts in the Epistle to the Galatians, iii. 13; ii. 19-20. From the former the author draws the conclusion that, according to St. Paul, Christ was accursed because He was crucified, not crucified because He was accursed; from the latter, that every believer in Christ is through the law dead to the law, inasmuch as he is crucified with Christ. The law says, every crucified man is ceremonially unclean. So be it, replies the Christian; I am crucified with Christ, therefore, with Him, ceremonially unclean; therefore, free from legal claims, dead to the law by the law's own act.

This is very ingenious, but critical doubts suggest themselves. My quarrel with the gifted author's interpretation chiefly concerns the second of the two proof texts. Against his interpretation of the first I have little to object. It is the fact that St. Paul affixes to the Saviour the epithet "accursed" simply because He suffered death in the form of crucifixion. Professor Everett states that he has nowhere found this view recognised by theologians. I have myself indicated it without being aware that he, as I suppose, had anticipated me. Thus far, therefore, I am happy to agree with him; but in his exegesis of the second text I think he errs by taking what St. Paul says of himself (I am crucified with Christ) as true of all Christians, and by holding ceremonial uncleanness to have been a *necessary* result of Christian faith. If this had been so, then all believers in Jesus would have been forthwith cast out of the synagogue and temple. Were they? On the contrary, the author of the Epistle to the Hebrews exhorts those to whom he writes to go forth without the camp bearing Christ's reproach, an exhortation which implies that they were still within, still clinging to synagogue and temple, and to companionship with unbelieving Jews.

If the theory in question were true, and the interpretation of *Gal.* ii. 20 valid, another inference would follow. All Christians would have understood their position as outlawed or "excommunicated" men. There would have been no Judaistic party, no controversy about the perpetual obligation of the law. They would have been compelled to understand their position by the treatment they received from unbelieving Jews. Professor Everett thinks that St. Paul before his conversion persecuted Christians, "because the pollution that came from the cross rested also upon them." For the same reason all non-Christian Jews ought to have been persecutors, at least to the extent of shunning with abhorrence all Christians; so educating the latter to understand thoroughly that to be a believer in Jesus was to be outside the commonwealth of Israel, dead to the law and free from its claims. How came it, then, that so few understood this, and that St. Paul had to fight a hard battle to gain for such ideas currency or even toleration within the Church?

The ideas expressed in *Gal.* ii. 19-20 are those of St. Paul the Christian theologian, not of Saul the Pharisee. They are, further, not ideas which St. Paul holds in common with Judaists, but which he cherishes as the advocate of a universal independent gospel, and employs in his controversy with Judaists, in opposition to their legalist propensities. The Judaists were not crucified with Christ in St. Paul's sense; if they had been, the controversy would have been at an end. They also, through the law, had been dead to the law.

The basis of Professor Everett's theory is too narrow. *Gal.* iii. 13 is only one of several texts of co-ordinate importance. Another of these is *Galatians* iv. 4, where it is stated that Christ redeemed men from the law by coming under the law. The principle is, that at whatever point Christ touched man in His state of humiliation, His touch had redemptive effect. And he touched us, not at one, but at many points. He came under the law, was circumcised, *e.g.* He endured death and so became in lot a sinner; He died on the cross, and so tasted the curse; in death His *blood* was shed, and so His death assumed the aspect of a sacrifice. All these points, and others not referred to, have to be taken into account in a scientific attempt to get at Paul's theory of atonement and his ways of thinking in general. This new contribution, while clever and interesting, makes the matter altogether too simple.

CHAPTER X

ADOPTION

THE idea of adoption, $υἱοθεσία$,[1] can hardly be said to occupy, in the Pauline system of thought, a place of importance co-ordinate with that of justification. It denotes a phase in the *blessedness of the Justified*, rather than an independent benefit of God's grace. It were, however, a mistake on this account to overlook the idea in an exposition of St. Paul's conception of Christianity. The "adoption of sons" conferred on believers demands prominent recognition were it only because of its connection with the justified man's felicity. For that topic, with all that belonged to it, bulked largely in the mind of the apostle. He descants thereon with evident delight in various places in his Epistles, especially in *Romans* v. 1–11, where he describes the justified state as one of triumphant joy, invincible buoyancy, and hopefulness; of joy in an anticipated future glory, in a present full of tribulation, but fruitful in spiritual discipline through that very tribulation, in God Himself the *summum bonum*. One cannot but note here how radically optimistic the apostle is; how truly joy is for him the keynote of the Christian life. "Rejoicing in hope, patient in

[1] *Gal.* iv. 4; *Rom.* viii. 15.

tribulation, continuing instant in prayer "—so he pithily defines the Christian temper in the hortatory part of his Epistle to the Romans,[1] and with this definition the whole strain of his religious teaching is in sympathy. And it is well, on so important a matter, to point out that St. Paul is here not only consistent with himself, but, what is of even greater moment, in thorough accord with the doctrine of Jesus, as when in a memorable utterance He likened the disciple-circle to a *bridal party*.[2] The harmony between apostle and Master in this respect points to and rests on a deeper harmony, an essential agreement in their respective conceptions of the relations between God and man.

St. Paul's letters being occasional and fragmentary, brief rapid utterances on urgent topics not necessarily or even probably revealing the full-orbed circle of his religious thought, it need not surprise us that we find nowhere in them a formal doctrine concerning God and man and their mutual relations. We can only expect hints, words which imply more than they say. Such a word is υἱοθεσία. It has for its presupposition Christ's characteristic conception of God as Father, and of men as His sons. Familiarity with Christ's doctrine of the Fatherhood, and more or less complete insight into and sympathy with its import, is to be presumed in all New Testament writers, who all use the new name for God which Jesus made current. The insight and sympathy need not be conceived of as complete: it is no reproach to the apostles to think it possible that in their insight

---

[1] *Rom.* xii. 12; with which compare 1 *Thess.* v. 16, 17.
[2] *Matt.* ix. 15.

into the spiritual essence of God, they came behind the only-begotten Son.¹ That St. Paul did so this very word υἱοθεσία may seem to prove. In Christ's doctrine God is always a Father, a Father even to the unthankful and evil, even to unfilial prodigals. In the apostle's doctrine, as commonly understood, God becomes Father by an act of adoption graciously exercised towards persons previously occupying a lower position than that of sons.

The difference is to a certain extent real, and it must be confessed that sonship in St. Paul's way of putting it appears an external and artificial thing compared to the aspect it assumes in the genial presentation of Jesus. Yet the divergence must not be exaggerated. For whatever may be said as to the form under which he conceives it, there can be no question that, for the apostle, the filial standing of a believer is a very real and precious thing. It is as real as if it were based on nature, and not on an arbitrary act of adoption. And it is by no means self-evident that the apostle thought of men as, antecedent to that act, in no sense sons of God. For we must note the connection in which he introduces the idea. In both the texts the state of adoption stands in antithesis to the state of legalism. The privilege consists in one being made a son who was formerly a slave. "Wherefore thou art no more a slave (δοῦλος) but a son."². But the two states are not absolutely exclusive. The slave might be a son who had not yet

---

[1] *Vide* Dr. Fairbairn in *Christ in Modern Theology*, p. 293, on this point.
[2] *Gal.* iv. 7. In *Romans* viii. 15, the Spirit of sonship is opposed to the spirit of bondage (δουλείας).

attained to his rights. So St. Paul actually conceived the matter when he wrote the Epistle in which the idea of adoption is first broached. Those who through the mission of Christ attain to the position of sons had been sons all along, only differing nothing from slaves because of their subjection to legalism.[1] The apostle had in view chiefly the religious condition of Israel under law and gospel—God's son from the first,[2] but subjected to legal ordinances, till Christ came and brought in the era of grace. But may not his thought be generalised so as to embrace the whole of mankind? Are not all men God's sons, reduced to a state of slavery under sin, and waiting consciously or unconsciously for the hour of their emancipation out of servitude into sonship by the grace of their heavenly Father?

It is only when we view the Pauline idea of adoption in connection with the antithesis between sonship and servitude that we can properly appreciate either its theological import or its religious value. Looked at apart therefrom, as an abstract theological term, the word may very readily foster inadequate conceptions of the Christian's privilege of sonship, and even give a legal aspect to his whole relation to God. It cannot be denied, that, to a certain extent, such results have actually followed the permanent use in theology of an expression which, as originally employed, was charged with a strong anti-legal bias. St. Paul's authority has gained currency in theology for a word which, as understood by theologians, has proved in no small

---

[1] *Gal.* iv. 1 : οὐδὲν διαφέρει δούλου.
[2] *Rom.* ix. 4 : "Israelites whose is the adoption" (υἱοθεσία).

measure antagonistic to his religious spirit. The fact raises the question, whether it would not be wise to allow the category of "adoption" to fall into desuetude, and to express the truth about the relation of man to God in terms drawn from our Lord's own teaching. Words used with a controversial reference do not easily retain their original connotation when the conflict to which they owe their origin has passed away. The primary antithesis is lost sight of, and new antitheses take its place. So in the case of υἱοθεσία. In the apostle's mind the antithesis was between a son *indeed*, and a son who is nothing better than a servant; in the mind of the systematic theologian it becomes sonship *of a sort* versus creaturehood, or subjecthood, the original relation of man to God as Creator and Sovereign. We are in a wholly different world of thought, while using the same phrases.

Adoption, in St. Paul's view, is, not less than justification, an objective transaction. It denotes the entrance into a new relation, being constituted sons. Adoption as a divine act must be distinguished from the *spirit* of adoption which is the subjective state of mind answering to the objective relation. The two things are not only distinguishable, but separable. All who are justified, all who believe in Jesus, however weak their faith, are in the Pauline sense sons of God, have received the adoption. But not all who believe in Christ have the Spirit of sonship. On the contrary, the fewest have it, the fewest realise their privilege, and live up to it; the greater number of Christians are more or less under the influence of a legal, fear-stricken spirit, which prevents them from regarding God as indeed their Father. The Spirit of sonship is therefore not identical with sonship; it is rather one of the benefits to which sonship gives right, and which, in a normal healthy state of the Christian life, follow in its train.

The really important contribution made by St. Paul to the doctrine of God's Fatherhood or man's sonship does not lie in his formal idea of adoption, but in the emphasis with which he insists on the filial spirit as that which becomes the believer in Jesus. In this whole matter of sonship we have to do, not with theological metaphysics, but with vital, ethical, and religious interests. What do we mean when we tell men they are sons of God? Not to flatter them or amuse them with idle phrases, or to teach them a pantheistic doctrine of the essential identity of the human and the divine. We mean to awaken in them an exacting sense of obligation, and a blessed sense of privilege. That was what Christ meant when He said to publicans and sinners, as He did in effect: Ye are God's sons. The statement signified: Because ye are sons ye may not live as ye have been living. God's sons must be Godlike. Because ye are sons ye may cherish high hopes in spite of your degradation. If ye return in penitence to your Father's house, He will receive you with open arms, as if ye had never done wrong; nay, with a warmer welcome, because ye are erring children returned. St. Paul deprived himself of the opportunity of enforcing the doctrine of sonship on the side of duty by failing to use the relation as one applicable to men in general; though this cannot be said without qualification, if we accept the discourse on

Mars' Hill as indicating the gist of what he said to the men of Athens. "Forasmuch as we are the offspring of God, we ought not to think that the Godhead is like unto gold, or silver, or stone, graven by art and man's device."[1] That is, it does not become God's sons to be grovelling idolaters; an excellent example of the *noblesse oblige* argument. But whatever historic value may be assigned to the Mars' Hill incident, it is certain at least that St. Paul did most vigorously enforce the filial dignity and privilege of Christians, and in connection therewith the duty incumbent on all believers to take out of their filial standing all the comfort and inspiration it was fitted to yield. Nothing is more fundamental in Pauline hortatory ethics than the exhortation: Stand fast in sonship and its liberties and privileges.

What then, according to the apostle Paul, are the privileges of the filial state? The catalogue embraces at least these three particulars—(1) freedom from the law; (2) endowment with the Spirit of sonship; (3) a right to the future inheritance, heirship. All these benefits are specified in the place in the Epistle to the Galatians which contains the apostle's earliest statement on the subject. That the privilege of sonship involves emancipation from the law is plainly taught in the words: "To redeem them that were under the law, that we might receive the adoption of sons." The second benefit is mentioned in the following verse: "And because ye are sons, God sent the Spirit of His Son into your hearts, crying, Abba, Father." The mission of the Spirit of sonship was a natural and necessary

[1] *Acts* xvii. 29.

sequel to the act of adoption. Of what avail were it to make one a son in standing unless he could be made to feel at home in the house? In order that sonship may be real, there must be a spirit answering to the state, that the adopted one may be no longer a slave in feeling, but a son indeed. The third benefit, right to the patrimonial estate, is pointed at in the words, " But if a son, then an heir, through God."

1. With regard to the first of these three privileges of sonship, St. Paul is very much in earnest. That the believer in Jesus is free from the law he again and again asserts. No better indication of the strength of his conviction on this point could be desired than the fact of his constructing no fewer than three allegorical arguments to establish or exhibit pictorially his view, those, viz., of the bondwoman and freewoman, the two husbands, and the veil of Moses. These allegories show at once what need there was for labouring the point, how thoroughly the apostle's mind had grasped it, so as to be fertile and inventive in modes of presentation, and how much he had the subject at heart, so as to be proof against the weariness of iteration.

In his doctrine of emancipation from the law, St. Paul had in view the whole Mosaic law without exception. The whole law as a code of statutes written on stone or in a book, put in the form of an imperative, " Thou shalt do this," " Thou shalt not do that," with penalties annexed, is, he holds, abolished for the Christian. Whatever remains after the formal act of abrogation, remains for some other reason than because it is in the statute-book. Some parts of the law may remain true for all time as revelation; some precepts may commend themselves to the human conscience in perpetuity as holy, just, and good; but these precepts will come to the Christian in a new form, not as laws written on stone slabs, but as laws written on the heart, as laws of the spirit of a new life. Summed up in love, they will be kept not by constraint, but freely; not out of regard to threatened penalties, but because the love commanded is the very spirit which rules in the heart.

One who dared to represent the state of the believer in Jesus as one of freedom from the Mosaic law, was not likely to have much hesitation in representing Christians as free from the commandments of men. This is rather taken for granted than expressly asserted. Of course all those passages in which St. Paul teaches that Christians are not bound by scruples as to meats and drinks point in this direction. And the general principle is very adequately stated in the words: "Ye are bought with a price; become not ye the servants of men."[1] For Rabbinical traditions, to which Saul the Pharisee had been a slave, Paul the Christian had no respect whatever. Even the Levitical law which appointed the sacred seasons and their appropriate ritual he characterised as "weak and poverty-stricken elements," to which it were as foolish in Christians to turn again, as it would be for a full-grown man to go back to an infant's school to learn the alphabet.[2] But for the

[1] 1 *Cor.* vii. 23.
[2] There has recently been a tendency among interpreters to revive the patristic view of στοιχεῖα, and to find in the word a reference to the heavenly bodies, sun, moon, and stars, conceived of as living

Rabbinical additions to the law he employed a much more contemptuous term. He called them σκύβαλα,[1] mere rubbish, never of any use save to puff up with empty pride, and now rejected by him, as a Christian, with loathing.

St. Paul found great difficulty in getting Christians to understand this doctrine of the liberty of a believer in all its comprehensiveness, and to sympathise with his passionate earnestness in maintaining it. He found men everywhere ready to relapse into legalism, and had thus occasion to address to many the warning, "return not again to the yoke of bondage." The history of the Church abundantly proves that there is no part of the apostle's teaching which the average Christian finds harder to understand. In every age, except at creative epochs like the Reformation, the legal spirit exercises extensive sway even over those who imagine themselves to be earnest supporters of Pauline doctrine, and emphatically evangelical in their piety, causing them to be afraid of new spiritual movements, though these may be but the new wine of the kingdom, and obstinately and indiscriminately conservative of old customs and traditions, though these may have lost all life and meaning. Such timidity and blind clinging to the past are not evangelic; they bear the unmistakable brand of legalism. Where the Spirit of the Lord is in any signal measure,

beings, by which the dates of holy seasons were fixed. Devotees who scrupulously observed holy times might very appropriately be represented as enslaved to the heavenly luminaries by whose positions these times were determined. This view is favoured by Lipsius in *Hand-commentar*.

[1] *Phil.* iii. 8

there will be liberty from bondage to old things, and from fear of new things; power to discern between good and evil, and courage to receive the good from whatever quarter it may come; there, in short, is not the servile spirit of fear, but the manly spirit of power and of love and of a sound mind. Such was the spirit of St. Paul, and it is much to be desired that his religious temper may ever be associated with profession of faith in his theological doctrine. The divorce of Pauline theology from the Pauline spirit is to be deplored as tending to create a prejudice not only against *Paulinism*, but even against what St. Paul loved more — evangelic piety; even against the word " evangelical." Yet what the Church really needs is not less evangelic life, but a great deal more, with all the breadth, strength, freedom, and creative energy that are the true signs of the presence in her midst of the spirit of sonship.[1]

2. This spirit is the second benefit which should accompany, and naturally springs out of, the true state of adoption. It is defined by certain attributes which may be taken as the marks of its presence. St. Paul describes it first, generically, as the Spirit of God's own Son, that is, of Jesus Christ. "Because ye are sons, He hath sent the Spirit of His Son into your hearts."[2] This might be taken as a summary reference to the history of Jesus as the source of the most authentic and reliable information

---

[1] Harnack (*Dogmengeschichte*, i. 129, 3te Aufl.) says: "Paulinism has acted as a ferment in the history of dogma, a basis it has never been." But if it has not been a basis in theology, still less has it in its religious spirit exercised a steady ascendency, to the great loss of the Church.

[2] *Gal.* iv. 6.

as to the true nature of the spirit of sonship. We may conceive the apostle here saying in effect: "If you want to know how the filial spirit behaves and manifests itself, look at Christ, and see how He bore Himself towards God. His personal piety is the model for us all: go to His school and learn from Him." Is this really what he had in his mind? Or is it merely an ontological proposition he offers us, to this effect: The Spirit who dwells in those who have a genuine filial consciousness is a Spirit sent by God and owned by Christ: the Spirit that proceedeth from the Father and the Son? I cannot believe it. The apostle's thought is dominated here throughout by the ethical interest. He thinks of the Spirit in the believer as a Spirit whose characteristic cry is *Father*, expressive of trust, love, loyal submission, and childlike repose. And when he calls that Spirit *Christ's*, he does not mean merely that He is Christ's *property*, but that He is Christ's own spiritual self. The Spirit of God's Son whom God sends into Christian hearts, and who reveals His presence by the child's cry, "Father," is the Spirit who in Him ever uttered that cry in clearest tone and with the ideal fulness of import.

We may, therefore, find in the expression, "the Spirit of His Son," an appeal to the evangelic history, and the recognition of Christ's personal relation to God as the norm of all Christian piety. How much knowledge of the earthly life of Jesus this presupposes cannot be determined. It may be taken for granted that St. Paul was aware that "Father" was Christ's chosen and habitual name for God. It may be regarded as equally certain that he knew the characteristics of Christ's personal religion to be such as justified reference to Him as the model Son, the pattern of filial consciousness as it ought to be. What historical vouchers for these characteristics were known to him we cannot say. We are not entitled to assume that he was acquainted with the prayer which begins, "I thank Thee, O Father,"[1] wherein the filial consciousness of Jesus found classic expression. But we certainly are entitled to affirm that there is no ground for the hypothesis recently put forth by Pfleiderer that this prayer is a composition of the Evangelists, made up of elements drawn from St. Paul's Epistles, or suggested by Paul's missionary career.[2] That such an utterance should fall from the lips of Jesus is intrinsically probable if the two inferences drawn from St. Paul's statement be allowed. If Jesus ever called God Father and bore Himself towards God so as to give the ideal expression to the filial consciousness, how natural that He should say in words on a suitable occasion what His whole life said in deed! Pfleiderer's scepticism is based on the assumption that St. Paul, not Jesus, was the originator of the religion of sonship. The assumption is contradicted by St. Paul's own testimony in the place before us, where he calls the Spirit of sonship the Spirit of Christ the Son. St. Paul being witness, it was Jesus who first introduced into the world the religious spirit whose characteristic cry Godwards is "Father."

It does not belong to my present task as the inter-

[1] *Matt.* xi. 25-27 ; *Luke* x. 21, 23.
[2] *Vide* his *Urchristenthum*, pp. 445, 446 ; and for a criticism of his view, *vide* my *Apologetics*, p. 454.

preter of Paulinism to offer an exposition, however brief, of the classic filial utterance of Jesus.[1] But it is competent to point out that the account given in the Pauline literature of the filial spirit in its practical manifestations is in full sympathy with the mind of Christ. The apostle sets forth the Spirit of sonship as a spirit of *trust* in *Romans* viii. 15, where it is put in contrast with the spirit of fear characteristic of legalism. In other places he gives prominence to *liberty* as an attribute of the Spirit of sonship. The most striking text in this connection is 2 *Corinthians* iii. 17 : "Where the Spirit of the Lord—liberty." It is a great word worthy to be associated with that of Jesus: "Ye shall know the truth, and the truth shall make you free," most comprehensive in scope, and susceptible of wide and varying application. Where the Spirit of the Lord, the Spirit of sonship, is, there is liberty even from the law of God, as a mere external commandment, with its ominous "Thou shalt not"; there is liberty from all commandments of men, whether written statutes or unwritten customs; there is liberty from the dead letter of truth which conceals from view the eternal spiritual meaning; there is liberty from the legal temper ever embodying itself in new forms and striving to bring human souls under its thraldom; there is liberty from the bondage of religious fear, which has wrought such havoc as the parent of superstition and will worship; there, finally, is liberty from fear with regard to the ills of life, and the uncertainties of to-morrow: for to one who knows God as a Father, what can there be to be afraid of ? "If God

[1] Vide *The Kingdom of God*, chap. vii.

be for us, who (or what) shall be against us?"[1] triumphantly asks St. Paul, echoing the thought of Jesus: "Fear not, little flock, it is your Father's good pleasure to give you the kingdom."

Here is an ample liberty, though the description is by no means exhaustive. But is it not too ample? men anxious for the interests of morality or of ecclesiastical institutions may be inclined to ask. The tendency has always been to be jealous of Christian liberties as broadly asserted by our Lord and St. Paul, and to subject them to severe restrictions lest they should become revolutionary and latitudinarian. Though not straitened either in Christ or in Paul, the Church has been much straitened in her own spirit. This jealousy of liberty has been to a large extent uncalled for, and has simply prevented the Church from enjoying to the full her privilege. That liberty may degenerate into licence is true. But where the Spirit of the Lord is, no such abuse can take place. For the Spirit of the Lord is a Holy Spirit as well as a free Spirit, and He will lead Christians to assert their liberty only for holy ends. What risk, *e.g.*, is there to the interests of holiness in the Pauline antinomianism? The law of God stands no more whip in hand saying, "Do this"; no, but the law of God is written on the heart, and the commandment is kept because it no longer is grievous by reason of the terrifying thunder and the threatened penalty. The only difference is, that obedience is made easy instead of irksome. Christ's yoke is easy, and His burden is light. Heavy is the burden when we carry the sense of duty

[1] *Rom.* viii. 31.

like the slabs on which the Decalogue was written on our back, but light is the burden when law is transmuted into love, and duty consists in becoming like our Father in heaven. What risk to the interests of religion in the Pauline disregard of ritual, in his doctrine that circumcision and everything of like nature is nothing? It is but getting rid of dead works in order the better to serve the living God, with a truly reasonable, spiritual service, in which all the powers of the inner man earnestly take part. What risk, finally, to the peace of the sacred commonwealth in the decided assertion of the liberty of the Christian conscience from the bondage of petty scrupulosity, when the Spirit of Jesus, who dwells in all the sons of God, is not only a Spirit of freedom, but not less emphatically a Spirit of charity, disposing all who are under its guidance in all things to consider their neighbour for their good unto edification, and also a Spirit of wisdom which can discern where concession and forbearance *are* for the good and edification of the whole body of Christ?

This reference to the body of Christ recalls to mind an important result flowing, according to Pauline teaching, from the Spirit of sonship. It is its tendency to remove barriers to Christian fellowship arising out of small matters to which the legal spirit attaches undue value. How closely sonship and brotherhood were connected in the apostle's mind appears from the fact that, on the first mention of the sonship of Christians in *Galatians* iii. 26, he proceeds immediately after to speak of the new society based on the Christian faith as one wherein is neither Jew nor Greek, neither bond nor free, neither male nor female, but all are one in Christ Jesus. It is easy to find the missing link which connects the two topics. In St. Paul's view, as we know, the first fundamental privilege of sonship is emancipation from the law. But the law was the great barrier between Jews and Gentiles; that removed, there was nothing to prevent them from being united in a Christian brotherhood on equal terms. The partition wall being taken down, the two separated sections of humanity could become one in a new society, having for its motto, "Christ all and in all." The accomplishment of this grand union, in which St. Paul took the leading part, was the first great historical exemplification of the connection between the Spirit of sonship and the Spirit of *catholicity*. It is obviously not the only possible one. The tendency of the legal spirit at all times is to multiply causes of separation, both in religious faith and in religious practice: in the former, increasing needlessly the number of fundamentals; in the latter, erecting every petty scruple about meats and drinks, and social customs, and forms of worship, to the dignity of a principle dividing from all whose practice is nonconformist. The legal spirit is essentially anti-catholic and separatist, and manifests itself as such in a thousand different ways. On the other hand, the filial spirit is not less essentially catholic: it craves for fellowship with all who are sons of God by faith in Jesus Christ, and has the impulse to sweep away the manifold artificial barriers which dogmatic, pragmatic, self-asserting legalism has set up to the dividing of those who are one in Christ. What a change would come over the face of Christendom if the Spirit of adoption were poured out in abundant measure on all who bear the Christian name!

3. The third benefit accruing from sonship is *heirship*. "If a son, then an heir";[1] "if children, then heirs; heirs of God, and joint heirs with Christ."[2] What is the inheritance, and when do the sons enter on it? Are they expectants only, or are they in possession already? Looking to the connection of thought in the Epistle to the Galatians, the sons, according to St. Paul, are in possession, at least in part. The adoption means that a son who in childhood differed nothing from a servant, becomes a son indeed at the time appointed. Objectively, that time arrived when Christ came; subjectively, it arrived then for all who, like St. Paul, understoood the significance of the Christian era. In natural life the heir enters on his inheritance at his father's death. God does not die, and there is no need to wait on that account. Rather Christians enter on their inheritance when they begin truly to live. The inheritance consists in *autonomy*, spiritual freedom; in *spiritual-mindedness*, which is life and peace; in *spiritual buoyancy*, victorious over all the ills of life, fearing nothing, rejoicing even in tribulation because of the healthful discipline and confirmation of character it brings. Truly no imaginary possessions, genuine treasures of the soul!

Yet, here, according to St. Paul, as we gather from the place in *Romans*, the Christian inherits only in part; he is largely an expectant, "saved by hope."[3] For the present is a scene of suffering. Doubtless the tribulations of the present afford the son of God opportunity for showing his heroic temper, and verifying the reality of his sonship.

[1] *Gal.* iv. 7.   [2] *Rom.* viii. 17.   [3] *Ibid.* viii. 24.

But on the most optimistic view of the present it must be admitted that groaning is a large element in human life. The Christian is often obliged to say to himself, " It is a weary world." Even the Divine Spirit immanent in him sympathetically shares in his groaning.¹ What is wrong? There is wrong within, defective spiritual vitality.² There is wrong in the body; it is still even for the redeemed man a body of death, and he will not be an effectively, fully-redeemed man till his body has shared in the redemptive process.³ There is wrong, finally, in the outside world, in the very inanimate, or lower animate creation, needing and crying for redemption from vanity, and travailing in birth pangs which shall issue in the appearance of the new heavens and of the new earth.⁴ In view of all these things, St. Paul seems half inclined to cancel his earlier doctrine of the era of sonship dating from the birth of Christ, and, regarding Christians as still sons who differ nothing from a slave, to project the *υἱοθεσία* forward to the era of consummation. For he applies the term, we note, to that era whereof the redemption of the body is the most outstanding feature and symbol. " Waiting for the adoption, the redemption of the body."⁵ In some codices the word *υἱοθεσίαν* is omitted,⁶ why, we can only conjecture. The copyists may have thought it strange that there should be two adoptions, or that a term denoting an imperfect kind of sonship should be applied to the final perfect state, wherein sonship

¹ *Rom.* viii. 26.
² *Ibid.* viii. 23. The believer has only the *first-fruits* of the Spirit; τὴν ἀπαρχὴν τοῦ πνεύματος.
³ *Ibid.* viii. 23.   ⁴ *Ibid.* viii. 19-22.
⁵ *Ibid.* viii. 23, last clause.   ⁶ D, F, G, omit it.

shall be raised to its highest power, its very ideal realised in fellowship with Christ in filial glory. No wonder they stumbled at the expression. For, in truth, the use of the word by the apostle in reference to the future consummation raises the doubt whether we have not been on the wrong track in imagining that, when he speaks of the υἱοθεσία in his Epistles, he has the Greek or the Roman practice of adoption in view. That use, at all events, shows that if, when it first entered into his mind to avail himself of the term, he was thinking of adoption as practised by either of the two classic nations, he was constrained by his Christian convictions to employ it in a manner which invested it with a new, nobler sense than it had ever before borne. Adoption in Roman law denoted the investment of persons formerly not sons with some measure of filial status; υἱοθεσία in St. Paul's vocabulary means the solemn investment of persons formerly sons in an imperfect degree with a sonship worthy of the name, realising the highest possibilities of filial honour and privilege.[1]

[1] Usteri (*Paulinischer Lehrbegriff*) thinks that as St. Paul uses the word the idea of adoption is not to be pressed. *Vide* note on υἱοθεσία at p. 194 of the work referred to.

CHAPTER XI

WITHOUT AND WITHIN

WE have now gained a tolerably definite view of St. Paul's way of conceiving the good that came to the world through Jesus Christ, that is to say, of his soteriological system of ideas. Our next task, in order, must be to make ourselves acquainted with the apologetic buttresses of that system. The Pauline apologetic, as we have already learned, relates to three topics: ethical interests, the true function of the law, and the prerogatives of Israel. We have now, therefore, to consider in detail what the apostle had to say on each of these topics in succession, and the value of his teaching as a defence against possible attacks in any of these directions.

The first of the three is a wide theme, and in the highest degree important. In reference to every religion it is a pertinent and fundamentally important question: What guarantees does it provide for right conduct? No religion has a right to take offence at such a question, or to claim exemption from interrogation on that score. Least of all Pauline Christianity; for, while Christianity as taught by Christ is conspicuously ethical in its drift, the same faith as presented by St. Paul seems on the face of it to be religious or even theological rather than ethical, so that the question as to moral tendency is in this case far from idle or impertinent. The point raised, it will be observed, does not concern the personal relation of the teacher to morality, about which there is no room for doubt, but the provision he has made in his doctrinal system for an interest which he obviously feels to be vital. Theoretic failure is quite conceivable even in the case of one who has a burning passion for righteousness.

Paulinism offers two guarantees for holiness in the Christian: *the moral dynamic of faith*, and *the influence of the Holy Ghost*. These, therefore, we shall consider, each in a separate chapter, with a view to ascertain their efficiency, and how they arise out of the system.

Despite the most circumspect theoretic provision, it is a familiar experience that the reality of conduct falls far below the ideal. The Christian religion is no exception to this observation, and the devout soul may well be moved to ask, Why, with such guarantees as the above named, should it be so? The question did not escape St. Paul's attention, and his thoughts about it shall be gathered together under the head of the *Flesh as a hindrance to holiness*.

It will help us to understand the doctrine of the apostle on these three themes if in a preliminary chapter we endeavour to ascertain what was the precise relation in his mind between the two sides of his soteriology as set forth in *Romans* i.–v. on the one hand, and in *Romans* vi.–viii. on the other. It is a question as to the connection in the apostle's thought between the objective and the subjective, the ideal and the real, the religious and the moral. This topic forms the subject of the present chapter.

On this question, then, various views may be and have been entertained.

1. The crudest possible solution of the problem would be to find in the two sections of the Epistle to the Romans two incompatible theories of salvation, the forensic and the mystical, the latter cancelling or modifying the former as found, on second thoughts, to be unsatisfactory and inadequate. This hypothesis, though not without advocates,[1] can hardly commend itself on sober reflection. That St Paul, like other thinkers, might find it needful to modify his views, and even to retract opinions discovered to be ill founded, is conceivable. But we should hardly look for retractations in the same writing, especially in one coming so late in the day. It may be taken for granted that the apostle was done with his experimental or apprentice thinking in theology before he indited the Epistle to the Romans, and that when he took his pen in hand to write that letter, he was not as one feeling blindly his way, but knew at the outset what he meant to say. He had thought out by that time the whole matter of objective and subjective righteousness; and if he keep the two apart in his treatment, it is not tentatively and provisionally, but as believing that each represents an important aspect of truth.

---

[1] Ritschl's treatment of St. Paul's view in *Die Entstehung der Alt-katholischen Kirche*, 2te Aufl., looks in this direction; *vide* pp. 87–90. *Vide* also his more recent work, *Die Christliche Lehre von der Rechtfertigung und Versöhnung*, ii. p. 224.

2. We may go to the opposite extreme, and find in the two sections not two incompatible theories, one superseding the other, not even two distinct while compatible aspects, but one train and type of thought running through the whole. And as the two parts of the Epistle certainly seem to speak in different dialects, it comes to be a question of interpreting either in terms of the other by ingenious exegesis. Which of the two apparently different types of thought is to be resolved into the other will depend on the interpreter's theological bias. One would gladly find in St. Paul's writings everywhere, and only, objective righteousness; another welcomes not less eagerly whatever tends to prove that subjective righteousness is the apostle's great theme. The latter bias, a natural reaction against the former, is the one most prominent in modern theology. Those under its influence read the doctrine of *Romans* vi.–viii. into *Romans* i.–v., and find in the Epistle one uniform doctrine of justification by faith as the promise and potency of personal righteousness, and one doctrine of atonement, not by substitute but by *sample*, Christ becoming a redeeming power in us through our mystic fellowship with Him in His life, death, and resurrection. Reasons have already been given why this view cannot be accepted.[1]

3. In the two foregoing hypotheses an earlier type of thought is sacrificed for a later, either by St. Paul himself or by his modern interpreter. A third conceivable attitude towards the problem is that of sturdily refusing assent to either of these modes of dealing with it, and insisting that the two aspects of the apostle's teaching

[1] *Vide* p. 157 f.

shall be allowed to stand side by side, both valid, yet neither capable of explaining, any more than of being explained into, the other. One occupying this attitude says in effect: "I find in the Epistle to the Romans a doctrine of gratuitous justification, to the effect that God pardons man's sin, and regards him as righteous, out of respect to Christ's atoning death. I find also, further on in the same Epistle, a doctrine of regeneration or spiritual renewal, to the effect that a man who believes in Christ, and is baptized into Him, dies to the old life of sin, and rises to a new life of personal righteousness." These two things, justification and regeneration, are two acts of divine grace, sovereign and independent. The one does not explain or guarantee the other. There is no nexus between them other than God's gracious will. Whom He justifies He regenerates, and that is all that can be said on the matter. There is no psychological bond insuring, or even tending to insure, that the justified man shall become a regenerate or righteous man. Faith is not such a bond. Faith's action is confined to justification; it has no proper function in regeneration; here baptism takes the place which faith has in justification.

4. So purely external a view of the relation between justification and regeneration, as handled in the Pauline literature, is not likely to be accepted as the last word, though spoken by a master of biblical theology, even by the most admiring of disciples. Accordingly, a fourth attitude falls to be discriminated; that recently taken up by Dr. Stevens, in his excellent work on *The Pauline Theology*, who in many respects is a follower of Dr. Weiss, the chief exponent of the theory stated in the

foregoing paragraph. The basis of the view espoused by this writer is the distinction between *form* and *essence* in Pauline thought. He holds that in form St. Paul's conception of justification is forensic, and that any attempt to eliminate this aspect from his system must be regarded as an exegetical violence. As a mere matter of historical exegesis, it is beyond doubt, in his judgment, that the apostle taught the doctrine of an objective righteousness. But this does not preclude the question, What is the eternal kernel of truth enclosed in this Jewish shell? The kernel the author referred to finds in the mystic doctrine of the more advanced portion of *Romans*. "In chap. iv. he (Paul) develops the *formal* principle of salvation, which is justification by faith, treated in a forensic manner, in accord with prevailing Jewish conceptions; in chaps. v., vi., and viii. he unfolds the real principle of salvation, which is moral renewal through union with Christ. The first argument is designed to parry a false theory, and meets that theory on its own juristic plane of thought; the second exposition is adapted to the edification and instruction of believers, and, mounting up into the spiritual realm, deals with the moral and religious truths, processes, and forces which are involved in justification."[1] The writer of these sentences, it seems to me, makes the mistake of imputing to St. Paul a distinction which exists only for the modern consciousness. It is one thing to insist on the need, and claim the right, to interpret Pauline forms of thought into eternally valid truth; quite another to ascribe to St. Paul our view of what is form and what

[1] *The Pauline Theology*, p. 275.

essence. For the apostle, objective righteousness was more than a form, it was a great essential reality, pardon of sin for Christ's sake; not a mere symbol of a higher truth, but an important member of the organism of Christian truth; not a mere controversial weapon, but a doctrine in which his own heart found satisfaction.

None of the foregoing hypotheses can be accepted as a satisfactory account of the way in which the two aspects of salvation were connected in the apostle's mind. How, then, are we to conceive the matter? Perhaps we shall best get at the truth by trying to imagine the psychological history of the apostle's thought on these themes. The first great stage in the process would be connected with his never-to-be-forgotten escape from *legalism* to a religion of faith in God's grace. What would be the attitude of his mind at that crisis? One of blissful rest in the ideal of righteousness as realised in Christ: "I have failed, but He has succeeded, and I am righteous in Him." That thought would undoubtedly give his eager spirit rest for a season. But only for a season. For the imperious hunger of the soul for righteousness is still there, and no mere pardon, or acceptance as righteous through faith, can satisfy permanently its longings. And as soon as the convert discovers that he has not yet attained, the cry will awake in his conscience, "How shall I become all I ought and desire to be?" It is not, like the old cry, "O wretched man that I am!" a despairing exclamation. It is the voice of Christian aspiration uttered in good hope, grounded on the consciousness of spiritual forces actually at work within the soul. What are these? There is faith incessantly active about Christ, constantly thinking of Him as crucified and risen, winding itself about Him, and extracting nourishment from every known fact in His earthly history. And there is the Holy Ghost, about whose mighty working in believers one living in those days could not fail to hear. How He revealed Himself in St. Paul's consciousness as a factor making for Christian holiness, distinct from faith, is a question that need not here be considered. Suffice it to say that, judging from his writings, the Spirit of Jesus did not leave Himself without a witness in his religious experience. These were two potent forces at work within him, filling him with high hope. But, alas, not they alone; along with them worked a sinister influence, seeming to have its seat in the *flesh*, possessing potency sufficient to disturb spiritual serenity, cloud hope, and introduce a tragic element of sadness into the new life. Here were conflicting powers supplying food for reflection: faith, the spirit, the flesh. How were those facts of the Christian consciousness to be formulated and correlated? The apostle's mind would not be at rest till it had got a way of thinking on these matters, and the results of his meditations, more or less protracted, lie before us in *Romans* vi.–viii., and in some other places in his Epistles. They consist of his doctrine of faith as a spiritual force, his doctrine of the Holy Spirit as the immanent source of Christian holiness, and his doctrine of the flesh as the great obstructive to holiness.

From the foregoing ideal history, it follows that St. Paul's doctrine of subjective righteousness, its causes and hindrances, was of later growth than his doctrine of objective righteousness. This was only what was to be expected. God does not reveal all things at once to truth-seeking spirits. He sends forth light to them just as they need it. Inspirations come piecemeal, in many parts and in many modes, to apostles as to prophets. System-builders may throw off a whole body of "divinity" at a sitting, but in a scheme of thought so originating there is little of the divine. The true divine light steals upon the soul like the dawn of day, the reward of patient waiting. So St. Paul got his doctrine of righteousness, not complete at a stroke, but in successive vistas answering to pressing exigencies. The doctrine of objective righteousness met the spiritual need of the conversion crisis; the doctrine of subjective righteousness came in due season to solve problems arising out of Christian experience.

The two doctrines, when they had both been revealed, lived together peaceably in St. Paul's mind. The latter did not come to cancel the earlier, or to put the Christian disciple out of conceit with his primitive intuitions. He conserved old views while gratefully welcoming the new. Why should he do otherwise? The two revelations served different purposes. They were not two incompatible answers to the same question, but compatible answers to two distinct questions. At his conversion, Saul, a despairing man, threw himself on the grace of God, crying, "God be merciful to me, the sinner, for Jesus Christ's sake," and in so doing found rest. On reflection this experience shaped itself intellectually into the doctrine of justification by faith: God regards as righteous any man, be he the greatest sinner, who trusts in His grace through Jesus Christ. At a later period, Paul, the believing man, on examining himself, discovered that what he had utterly failed to accomplish on the method of legalism, he was now able approximately to achieve, the realisation of the moral ideal even as interpreted by the Christian conscience, an ideal infinitely higher than the Pharisaic. The righteousness of the law, spiritualised and summed up in love, was actually being fulfilled in him. A marvellous contrast; whence came the striking moral change in the same man? The earlier question had been, How can I get peace of conscience in spite of failure? The question now is, Why is it that I no longer fail? how comes it that, notwithstanding my greatly increased insight into the exacting character of the divine law, I have a buoyant sense of moral ability and victory? St. Paul sought and found the answer through observation of the forces which he perceived to be actually at work within him.

In making this statement I have answered by anticipation the question, Whence did St. Paul get the mystic element which formed the later phase in his composite conception of salvation as unfolded with exceptional fulness in the Epistle to the Romans? According to some he was indebted for this, directly or indirectly, to the Alexandrian Jewish philosophy. Certain modern theologians, while ascribing to the apostle a preponderant influence in determining the character of Christianity, seem disposed to reduce his originality to a minimum. They will have it that in no part of his system was he much more than a borrower. He got his forensic doctrine of imputed righteousness from the Pharisaic schools, and his mystic doctrine of imparted righteousness from Philo possibly, or more probably from the Hellenistic *Book of Wisdom*. So Pfleiderer, for example, in his *Urchristenthum*, and in the new edition of his *Paulinismus*. Men of sober judgment will be very slow to take up with such plausible generalisations. They rest upon an extremely slender basis of fact, and they are *à priori* improbable. That St. Paul, after he became a Christian, wholly escaped from Rabbinical influence, I by no means assert; but I am very sceptical as to the wholesale importation into his system of Christian thought of the stock ideas of the theology of the Jewish synagogue. There is truth in the remark of Beyschlag, that it does too little honour to the creative power of the Christian spirit in St. Paul to lay so much stress on the points of resemblance between his views and the Pharisaic theology.[1] Still less justifiable is the hypothesis of dependence in reference to Hellenism. Even Pfleiderer admits that possibly St. Paul was not acquainted with Philo, and his contention is not that the

[1] *Neutestamentliche Theologie*, vol. ii. p. 23. Interesting in this connection are the remarks of C. J. Montefiore in a recent article in the *Jewish Quarterly Review* (April 1894), on "First Impressions of Paul." "The Epistles of Paul," he says, "fill a newcomer with immense astonishment. They are so unique. They are so wholly unlike anything else he ever read. When I read the Synoptical Gospels I do not feel this utter unlikeness. . . . But Paul—even if, as Pfleiderer so ably argues, he is a mixture of Greek and Hebrew—still why should any such mixture produce *him*? His conception of the law, his theory of Christ, his view about Israel, his doctrine of justification, seem all not only original, but utterly strange and unexpected. His break with the past is violent. Jesus seems to expand and spiritualise Judaism. Paul in some senses turns it upside down."

apostle drew from the great Alexandrian philosopher, but that he derived some of his characteristic doctrines from the *Book of Wisdom*, which is a literary product of the same Greek spirit. It is in the power of anyone by perusal of the book to test the value of the assertion, and for myself I put it at a low figure. Speaking generally, I distrust this whole method of accounting for Paulinism by eclectic patchwork. It attaches far too much importance to contemporary intellectual environment, and far too little to the creative personality of the man. The true key to the Pauline theology is that personality as revealed in a remarkable religious experience. And if we are to go outside that experience in order to account for the system of thought, I should think it less likely to turn out a wild goose chase to have recourse to the Hebrew Scriptures, and especially to *the Apostolic Church*, than to the Jewish synagogue or the literature of Hellenism.[1]

For, while the originality of St. Paul in his doctrines of faith and of the Holy Spirit is by all means to be insisted on, it is at the same time to be remembered that he did not need to be original in order to recognise the existence of faith and the Holy Spirit as real and potent factors in the Christian life. One could not live within the Church of the first generation without hearing much of faith as a great spiritual force from the men who were acquainted with the tradition of Christ's teaching,

---

[1] On the dependence of St. Paul on the Hellenistic *Book of Wisdom*, vide Dr. Edmund Pfleiderer, *Die Philosophie des Heraklit von Ephesus* (1886), p. 296, where it is contended that 2 *Corinthians* v. 1-9 bears unmistakable traces of intimate acquaintance with that book.

and without witnessing remarkable phenomena which
believers were in the habit of tracing to the mighty
power of the Holy Ghost. Faith and the Divine Spirit
were universally regarded in the primitive Church as
veræ causæ within the spiritual sphere. This common
conviction was a part of the inheritance on which St.
Paul entered on becoming a Christian. His originality
came into play in the development which the common
conviction underwent in his mind. In his conception of
the subtle, penetrating nature of faith and its irresistible
vital power he distanced all his contemporaries. The
faith-mysticism is all his own; there is nothing like it
elsewhere in the New Testament. The apostle Peter
comes nearest to it when he exhorts Christians to arm
themselves with the mind exemplified by Christ in
suffering for men in the flesh.[1] But St. Peter's point of
view is comparatively external. The suffering Christ is
for him simply exemplary: "Christ also suffered for us,
leaving us an example, that ye should follow His steps."[2]
There is no co-dying and co-rising here, as in the Pauline
Epistles. So peculiar is this to the Gentile apostle that
it might be made the test of genuineness in reputedly
Pauline literature. On this ground alone there is a
strong presumption in favour of the Pauline authorship
of the Epistle to the Colossians, wherein we find an
exhortation to Christians who have risen with Christ to
complete the process of mystic identification by ascending with Him to heaven.[3] If some unknown disciple of
the Pauline school wrote the letter, he had caught the
master's style very well, and had noted the faith-

[1] 1 *Peter* iv. 1.   [2] *Ibid.* ii. 21.   [3] *Col.* iii. 1.

mysticism as specially characteristic. It is indeed very doubtful if any imitation, conscious or unconscious, would have reproduced that trait. It was too peculiar, too poetic, too much the creation of individual idiosyncrasy. The ordinary man would be afraid to meddle with it, and inclined to leave it alone, or to translate it into more prosaic and generally intelligible phraseology, like that in which St. Peter held up Jesus for imitation as the great exemplar.

For a similar reason it may be regarded as certain that St. Paul did not borrow the faith-mysticism from any foreign source. The mind which could not produce it would not borrow it. The presence of that element in St. Paul's letters is due to his religious genius. No other psychological explanation need be sought of his great superiority to his fellow-writers of the New Testament as an assertor of faith's powers. He was a far greater man, incomparably richer in natural endowment, than St. Peter or St. James, or even than the author of the Epistle to the Hebrews, though in some respects the latter excelled him. He was gifted at once with an original intellect, an extraordinary moral intensity, and a profoundly mystical religious temperament. To the united action of these characteristics we owe his doctrine of the believer's fellowship with Christ. As he states the doctrine, that fellowship was a source of ethical inspiration, and so doubtless it was; but it is equally true that it was an effect, not less than a cause, of exceptional moral vitality. St. Paul's whole way of thinking on the subject took its colour from his spiritual individuality. This statement does not mean that his views are purely subjective and personal, and of no permanent objective value to Christians generally. But it does imply that the Pauline mysticism demands moral affinity with its author for due appreciation, and that there must always be many Christians to whom it does not powerfully appeal.

One point more remains to be considered, viz., the mode in which the two aspects of the apostle's double doctrine of righteousness are presented in his Epistles in relation to each other. There is no trace of the gradual development implied in the psychological history previously sketched beyond the fact that the subjective aspect, the later, according to that history, in the order of development, comes second in the order of treatment, both in *Romans*, where it is handled at length, and in *Galatians*, where it is but slightly touched on. In both Epistles the doctrine of subjective righteousness is introduced with a polemical reference. In *Romans* it is set in opposition to the notion that reception of "the righteousness of God" by faith is compatible with indifference to personal holiness; in *Galatians* it is exhibited as the true method of attaining personal holiness as against a false method which is declared to be futile. "Shall we continue in sin that grace may abound?"[1] is the question to which the doctrine is an answer in the one case; "Shall we supplement faith in Christ by circumcision and kindred legal works?" is the question to which it is an answer in the other.[2] Over against the patchwork programme of Judaistic Christianity the apostle sets the thorough-going self-consistent

[1] *Rom.* vi. 1.   [2] *Gal.* v. 2–6.

programme of a Christianity worthy of the name: "We in the Spirit from faith wait for the hope of righteousness," where, as we shall see more fully hereafter, righteousness is to be taken *subjectively*, and the two great guarantees for the ultimate attainment of personal righteousness, faith and the Spirit, are carefully specified. His whole doctrine of sanctification, as fully unfolded in the Epistle to the Romans, is contained in germ in this brief text in his earlier Epistle to the Galatians. As here stated, the Pauline programme is sanctification by faith not less than justification—faith good for all purposes, able to meet all needs of the soul.

In some respects the earlier formulation is to be preferred to the later. If briefer, it is also simpler, gives less the impression of abstruseness and elaboration, wears more the aspect of a really practicable programme. It makes Paulinism appear one uniform self-consistent doctrine of righteousness by faith, not as in *Romans*, on a superficial view at least, a doctrine of objective righteousness imputed to faith, supplemented by a doctrine of subjective righteousness wrought out in us by the joint operation of faith and the Holy Spirit. It addresses itself to a nobler state of mind, and moves on a loftier plane of religious feeling. St. Paul's ideal opponent in *Galatians* is a man who earnestly desires to be righteous in heart and life, and fails to see how he can reach that goal along the line of faith. In *Romans*, on the other hand, he is a man who conceives it possible to combine reception of God's grace with continuance in sin, and even to magnify grace by multiplying sin. Against the latter, the apostle has to plead that his gospel *is* a way to holiness; against the former, that it is the *only* way to holiness. That it tends that way the legalist does not dispute; he only doubts its ability by itself to bring men to the desired end. Such an one an apostle may, without loss of dignity, seek to instruct. But how humiliating to argue with one who cares nothing for holiness, but only for pardon; and how vain! What chance of such an one understanding, or sympathising with, the mystic fellowship of faith with Christ? Is it not casting pearls before swine to expound the doctrine to so incapable a scholar? Perhaps, but St. Paul's excuse must be that he cannot bring himself to despair of any who bear the Christian name. He wishes to lead into the school of Jesus all who have believed in Him, whether they be honest but ill-instructed legalists, or low-minded sensualists. Therefore, to the one class, he says: "If ye be circumcised, Christ shall profit you nothing";[1] and to the other: "Let not sin reign in your mortal body, that ye should obey it in the lusts thereof."[2]

[1] *Gal.* v. 2   [2] *Rom.* vi. 12.

CHAPTER XII

THE MORAL ENERGY OF FAITH

EARNESTLY bent on reconciling his gospel with all the three interests covered by his apologetic, the apostle was specially anxious to show that his doctrine was not open to objection on the score of moral tendency. It was quite natural that he should be exceptionally sensitive on this subject, not only because he was himself a morally earnest man, keenly alive to the supreme importance of right conduct as the ultimate test of the truth of all theories, and of the worth of all religions, but more especially because it was at this point that his system might plausibly be represented as weakest. How easy to caricature his antinomianism as a licentious thing which cancelled all moral demands, and set the believer in Jesus free to do as he liked, to sin if he pleased, without fear, because grace abounded! It is not improbable that such misconstruction was actually put by disaffected persons on the Pauline gospel; it is only too likely that some members of the various churches founded by the apostle's preaching, by the unholiness of their lives, supplied a plausible excuse for misrepresentation. In any case both these phenomena were *à priori* to be expected. On all grounds, therefore, it was most needful that the doctrine of justification by faith in God's free grace should be cleared of all suspicion in reference to its practical tendency.

As already pointed out, the Pauline apologetic offers two lines of defence for this purpose—the one based on the moral energy of faith, the other on the sanctifying influence of the indwelling Holy Spirit. The first line of defence falls now to be considered.

Faith, as St. Paul conceives it, is a mighty principle, possessing a plurality of virtues, and capable of doing more things than one. For him, as for the author of the Epistle to the Hebrews, it is the mother of heroic achievements, and can not only please God, but enable men to make their lives morally sublime. It is, in his view, as good for sanctification as for justification. Therefore, his programme, as formulated in *Gal.* v. 5, is: faith alone for all purposes, for the obtainment of righteousness in every sense; not merely righteousness objective, or God's pardoning grace, but righteousness subjective, or personal holiness. In this notable text δικαιοσύνης is an objective genitive—" the hope whose object is righteousness "—and the righteousness hoped for is *subjective*, an inward personal righteousness realising the moral ideal. That the apostle does sometimes use the term δικαιοσύνη in a subjective sense is unquestionable. We have clear instances of such use in *Rom.* viii. 10: "If Christ be in you, the body is indeed dead on account of sin, but the spirit is life on account of righteousness"; and *Rom.* vi. 16–20, especially ver. 18: "Being freed from sin, ye became the servants of righteousness." On inquiry it will be found that the subjective sense prevails chiefly, as we might expect, in apologetic passages, where the apostle is concerned to vindicate for his doctrine a wholesome ethical tendency. On this principle *Gal.* v. 5 must be regarded as one of the texts in which δικαιοσύνη bears a subjective meaning. For in the context the writer is engaged in combating a religious theory of life on which the Galatian churches seem to have been, perhaps half unconsciously, acting, viz., that while faith might be good for the initial stage of the Christian life, it was of little or no avail for the more advanced stages, the needs of which must be met by a methodised system of legal observances. Against this patchwork theory what should we expect the champion of anti-legalist Christianity to say? This: "Faith is good for all stages, beginning, middle, and end; for all purposes, to make us holy, as well as to obtain pardon; it is the only thing that is good for holiness. Circumcision is good for nothing, and of equally little avail is the whole elaborate system of ritual, which legal doctors inculcate upon you." This accordingly is just what the apostle does say in the text *Gal.* v. 5, 6, if we take righteousness in a subjective sense as equivalent to holiness: "We, right-minded, right-thinking Christians, in the spirit, from faith, expect the hope of holiness; for in Christ neither circumcision availeth anything, nor uncircumcision, but faith working by love." It tends to confirm this interpretation that righteousness is here represented as an object of hope. Righteousness is set forth as the goal of Christian hope, which the apostle and all who agree with him expect to reach from faith, that is on the footing of faith, with faith as their guide all through. Obviously this goal of righteousness is synonymous with Christian holiness, conformity to the moral ideal. One other fact supporting the foregoing interpretation is, the description of faith in the last clause of ver. 6, as *energising through love* (δι' ἀγάπης ἐνεργουμένη). How far the description is true is a question to be considered; the point now insisted on is, that such an account of faith is relevant only if faith be viewed as a sanctifying influence, as conducive to *subjective* righteousness.[1]

This, then, is the Pauline programme: from faith *justification, i.e.* righteousness in the objective sense; from faith also the hope of *holiness, i.e.* righteousness in the subjective sense. But by what right does the apostle repose such unbounded confidence in faith as the principle of a new life of Christian sanctity? He gives two answers to this question at least formally distinct; one in the text just quoted, wherein faith is described as energetic through love; the other in that earlier text in *Galatians*, wherein faith is also described as making the believer one with Christ,[2] a line of thought which is resumed and expanded in *Rom.* vi.

The former of these two views of faith exhibits it as a powerful, practical force, which works mightily, and in the best way, from the highest motive, love. The attribute denoted by ἐνεργουμένη, guarantees the requisite life force, the motive denoted by the expression δι' ἀγάπης insures the pure quality of the action produced thereby.

[1] Holsten (*Das Evangelium des Paulus*) endorses this view. He says "that here δικαιοσύνη refers not to objective righteousness but to subjective righteousness of life is shown by the connection, and the grounding of δικαιοσύνη on the spirit," p. 173.
[2] *Gal.* ii. 20.

The allegations are obviously most relevant to the argument. For if faith be really an energetic principle, and if it do indeed work from love as its motive, then we may expect from its presence in the soul right conduct of the highest order. Out of the energy of faith will spring all sorts of right works, and those works will not be vitiated by base motives, as in religions of fear, in connection with which superstitious dread of God proves itself not less mighty than faith, but mighty to malign effects, making men even give of the very fruit of their body for the sin of their soul. The only question therefore remaining is: Are the apostle's statements concerning faith true? is faith an energetic force? does it work from love as its motive?

There should be no hesitation in admitting the truth of both statements. That faith is an energetic principle all human experience attests. Faith, no matter what its object, ever shows itself mighty as a propeller to action. If a man believes a certain enterprise to be possible and worthy, his faith will stir him up to persistent effort for its achievement. The eleventh chapter of the Epistle to the Hebrews settles the question as to the might inherent in faith. In this might all faith shares, therefore the faith of Christians in God. But why should the faith of Christians work by *love?* Why not by some other motive, say fear, which has been such a potent factor in the religious history of mankind? Is there any intrinsic necessary connection between Christian faith and love? There is, and it is due to the Christian idea of God. *All turns on that.* The God of our faith is a God of *grace*. He is our Father in heaven, and we, however unworthy, are His children. Therefore our faith inevitably works by love. First and obviously by the love of gratitude for mercy received. For, whereas the question of a religion of fear is: "Wherewithal shall I come before the Lord that I may appease His wrath," faith speaketh in this wise: "What shall I render unto the Lord for all His benefits?" But not through the love of gratitude alone; also through the love of adoration for the highest conceivable ethical ideal realised in the divine nature. God is love, benignant, self-communicating, self-sacrificing. To believe in such a God is to make love, similar in spirit if limited in capacity, the law of life. Hence the necessity for taking care that our developed theologies and our theories of atonement do not make whole-hearted faith in such a God difficult or impossible. All theologies which have this result are suicidal, and secure a barren orthodoxy at the expense of Christlike heroic character and noble conduct.

The apostle's conception of the Christian faith, as energetic through love, is thus in harmony at once with the general nature of faith as a principle in the human mind, and with the specific nature of the Christian religion. But the boldness with which he gave utterance to this conception really sprang out of his own experience. His own faith was of this description; hence his unbounded confidence in the power of faith to work out the problem of salvation from sin. And his life as a Christian is the justification of his confidence; for if we may judge of faith's sufficiency for the task assigned to it in the Pauline system by the character and career of the apostle to the Gentiles, then we may, without hesitation, give in our adherence to the watchword, FAITH ALONE. Testing the formula by the common phenomena of religious life, we might very excusably pause before adopting it. Two classes of phenomena are of frequent occurrence. One is, the combination of the standing-ground of faith with various forms of legalism. The other is, the more incongruous combination of evangelic faith with vulgar morality or, worse still, with immorality. The former combination, exhibited in one form or another in every generation, and in every branch of the Church, may seem to prove that the programme, Faith alone for all purposes, is generally found by devout souls unworkable. From the latter combination it may plausibly be inferred that the proclamation from the housetop of the Pauline programme is dangerous to morals.

Now, as to the combination of faith and legalism, it must be sorrowfully admitted that it always has been, and still is, very prevalent. History attests that it has ever been found a hard thing to remain standing on the platform of free grace. Downcome from that high level to a lower, from grace to law, from faith to technical "good works," from liberty to bondage, seems to be a matter of course in religious experience, individual and collective. What happened in Galatia repeats itself from age to age, and in all churches. Legalism in some form recurs with the regularity of a law of nature. The fact raises a preliminary presumption against the Pauline programme which must be faced. How, then, are we to reconcile the fact with the all-sufficiency of faith? We shall best do this by taking into account the law of growth in the kingdom of God, enunciated by our Lord in the parable of the blade, the ear, and the ripe corn. Legalism is a characteristic of the stage of the green ear, in the spiritual life of the individual and of the community. The blossom and the ripe fruit, the beginning and the end of a normal Christian experience, exhibit the beauty of pure evangelic faith. The green fruit is a lapse from the simplicity of the beginning, a lapse which is at the same time a step in advance, as it prepares the way for a higher stage, in which evangelic faith shall reappear victorious over the legal spirit of fear, distrust, and self-reliance. If this be true, and it is verified at once by church history and by religious biography, then the apostle's programme is vindicated; for we must test his principle by the end of Christian growth, and by the beginning, which is a foreshadowing of the end, not by the intermediate stage, in which morbid elements appear, the only value of which is that they supply a discipline which makes the heart glad to return again to the simplicity of trust. Judge Paulinism by its author, not by his degenerate successors; by the Reformers, not by the scholastic theologians of the seventeenth century; by the men in whom the spirit of the Reformation reappeared at the close of the dreary period of Protestant scholasticism, terminating in universal doubt; by men like Bengel in Germany, and Chalmers in Scotland, whose faith was not a mere tradition from the fathers, and, as such, a feeble degenerate thing, but a fresh revelation from heaven to their own souls. True evangelic faith cannot be a tradition; in the very act of becoming such, what passes for evangelic faith degenerates into a legalism which brings the way of faith into discredit.

Passing now to the other phenomenon, the combination of evangelic faith, so-called, with a low moral tone, what shall we say of it? Does it not prove that there is a real risk of the Pauline doctrine not only failing to promote sanctification, but even becoming perverted into a corrupting, demoralising influence? It certainly does show that there is serious risk of abuse, through the unworthiness of men who turn the grace of God into licentiousness. But divine grace is not the only good thing that is liable to be abused. And in other matters men guard against abuse as best they can, still holding on to the legitimate use. Even so must we act in reference to the matter of salvation by faith in divine grace. We must refuse to be put out of conceit with that way to spiritual life and health by a counterfeit, hypocritical, immoral evangelicism. We must reckon the principle of the Pauline gospel a thing so good as to be worth running risks for, and continue to adhere to it in spite of all drawbacks. We must not be ashamed of the motto on our banner because a rascally mob follows in the rear repeating our watchword, and shouting, "We will rejoice in Thy salvation." Think of the men who constitute the real body of the army, the people who give themselves willingly to the noble fight against evil, clothed in the beauties of holiness from the womb of the morning; men of the stamp of Luther, Knox, Wishart, who were as the dew of Christ's youth in the morning of the Reformation. May we not bear with equanimity the presence in the Church of some worthless counterfeits, orthodox worldlings, selfish saints, hypocritical schemers, and the like, for the sake of such a noble race of men? May we not patiently see some using Christian liberty for an occasion to the flesh, when we recognise in such simply the abuse of a principle whose native tendency is to produce men like-minded with St. Paul: men taking their stand resolutely on grace, not because they desire to evade moral responsibilities, but because they hope to get the hunger of their spirit for righteousness filled, and to be enabled to rise to heights of moral attainment otherwise inaccessible; men passionately bent on being freed from every species of degrading, hampering bondage, specially jealous of all religious fetters, yet desiring freedom only for holy ends; ridding themselves of "dead works" that they may serve God in a new, living, devoted way? Such, beyond doubt, is the kind of men thoroughgoing faith in divine grace tends to produce; and if there are fewer such men in the Church than one could wish, it is because the faith professed is not earnestly held, or held in its purity, but is mingled with some subtle element of legalism which prevents it from having its full effect.

After what has been said in a former chapter,[1] it will not be necessary to expatiate on the other source of faith's sanctifying power, the fellowship which it establishes between the believer and Christ. However mystic and transcendental this fellowship may appear to some minds, it will not be denied that in proportion as it is realised in any Christian experience it must prove a powerful stimulus to Christlike living. No man can, like the apostle, think of himself as dying, rising, and ascending with Christ without being stirred up to

[1] *Vide* chap. ix.

strenuous effort after moral heroism. The "faith-mysticism" is the stuff out of which saints, confessors, and martyrs are made. The only point on which there is room for doubt is whether, under this form of its activity, faith be a sanctifying power to any considerable extent for all, or only for persons of a particular religious temperament. Under the aspect already considered, faith is a universal moral force. No man, be his temperament what it may, can understand and believe in the loving-kindness of God, as proclaimed in the gospel, without being put under constraint of conscience by his faith. The man who earnestly believes himself to be a son of God must needs try to be Godlike. Even if in spiritual character he be of the unimaginative, unpoetic, matter-of-fact type, he will feel his obligation none the less; it will appear to him a plain question of sincerity, common honesty, and practical consistency. In comparison with the mystic, he may have to plod on his way without aid of the eagle wings of a fervid religious imagination; nevertheless observe him, and you shall see him walk on persistently without fainting. He knows little of devotee raptures; St. Paul's way of thinking concerning co-dying and co-rising is too high for him. He does not presume to criticise it, or depreciate its characteristic utterances as the extravagant language of an inflated enthusiasm; he simply leaves it on one side, and, renouncing all thought of flying, is content with the pedestrian rate of movement. But the steadiness of his advance approves him also to be a true son of faith.

The wings of the mystic are essentially one with the feet of the plain Christian man. Fellowship with Christ is only a form which the moral energy of faith takes in certain types of spiritual experience. In a low degree it is known to all, but in signal measure it is exhibited only in the lives of saints like St. Bernard and Samuel Rutherford. Translated into ethical precepts directed against fornication, uncleanness, and covetousness, to rise with Christ is a universal Christian duty;[1] but to clothe duty in that imaginative garb, and to realise it emotionally under that aspect, is, at the best, a counsel of perfection.

From all that precedes, it will be apparent that I regard St. Paul as teaching that sanctifying power is inherent in faith. It is not an accident that it works that way, it cannot but so work. Given faith, Christian sanctity is insured as its fruit or natural evolution. This view, if well founded, supplies a satisfactory connection between justification and sanctification, between religion and morality. Faith is the sure nexus between the two. But some writers on Paulinism demur to such prominence being given to the moral energy of faith. One can understand how Protestant orthodoxy, in its jealousy of Romish views, should be tempted to minimise faith's ethical virtue, with the result of failing to insure a close, genetic connection between justification and sanctification; but modern commentators might have been expected to rise above such one-sidedness. Yet so weighty a writer as Weiss, under what influences one can only conjecture, completely disappoints us on this score. He maintains that such a view of faith's function as I have endeavoured to present is un-Pauline. The true account

[1] *Col.* iii. 1-5.

of the apostle's doctrine, he thinks, is, that justification and the communication of new life are two distinct divine acts, independent of each other, and connected together only in so far as faith is required in receiving both. Far from producing the new life by its moral energy, faith, according to this author's reading of Paulinism, is hardly even the main condition of our receiving that life from God. In this connection, baptism is supposed to come to the front as a second great principle of salvation, not less indispensable for regeneration, or the reception of the Holy Spirit, than faith is for justification.

Is this really Paulinism? I should be slow and sorry to believe it. This minimising of faith's function is hardly in the great apostle's line. He was more likely to exaggerate than to under-estimate the extent and intensity of its influence. We should not, indeed, expect from him any doctrine of faith which ascribed to it, conceived as a purely natural faculty of the human soul, power to renew character apart altogether from the grace of God. But he nowhere conceives of faith after this manner. He regards it as due to the action of the Divine Spirit in us that we know, have the power to appreciate, the things that are freely given to us of God.[1] And no other view of the matter is reasonable. Faith, even in its justifying function, is a fruit of the Divine Spirit's influence. It is the act of a regenerate soul. How much is implied even in the faith that justifies! A sense of sin and of the need of salvation, self-distrust, trust in God, victory over the fear engendered by an

[1] 1 *Cor.* ii. 12.

evil conscience, and courage to believe in God's goodwill even towards the guilty; instinctive insight into the magnanimity of God, in virtue of which He most readily gives His grace to the lowest, with resulting boldness to conceive and utter the prayer, " Pardon mine iniquity, for it is *great*." Surely the Divine Spirit is in this initial faith, if He be anywhere in our religious experience; and surely the faith which at its birth is capable of such achievements will, as it grows and gains strength, prove itself equal to all the demands of the spiritual life! And because both these things are true, the whole Christian life, from beginning to end, must be conceived of as an organic unity, with faith for its inspiring soul. The rupture of that unity, by the dissection of experience into two independent experiences, justification and renewal, is a fatal mistake on the part of anyone who undertakes to expound the Pauline theology. The resulting presentation is not Paulinism as it lives and breathes in the glowing pages of the four great Epistles, but the dead carcase of Paulinism as anatomised by scholastic interpreters.

And what is to be said of the theory which gives to baptism, in reference to the new life of the Christian man, a function parallel in importance to that of faith in reference to justification? Many reasons can be given why it cannot be accepted as resting on the authority of St. Paul. It would require very clear and strong texts to overcome the antecedent unlikelihood of any such theory receiving countenance from him. Think of the man who so peremptorily said, " Circumcision is of no avail," assigning to baptism not merely symbolical, but essential significance in reference to regeneration. Then how weak his position controversially, if this was his view! How easy for Judaistic opponents to retort: "What better are you than we? You set aside circumcision, and you put in its place baptism. We fail to see the great advantage of the change. You insist grandly on the antithesis between letter and spirit, or between flesh and spirit. But here is no antithesis. Baptism, not less than circumcision, is simply a rite affecting the body. You charge us with beginning in the spirit and with faith, and ending in the flesh. How do you defend yourself against the same charge?" It is not likely that the apostle would teach a doctrine that made it possible for foes to put him in so narrow a corner. But consider further his position as an apologist for his gospel, as not unfavourable to ethical interests. It is in this apologetic connection that he refers to baptism in *Romans* vi., and, on the hypothesis as to the significance of that rite now under consideration, what we must hold him to say is in effect this: "No fear of my doctrine of justification by faith compromising ethical interests; every believer is baptized, and baptism insures a new life of holiness." This defence is open to criticism in two directions. First on the score of logic. Opponents might bring against it the charge of *ignoratio elenchi*, saying: "We questioned the moral tendency of your doctrine of justification by *faith*, and we expected to hear from you something going to show that the faith that makes a man pass for righteous can, moreover, make him really righteous. But lo! you bring in as *deus ex machinâ* this baptism which you never mentioned before. Is this not really an admission that your doctrine of justification is morally defective?" On the other hand, the hostile critic might assail the supposed Pauline apologetic on the ground of fact, by enquiring, "Is, then, baptism an infallible specific for producing holiness? Do you find that all baptized persons live saintly lives? It is incumbent on you, who have been so severe a critic of heathenism and Judaism, to be scrupulously candid and truthful in your answer." Who does not feel that the very conception of this ideal situation is a *reductio ad absurdum* of the sacramentarian theory? After pronouncing heathenism and Judaism failures, as tested by morality, the apostle Paul, in the face of the world, in a letter addressed to the metropolis of universal empire, declares his faith in Christianity as a religion that will stand the severest moral tests, and the ground of his confidence is—the rite of baptism![1]

[1] The view has lately been propounded that the Lord's Supper owed its origin to St. Paul. It was revealed to him, such is the hypothesis, in one of those visions he was constitutionally liable to have, after he had seen or heard of the celebration of the Mysteries of Demeter at Eleusis near Corinth, during his stay at the latter city. The vision was the result of a desire to turn the pagan ceremony to Christian use. The vision he turned into a history of something Jesus had actually done, and from him the story passed into the Gospels. The institution at least of the Lord's Supper as a sacrament, if not the whole transaction as recorded in the Gospels, originated in this way. Vide *The Origin of the Lord's Supper*, by Piercy Gardner, Litt.D. (Macmillan & Co. 1893). Apart from other considerations the theory appears to me improbable in view of St. Paul's whole religious attitude. A vision presupposes a mood to which it corresponds. The apostle's anti-Judaistic bias would disincline him from attaching importance to religious ritual. He was the last man to create sacraments, and he would accept either Baptism or the Lord's Supper only because he believed Christ had instituted it

The theory is without exegetical foundation. It is not necessary, in order to do full justice to the apostle's argument in *Romans* vi., to assign to baptism more than symbolical significance. We can, if we choose, ascribe to the rite essential significance, and bringing that view to the passage, ingeniously interpret it in harmony therewith. But it cannot be shown that baptism is for the apostle more than a familiar Christian institution, which he uses *in transitu* to state his view of the Christian life in vivid, concrete terms, which appeal to the religious imagination. He employs it in his free, poetic way as an aid to thought, just as elsewhere he employs the veil of Moses, and the allegory of Sarah and Hagar. But, alas! what with him was a spirited mystic conception has become a very prosaic dogma. It is a fatality attending all religious symbolism. An apostle cannot say, "We were baptized into Christ's death," but he must be held to mean that the rite not only symbolises, but causes death to sin and resurrection to righteousness. Christ Himself cannot say, "This is My body," but He must be held to mean: This bread is changed into My body. Yet, in the case of the apostle, the very manner in which he expresses himself as to the prevalence of the rite might put us on our guard against ascribing to him a theory of sacramental grace. "So many of us as were baptized" (ὅσοι ἐβαπτίσθημεν). He leaves it doubtful whether all bearing the Christian name were baptized. Bengel appends to the word ὅσοι the remark: "Nemo Christianorum jam tum non baptizatus erat." It may have been so as a matter of fact, but it cannot be inferred from the apostle's language that every Christian, without exception, was baptized. There may have been some who remained unbaptized, for anything he says to the contrary; just as the statement of the evangelist, that "as many as touched were made perfectly whole," [1] leaves it doubtful whether all who desired to touch the hem of Christ's garment succeeded in gratifying their wish. If St. Paul had been a sacramentarian, he would have taken care to exclude the possibility of doubt.[2]

[1] *Matt.* xiv. 36.
[2] A slight tinge of Bengel's dogmatism is discernible in the Revised Version, which substitutes at this point for the words of the A.V. quoted above, "All we who were baptized."

CHAPTER XIII

THE HOLY SPIRIT

IN no subject connected with Paulinism is it more necessary to be on our guard against a purely speculative or theoretic treatment than in that of the Holy Spirit. On this solemn theme, above all, the apostle's utterances are the echoes of a living experience, not the lucubrations of a scholastic theologian. The great question for him was not, what the Holy Spirit is, but what He does in the soul of a believing man; and, to be faithful interpreters of his mind, we must follow the guidance of the same religious interest. In the light of this consideration one can see the objection which lies against allowing the discussion of the present topic to be dominated, as it is in some recent monographs, by the antithesis between spirit and flesh. It is true that this is a very prominent Pauline antithesis, and it is also true that handling the *locus* of the Holy Spirit in connection therewith need not lead us away from the practical, inasmuch as the antithesis, as presented in the Pauline literature, signifies that the Holy Spirit is the antagonist and conqueror of the flesh as the seat of sin. But all antitheses tend to provoke the intellectual impulse to abstract definition, and this one in particular readily raises questions as to what spirit is and what flesh is, and draws us into abstruse discussions as to what ideas are represented by the terms, and what theory of the universe underlies their use.

No such objection can be taken to the place here assigned to the doctrine of the Spirit as a topic coming under the general head of the Pauline apologetic, and more particularly under that part of it which has for its aim the reconciliation of the Pauline gospel with ethical interests. For this setting of the doctrine not only allows but compels us to give prominence to that which forms the distinctive contribution of St. Paul to the New Testament teaching on the subject, the great and fruitful thought that the Holy Spirit is the ground and source of Christian sanctity—a commonplace now, but by no means a commonplace when he wrote his Epistles. Only one drawback is to be dreaded. The position of the doctrine of the Spirit's work in the Pauline apologetic rather than in the heart of the Pauline gospel might create in ill-informed minds an erroneous impression as to its importance, as if it were an afterthought to meet a difficulty, instead of being, as it is, a central truth of the system.

That the Divine Spirit was present in the community of believers, revealing there His mighty power, was no discovery of the apostle Paul's. The fact was patent to all. By all accounts the primitive Church was the scene of remarkable phenomena which arrested general attention, and bore witness to the operation of a cause of a very unusual character to which beholders gave the name of the Holy Ghost. The Pauline Epistles,[1] the Epistle to the

[1] *Vide* especially 1 *Cor.* xii. and xiv.

Hebrews,[1] and the Acts of the Apostles, all refer to these phenomena in terms which show what a large place they held in the consciousness of believers. Among the manifestations of the Spirit's influence, the most common and the most striking appears to have been *speaking with tongues*. The nature of this phenomenon has been a subject of discussion, chiefly on account of the difficulty of reconciling the narrative in *Acts* ii. with the statements of St. Paul in his First Epistle to the Corinthians. But following him, our most reliable authority, we arrive at the conclusion that the gift consisted in ecstatic utterance, not necessarily in the words of any recognised language, and not usually intelligible to hearers. "He that speaketh in a tongue speaketh not unto men but unto God."[2] The speaker was not master of himself; he was carried headlong, as if driven by a mighty wind; he was subject to strong emotion which must find vent somehow, but which could not be made to run in any accustomed channel. To the onlooker the state would present the aspect of a possession overmastering the reason and the will.

It was in phenomena of this sort, preternatural effects of some great power, that the first Christians saw the hand of God. The miraculousness of the phenomena was what they laid stress on. The more unusual and out of the ordinary course, the more divine. In accordance with this view, the Spirit's work was conceived of as transcendent, miraculous, and charismatic. The power of the Holy Ghost was a power coming from without, producing extraordinary effects that could arrest the

[1] Vide *Heb.* vi. 4, 5.   [2] 1 *Cor.* xiv. 2.

attention even of a profane eye—perceptible to a Simon
Magus, *e.g.*,[1] communicating charisms, technically called
"spiritual," but not ethical in nature; rather consisting
in the power to do things marvellous and create astonishment in vulgar minds. The fact that so crude an idea
prevailed in the apostolic Church bears convincing testimony to the prominence of the preternatural element in
the experience of that early time. And, of course, that
prominence had for its natural consequence a very partial
one-sided view of the office of the Holy Spirit. His
renewing, sanctifying function seems to have been left
very much in the background. He was thought of as
the author not of grace ($\chi\acute{\alpha}\rho\iota\varsigma$) as we understand the
term, but of charisms ($\chi\alpha\rho\acute{\iota}\sigma\mu\alpha\tau\alpha$), and "spiritual" in the
vocabulary of the period was an attribute ascribed to the
effects of a Spirit of *power*, not to those of a Spirit of
holiness. This statement is warranted by some narratives
of apostolic church history in the Book of Acts, in which
the communication of the Holy Ghost is represented as
following, not preceding, the believing reception of the
gospel. So, *e.g.*, in the account of the evangelistic movement in Samaria.[2] It was after the Samaritans had
received the word of God that Peter and John, commissioned by the apostles in Jerusalem, went down and
prayed for them that they might receive the Holy
Ghost. It is indeed expressly stated, as a reason for the
prayer, that "as yet He was fallen upon none of them;
only they had been baptized into the name of the Lord
Jesus." And to what effect they received the Holy Ghost
in answer to prayer may be inferred from the fact that

[1] *Acts* viii. 18.   [2] *Acts* viii. 14–24.

the result was immediately obvious to Simon the sorcerer. They must have begun to speak with tongues and to prophesy, as happened in the case of the disciples at Ephesus, who had lived in ignorance of the gift of the Spirit till St. Paul came and laid his hands on them.[1] In these naive records, which have every appearance of being a faithful reflection of the spirit of the early Jewish Church, faith, conversion, is not thought of as a work of the Spirit, but rather as the precursor to His peculiar operations, which in turn are regarded as a seal set by God upon faith. We are not to suppose that anyone meant deliberately to exclude the Holy Ghost from the properly spiritual sphere, and to confine His agency to the charismatic region. That the author of *Acts* had no such thought may be gathered from the fact that he ascribed Lydia's openness of mind to the gospel to divine influence.[2] Possibly, if the matter had been plainly put before them, all the members of the apostolic Church would have acknowledged that the Holy Spirit was the source of faith, hope, and love, as well as of tongues, and prophesyings, and miraculous healings. Only the latter phenomena appeared the more remarkable, and the former appeared a matter of course; whence it resulted that the gift of the Holy Spirit came in ordinary dialect to mean, not the power to believe, hope, and love, but the power to speak ecstatically, and to prophesy enthusiastically, and to heal the sick by a word of prayer.

Very natural then and always; for the same tendency exists now to prefer the charismatic to the spiritual, and to think more highly of the occasional stormy wind of

[1] *Acts* xix. 1-7.   [2] *Ibid.* xvi. 14.

preternatural might than of the still, constant air of divine influence. But the tendency has its dangers. What if these marvellous gifts become divorced from reason and conscience, and the inspired one degenerate into something very like a madman; or, still worse, present the unseemly spectacle of high religious excitement combined with sensual impulses and low morality? Why, then, there will be urgent need for revision of the doctrine of the Holy Spirit, and for considering whether it be wise to lay so much stress on charisms, as distinct from graces, in our estimate of His influence. This was probably one of the causes which led St. Paul to study carefully the whole subject. For the possibilities above pointed out were not long of presenting themselves as sorrowful realities. Ananiases and Sapphiras and Simons,—the whole fraternity of people who can be religious and at the same time false, greedy, sensual, bending like reeds before the swollen stream in a time of enthusiasm without radical change of heart,—soon began to swarm. They appeared everywhere, tares among the wheat of the kingdom; they were unusually abundant in the Corinthian Church, where everybody could speak in one way or another, and virtue was at a discount—a Church mostly gone to tongue. Phenomena of this sort, familiar to him from the beginning of his Christian career, would set the apostle on musing, with the result of a deepened insight into the nature, scope, and great aim of the Spirit's function among those who believed in Jesus.

These phenomena would give a thoughtful man food for reflection in a direction not yet indicated. They showed very clearly that Christian sanctity was by no means so much a matter of course as antecedent to experience many might be inclined to suppose. At first it was thought that the great thing was to get the charisms, and that the graces might be left to look after themselves. But when men arose who could prophesy in Christ's name, and by His name cast out devils, and do many other wonderful works, and yet remain bad in heart and in life,[1] then the wise would begin to see that Christian goodness was the important thing, and also the most difficult, and that the Holy Ghost's influence was more urgently needed as an aid against the baser nature of man than as a source of showy gifts of doubtful utility.

In some such way we may conceive the apostle Paul to have arrived at his distinctive view of the Holy Spirit, according to which the Spirit's function is before all things to help the Christian to be holy. At all events, however he reached it, this undoubtedly is his view. By this statement it is not intended to suggest that the apostle broke entirely away from the earlier charismatic theory. He not only did not doubt or deny, he earnestly believed in the reality of the miraculous charisms. He even sympathised with the view that in their miraculousness lay the proof that the power of God was at work. He probably carried this supernaturalism into the ethical sphere, and saw in Christian holiness a work of the Divine Spirit, because for him it was the greatest of all miracles that a poor sinful man was enabled to be holy. This may have been the link of connection between his theory of the Spirit's influence and that of the primitive Jewish Church; the common element in both theories

---

[1] *Matt.* vii. 22.

being the axiom that the supernatural is divine, the element peculiar to his that the moral miracle of a renewed man is the greatest and most important of all. But while giving the moral miracle the first place, he did not altogether despise the charismatic miracle. He criticised the relative phenomena, as one aware that they were in danger of running wild, and that they very much needed to be brought under the control of the great law of edification.[1] But he criticised in an ethical interest, not with any aversion to the supernatural. His criticism doubtless tended to throw the charisms into the shade, and even to bring about their ultimate disappearance. But there is nothing in his letters to justify the assertion that he desired their discontinuance, or deliberately worked for it.[2] Even his supreme concern for edification would not lead him to adopt such a policy. For the charisms were not necessarily or invariably non-edifying. The power to heal[3] could not be exercised without contributing to the common benefit. Even speaking with tongues might occasionally be edifying, as when one here and there in an assembly cried out ecstatically, "Abba, Father," or uttered groans expressive of feelings that could not be embodied in articulate language.[4] The one phenomenon,

---

[1] 1 *Cor.* xiv. 26; πάντα πρὸς οἰκοδομήν.

[2] On the two conceptions of the Spirit's influence, as transcendent and immanent, *vide* Harnack, *Dogmengeschichte*, 3rd Aufl. vol. i. p. 49, Note 1, where St. Paul is represented as vibrating between the two. Harnack refers to Gunkel and reflects his point of view.

[3] 1 *Cor.* xii. 9; ἄλλῳ δὲ χαρίσματα ἰαμάτων.

[4] Gunkel (*Die Wirkungen des heiligen Geistes*, p. 67) suggests that both these phenomena belong to the category of "Glossolalie." It is one of many fruitful fresh suggestions to be found in this book, to which I gladly acknowledge my obligations.

even if it stood alone without any added prayer, was a witness of the Divine Spirit to the sonship of the believer. It was but a child's cry, uttered in helpless weakness, but the greater the helplessness the more conclusive the witness; for who could teach the spiritual babe to utter such an exclamation but the Spirit of its Heavenly Father? The other phenomenon was but a speechless sound, a groan *de profundis*, but then it was a groan of the Holy Ghost, and as such revealed His unspeakably comforting sympathy with the sighing of the whole creation, and of the body of believers in Jesus for the advent of the new redeemed world.

Yet, withal, the apostle believed that there were better things than charisms, and a better way than to covet them as the *summum bonum*. It was better, he held, to love than to prophesy or to speak with tongues; and to help a man to love, a more worthy function of the Spirit than to bestow on him all the charisms. For in the charity extolled in 1 *Corinthians* xiii. he did recognise an effect of the divine activity, as we learn from the Epistle to the Galatians, where $\dot{a}\gamma\dot{a}\pi\eta$ heads the list in the catalogue of the fruit of the Spirit.[1] What an immense step onwards in the moral education of the world this doctrine, that love and kindred graces are the best evidence that a man is under the inspiration of the Holy Ghost, and that only they who love deserve to be called *spiritual*! In the Epistle to the Galatians love, joy, peace, long-suffering, gentleness, goodness, faith, meekness, and self-control are set in antithesis to the works of the flesh, as the proper fruit of the Spirit. It

[1] *Gal.* v. 22.

is an instructive contrast; but even more significant, because more unexpected, is it to find the apostle in effect setting these virtues in contrast to the charisms, and saying to the Church of his time: "The true proper fruit of the Spirit is not the gift of healing, or of working miracles, or of speaking with tongues, or of interpreting tongues; it is love that suffereth long and is kind, that envieth not, and boasteth not; that beareth all things, believeth all things, hopeth all things, endureth all things."[1] No one possessing ordinary moral discernment can mistake the works of the flesh for the fruit of the Spirit, though here also mistakes are possible, even in the case of religious men who confound their own private resentments with zeal for the glory of God. But how easy to imagine oneself a spiritual, Spirit-possessed man, because one has prophesied, and cast out devils in Christ's name; and how hard on such a self-deceived one the stern repudiation of the Lord, "I know you not," and the withering contempt expressed in the words of his apostle, "If a man thinketh himself to be something, when he is nothing, he deceiveth himself."[2]

Divine action, when transcendent and miraculous, is intermittent. The speaker in a tongue does not always speak ecstatically, but only when the power from on high lays hold on him. In the case of the charisms it does not greatly matter. But in the case of the graces it matters much. Here intermittent action of the Spirit means failure, for a man cannot be said to be sanctified unless there be formed in him fixed habitudes of grace,

[1] 1 *Cor.* xiii. 4–7.   [2] *Gal.* vi. 3.

manifesting themselves with something like the regularity of a law of nature. But where the action of the Spirit is intermittent there can be no habits or abiding states, but only occasional elevations into the third heaven of devout thought and holy emotion, followed by lapses to the lower levels in which unassisted human nature is at home. We can see what is involved by reference to the case of those who cried in ecstatic moods, Abba, ὁ πατήρ. While they were in the mood they realised that God was their Father, that they were His sons. But the filial consciousness was not established in their hearts; when the transcendent influence out of which they spoke for the moment passed away, they sank down from the filial spirit to the legal, from trust to fear. To eliminate this fitfulness, and secure stable spiritual character, transcendency must give place to immanence, and preternatural action to action in accordance with spiritual law. The Divine Spirit must cease to be above and outside, and take up His abode in our hearts, and His influence, from being purely mysterious and magical, must be exerted through the powers, and in accordance with the nature, of the human soul. Without pretending that the apostle anticipated the modern doctrine of divine immanence, it must be said that an indwelling of the Holy Spirit in man finds distinct recognition in his pages. He represents the Christian man as a temple in which the Spirit of God has His abode.[1] Even the body of a believer he conceives of under that august figure; as if the Divine Spirit had entered into as intimate a connection with his material

[1] 1 Cor. iii. 16.

organism as that which the soul sustains to the body.¹ And from that indwelling he expects not only the sanctification of the inner spiritual nature, but the endowment of the mortal body with unending life.² The idea of the believing man as the temple of the Spirit is introduced by the apostle as a motive for self-sanctification, as if out of respect for our august tenant. But the same idea may be held to teach by implication the unintermitting, sanctifying influence of the immanent Spirit, whose constant concern it must be to keep His chosen abode worthy of Himself. His honour is no wise compromised by withholding for a season, or permanently, from any believer charismatic power. The withdrawal may even be an index of spiritual advance from the crudity of an incipient religious enthusiasm to the calm of self-control. But the temple of God cannot be defiled by sin without injury to His good name, therefore for His own sake He is concerned to be constantly active in keeping the sanctuary holy.

The immanency of the Holy Spirit carries further along with it, as has been stated, that His influence as a sanctifier is exerted in accordance with the laws of a rational nature. His instrument must be truth, fitted, if believed, to tell upon the conscience and the heart. This fact also finds occasional, though not very elaborate recognition, in the Pauline Epistles. It is broadly indicated in the text in which the apostle tells the Thessalonians that God had chosen them unto salvation, in sanctification of the Spirit and belief of the truth.³ From this text the fair inference is, that the Spirit

[1] 1 *Cor.* vi. 15.   [2] *Rom.* viii. 11.   [3] 2 *Thess.* ii. 13.

sanctifies through Christian truth believed. We naturally expect to find useful hints on this topic in the Epistles written to the church in which the charismatic action of the Spirit was specially conspicuous, and in which at the same time there was a great need for sanctification. And we are not disappointed. And it is noteworthy that the hints we do find connect sanctification closely with Christ. "Sanctified in Christ Jesus,"[1] "Sanctified in the name of the Lord Jesus Christ,"[2] "Christ made unto us sanctification."[3] The idea suggested in the second of these phrases may be, that by the very name he bears the Christian is consecrated to God. But this ideal sanctification is of value only on account of the real sanctification of which it is the earnest. And the other two phrases teach that the material conditions of such sanctification are provided in Christ as an object of knowledge and faith. Christ fully taken advantage of in these ways will completely insure our sanctification. The Spirit dwelling in the heart sanctifies through Christ dwelling in the heart by faith, and by *thought* in order to faith. Hence it comes that the Spirit and Christ are sometimes identified, as in the sentence, "The Lord is the Spirit,"[4] and the expression, "The Lord the Spirit."[5] As a matter of subjective experience the two indwellings cannot be distinguished; to consciousness they are one. The Spirit is the *alter ego* of the Lord.

The truth as it is in Jesus, the idea of Christ, is the Spirit's instrument in sanctification. And whence do we

[1] 1 *Cor.* i. 2.   [2] *Ibid.* vi. 11.   [3] *Ibid.* i. 30.
[4] 2 *Cor.* iii. 17.   [5] *Ibid.* iii. 18.

get our idea of Christ? Surely from the earthly history of our Lord! It has been supposed that the apostle means to cast a slight on that history as of little value to faith when he says: "Even though we have known Christ after the flesh, yet now we know Him so no more."[1] But what he here says, like much else in his principal Epistles, must be looked at in the light of his controversy with the Judaists. His opponents attached great importance to mere external companionship with Jesus, and because he had not, like the Eleven, enjoyed the privilege of such companionship, they called in question his right to be an apostle. His reply to this in effect was, that not outside acquaintance, but insight was what qualified for apostleship. The reply implies that the former may exist without the latter, which from familiar experience we know to be true. How ignorant oftentimes are a man's own relations of his inmost spirit! What is the value of any knowledge which is lacking in this respect? Knowledge of a man does not mean knowing his clothes, his features, his social position. I do not know a man because I know him to be a man of wealth, who resides in a spacious dwelling, and is surrounded with many comforts, and adorned with many honours. Some are very ambitious to know a person of whom these things are true, and they would cease to know him if he were deprived of these advantages. This is to know a man after the flesh, in Pauline phrase; and if the man so known be a man of moral discernment, as well as of means and position, he will heartily despise such snobbish acquaintances who are friends of

[1] 2 *Cor.* v. 16.

his good fortune rather than of himself. Somewhat similar was the apostle's feelings in regard to the stress laid by the Judaists on acquaintance with Jesus after the manner of those who were with Him during the years of His public ministry. To cast a slight on the words and acts spoken and done in that ministry, and on the revelation of a character made thereby, was not, I imagine, in all his thoughts.

Of systematic absolute neglect of the history of Jesus the apostle cannot be charged, in view of the importance he attaches to one event therein, the crucifixion, and that in connection with the work of the Holy Spirit. The Spirit he represents as shedding abroad in our hearts the love of God, as manifested in the death of Christ,[1] overwhelming us, as it were, with a sense of its grandeur and graciousness, and so materially contributing to our sanctification through the strong hope it inspires and the consciousness of obligation it creates. One fails to see why every other event and aspect of Christ's earthly life should not be made to contribute its quota towards the same great end, and the whole evangelic story turned into motive power for sanctification. It is quite true that St. Paul has not done this, and that he has restricted his attention very much to the death and resurrection. But that is no reason why we should draw our idea of the Christ, by whose indwelling we are to be sanctified, exclusively from these two events. The fuller and more many-sided our idea the better, the more healthy the resulting type of Christian piety. The entire gospel story is needed and useful. To those who believe in an

[1] *Rom.* v. 5; cf. v. 8.

inspired New Testament no further proof of this statement should be necessary than the simple fact that the Gospels are there. The Gospels say little about the Spirit, at least the Synoptical Gospels, but they supply the data with which the Spirit works. The Pauline Epistles say much about the Spirit and His work, but comparatively little about His tools. Gospels and Epistles must be taken together if we wish to construct a full wholesome doctrine of sanctification. No good can ultimately come to Christian piety from treating the evangelic history as a scaffolding which may be removed after the edifice of faith in a risen Lord has been completed. Antæus-like faith retains its strength by keeping in touch with the ground of history. The mystic's reliance on immediate influence emanating from the ascended Christ, or from the Holy Spirit at His behest, without reference to the Jesus that lived in Palestine, exposes to all the dangers connected with vague raptures, lawless fancies, and spiritual pride. That the divine Logos, or the eternal Spirit of truth and goodness, can and does work on the human mind outside Christendom is most certainly to be believed. But that fact is no valid reason why endeavours should not be made to propagate Christianity among the heathen by missionary agencies, still less why there need have been no historical Christianity to propagate. In like manner it may be affirmed that, while it may be possible for the Divine Spirit in a transcendental way to exert an influence on Christians without the aid of the "Word," the results of such action are not likely to be of a kind to compensate for the loss of knowledge of the historical Christ. It is true, indeed, that the historicity of the Gospels may be more or less open to question. In so far as that is the case, it is our loss. The cloud of uncertainty enveloping the life of Jesus is matter of regret, not a thing to be taken with philosophical indifference as if it were of no practical consequence.

An apology is needed for making these observations, which to men of sober judgment will appear self-evident, but some present-day tendencies must be my excuse. And it is not irrelevant to offer such remarks in connection with the Pauline doctrine of the Spirit and the circumstances amidst which it was formulated. There can be little doubt that the religious enthusiasm of the apostolic age tended to breed indifference to the historical Christ. What need of history to men who were bearers of the Spirit, and were in daily receipt of revelations? I should be sorry to believe that the apostle sympathised with this tendency, though some have supposed that he did.[1] Be that as it may, what is certain is, that the tendency was unwholesome. It was well that it had not the field altogether to itself, and that in spite of it the memory of Jesus was lovingly preserved. That memory saved Christianity.[2]

To rescue the name of St. Paul from being used as an authority for contempt of the historical, it may be well to cite another text, in which he connects the work of

[1] On this point Gloël (*Der Heilige Geist*, 173) remarks: "Paul is far removed from an enthusiastic subjectivism which consoles itself with personal experiences, but loses out of sight the historical foundations of the faith."

[2] Gunkel says: "Not a pneumatic speculation like that of St. Paul, which offered no security that Christianity should keep in the

the Spirit with the example of Christ. In *Galatians* vi. 1 he exhorts to considerate, gentle treatment of such as have been overtaken in a fault. The exhortation is addressed to the πνευματικοί, *i.e.* those who are supposed to be specially filled with the Spirit, as if they were in danger of assuming a tone of severity, and so of reviving in the Church, under a new Christian guise, the Pharisaic type of character. Forbearing conduct towards offenders is then enforced by the consideration, that it is in accordance with "the law of Christ." No facts are specified to justify the title, but the reference is evidently to a manner of action on the part of Jesus with which it was possible for the Galatians to make themselves acquainted through available sources of information. Christ's endurance of death on the Cross was the most signal instance of His bearing the burdens of others; but there is no reason for limiting the reference to it. The apostle doubtless writes as one familiar with the fact that Jesus detested the inhumanity of the Pharisees, as represented in the behaviour of the elder brother of the parable, and in contrast to them pitied straying sheep and prodigal sons. In effect he sets before the Galatians as their model the Jesus of the Gospels, at once in His sympathies with the sinful, and in His antipathies towards the character of spurious saints, who, while boasting many virtues, lacked the cardinal grace of

tracks of the historically given gospel, but the infinitely imposing impression of the historical Christ has brought about that Christianity has not lost its historical character. The memory of Jesus has in this respect paralysed the pneumatic phenomena of the apostolic age, and survived them for more than a millennium."—*Die Wirkungen des heiligen Geistes*, p. 61.

charity. The true πνευματικὸς, therefore, in his view, is the man before whose conscience the enlightening Spirit of truth keeps the Christlike ethical ideal as an object of ardent admiration and earnest pursuit. If this be indeed the way the Spirit takes to make the Christian holy, then it cannot be doubted that His influence makes for real sanctity. His power may seem small, its very existence as something distinct from our personal effort may appear questionable—all immanent divine action is liable to this doubt—but at all events it works in the right direction. In view of the extent to which the gracious spirit of Jesus has grown in the community, and of the deepened sense of responsibility for the welfare of others visible on all sides in our time, why should we have difficulty in believing that the power of the Holy Ghost is as mighty as it is beneficent? At last the Spirit of truth has come to show us what Jesus was, and what true religion is: to teach us that orthodox faith by itself is nothing, and that Christlike love is all in all.

It cannot be said that the apostle has laid undue stress on the work of the Spirit in his apologetic, as if taking refuge in a supernatural power, in absence of any other adequate guarantee in his system for holy living. It may be asked, Why should the Divine Spirit be available for the enlightenment or renewal of Christians exclusively, or even more than for that of other men? The reply must be, in the first place, that neither in the Pauline Epistles, nor anywhere else in the New Testament, is it said or assumed that the Holy Spirit's presence is confined to Christendom. The underlying postulate rather is, that the Spirit of God, like God Himself, is everywhere, even in the inanimate creation, working towards the birth of a new world wherein dwelleth righteousness. He is the atmosphere of the moral world, ready to enter into every human heart wherever He finds an opening. If, therefore, He is in the Christian world more than in other parts of humanity, it must be because He finds there a more abundant entrance. And that, again, must be due to the intrinsic and superior excellence of the Christian faith. The Spirit of God is a sanctifier in Christendom more than elsewhere, because He there has at command the best material for His purpose.[1]

[1] The question how far St. Paul recognised a law of growth in sanctification will be considered in another connection.

CHAPTER XIV

THE FLESH AS A HINDRANCE TO HOLINESS

THE title of this chapter indicates correctly the point of view from which the flesh is regarded in the Pauline Epistles. It is not with an abstract doctrine or theory of the flesh that we have to do, but with an unhappy, untoward fact of Christian experience—a stubborn resistance offered by a power residing in the flesh to the attainment of that entire holiness after which every sincere Christian earnestly aspires. The point of view is clearly indicated in this exhortation to the Galatian Church: "Walk in the Spirit, and do not fulfil the lusts of the flesh. For the flesh lusteth against the Spirit, and the Spirit against the flesh; for these are contrary to each other; so that ye may not do the things that ye would."[1] That the flesh is an obstructive in the way of holiness could not be more distinctly stated. And yet in the Epistle to the Romans the same truth is proclaimed, if not with greater plainness, at least with more marked emphasis. "Therefore, brethren," writes the apostle, "we are debtors, not to the flesh, to live after the flesh. For if ye live after the flesh, ye must die: but if by the Spirit ye mortify the deeds of the

[1] *Gal.* v. 16, 17.

body, ye shall live."[1] Here to fight with the flesh is represented as a positive duty. We are "debtors" to this intent. And the fight is urgent, a matter of life and death. The state of the case is that we must kill the flesh, or it will kill us.

We, *Christians*, have to wage this war as we value our salvation. In the seventh chapter of *Romans* mention is made of a tragic struggle with the flesh, which might, on fair exegetical grounds, be relegated to the pre-regenerate or pre-Christian state. But the fight is not over when one has become a believing man, and has begun effectively to walk in the Spirit. Thenceforth it is carried on with better hope of success, that is all the difference. It is to believing men, Christians, regenerate persons, that the apostle addresses himself in the above-cited texts. And he speaks to them in so serious a tone, because he knows the formidable nature of the foe from *present, chronic, personal experience*. This we know from that extremely significant autobiographical hint in 1 *Corinthians*: "I buffet my body, and bring it into bondage; lest by any means, after having preached to others, I myself should become a rejected one."[2] Depend upon it, this buffeting or bruising of the body was for St. Paul a serious business. He found it necessary for spiritual safety to be in effect an ascetic, not in any superstitious sense, or on a rigid system, but in the plain, practical sense of taking special pains to prevent the body, with its clamorous passions, from getting the upper hand.

One thing we may note here by the way. Comparing

[1] *Rom.* viii. 12, 13.   [2] 1 *Cor.* ix. 27.

these three texts one with another, we gather that *body* and *flesh*, so far as obstructing holiness is concerned, are for the apostle synonymous terms. It is against the *flesh* he warns fellow-Christians; the *body* is the foe he himself fears. Those who are familiar with the recent literature of Paulinism will understand the bearing of this remark. Some writers will have it that the two terms bear widely different senses in the Pauline letters. Σάρξ, they say, is a *Substanzbegriff*, and σῶμα a *Formbegriff*: the word "flesh" points to the material of which the body consists, the word "body" to the form of our material organism. The distinction is made in the interest of a theory to the effect that St. Paul shared the Greek view of flesh and of all matter—that it is inherently evil. This theory will come up for consideration at a later stage. Meantime we have to remark, that so far as we have gone we have found no reason to suppose that the conceptions of "flesh" and "body" lay so far apart in the Pauline system of thought as is alleged.

It may surprise some that so good and saintly a man as the apostle Paul should have found in the body or the flesh so much of a hindrance to the spiritual life. Surprising or not, we may take it for certain that such was the fact. In spite of his passion for holiness, the flesh was constantly and obstinately obstructive. Nay, may we not say that it was obstructive not merely in spite, but in consequence of his passion for holiness? None knows better than the saint what mischief the flesh can work. Let the tragedies which have been enacted in the cells of holy monks bear witness. There is a mysterious, subtle, psychological connection between spiritual and sensual excitements, which some of the noblest men have detected and confessed. Hence it comes to pass, paradoxical as it may seem, that most earnest and successful endeavours to walk in the Spirit, or even to fly under His buoyant inspiration, may develop, by way of reaction, powerful temptations to fulfil the grossest lusts of the flesh. Eloquent preachers, brilliant authors, know that this is no libel. Times of widespread religious enthusiasm make their contribution to the illustration of this same law. Powerful breezes of the Spirit are followed by outbreaks of epidemic sin, in which the works of the flesh are deplorably manifest.

Whatever surprise or disappointment it may awaken in us that the flesh should give trouble to such an one as St. Paul, we are quite prepared to discover in his writings traces of a subtle insight into the nature and varied manifestations of its evil influence. Such insight formed an essential feature of his spiritual vitality. It was what was to be expected from one who, even before he became a Christian, and in spite of a Pharisaic training, which taught him to regard the outward act as alone important, made the great discovery that *coveting* was a sin. It would be only an extension of that discovery if Paul, the Christian and the apostle, found in himself much of the evil working of the flesh when there was nothing in his outward conduct on which the most unfriendly critic could fasten. "Thou shalt not commit adultery,"—that is a commandment forbidding a definite outward act. But Jesus, on the Mount, had said, "Whosoever looketh on a woman to lust after her, hath committed adultery with her already in his heart,"[1] and Paul's Christian conscience endorsed the sentiment as, however severe and searching, nothing but the truth. And who can tell what painful inner experiences this saintly man passed through in this direction? That the flesh meant for him very specially, though not exclusively, sexual impulse, may be inferred from the prominent position given to sins of impurity in his catalogues of the works of the flesh.[2] A voluntary abstainer from marriage relations that he might the better perform the duties of his apostolic calling, a veritable "eunuch for the kingdom of heaven's sake,"[3] he rightly appears to the spectator of his great career a devoted, saintly, heroic man. But what, just because of the loftiness of his moral ideal, and the keenness of his insight, may he sometimes have appeared to himself? Less than the least of all saints; nay, no saint at all, but a poor, vile, self-humiliated sinner, actually within measurable distance of being a "castaway." Does this language shock pious readers? It certainly costs this writer an effort to put such words on paper. But he forces himself to do so, because he believes that it is along this road we shall most readily arrive at an understanding of what St. Paul means by his many strong words concerning the flesh, rather than through learned lucubrations concerning the meaning of the Hebrew word for flesh in the Old Testament Scriptures, or as to the probability of the apostle having got his doctrine of the σάρξ from Philo or some other representative of Hellenistic philosophy. That one statement, "I buffet my body," is of more value to me as a guide to his thought than all

[1] *Matt.* v. 28.   [2] *Gal.* v. 19.   [3] *Matt.* xix. 12.

the monographs on the subject. It tells me that *Saint Paul*, while a true saint, was also a man of like passions with ourselves, that he had his desperate struggles with the flesh under very common forms of temptation, and that his sanctity was a victory achieved in that fell war by one who was prepared to sacrifice an offending member that the whole body might not be cast into hell. For the comfort of those who are manfully, though, as it appears to themselves, with very indifferent success, fighting the same battle, it is well to make this plain.

In the foregoing remarks I have virtually forestalled the question, What is meant by the flesh in the Pauline letters, and on what ground is it there represented as the very seat of sin? An unsophisticated reader, confining his attention to these Epistles, would probably gather from them an answer to this question somewhat to the following effect. The flesh means, of course, primarily the material substance of the body, and its ethical significance in the Pauline Epistles, as representing the sinful element in general, is due to the fact of its being the seat of appetites and passions of a very obtrusive character, which, though neither in themselves nor in their effects the whole of human sin, yet constitute its most prominent part, especially in the case of a Christian. Take the case of St. Paul himself, once more, as our example. He is conscious that with his mind and heart he approves, loves, and pursues the good; that he is a devoted follower of the Lord Jesus Christ, and a single-minded servant of the kingdom of God. But he is conscious of distractions, temptations, hindrances, and on reflection these appear to him to arise out of his body. He sees still, as of old, a law in his members warring against the law of his mind. This body of death, therefore, this flesh, becomes to him the symbol of sin generally; he speaks of it as if it were the one fountain of sin, tracing to its evil influence not merely sensual sins, properly so called, though these are generally placed first in enumerations, but sins of the spirit likewise, such as pride, envy, hatred. This *primâ facie* answer is, I believe, not far from the truth. But it raises other questions not to be disposed of so easily. How does it come to pass that the *flesh* causes the saint so much trouble ? why does it lag so far behind the *mind* in the path of sanctification ? We know what Philo and the author of the *Book of Wisdom,* and the Greeks from whom they drew their inspiration, thought on that subject. They deemed matter generally, and especially the fleshly part of human nature, to be inherently and incurably evil. The animated matter which we call our bodies was in their view necessarily, inevitably, universally a source of evil impulse; the problem of the spirit being to trample its unworthy companion under foot, and its hope to get finally rid of it by death.

Was this St. Paul's view ? Many modern theologians think that it was, and that on this important subject he was a disciple of the Alexandrian or Judæo-Greek philosophy. On this question it is needful to speak with care and discrimination. St. Paul might hold the Greek view without getting it from the Greeks or from any external source. Again, he might go a considerable way with the Greeks in his thoughts concerning the flesh, without having any cut-and-dried theory regarding it, such as speculative minds loved to elaborate. As a matter of fact, I believe the latter supposition to be pretty nearly correct. A reader of the Pauline Epistles gets the impression that the writer thought as badly of the flesh, that is of the material part of man, as did Philo, who beyond doubt was in entire sympathy with the Greek view of matter. And I apprehend that Paul and Philo thought so badly of the flesh for very much the same reason—not to begin with at least on à *priori* grounds of theory, but on practical grounds of experience. Philo's writings, just like those of St. Paul, are full of allusions to the temptations which assail the saint or sage arising out of the appetites and passions that have their seat in the flesh. But the difference between the two men lay here. Philo, with his leaning towards Greek philosophy, theorised on the subject of the flesh and its evil proclivities, to the effect already indicated. St. Paul, on the other hand, did not theorise. He contented himself with stating facts as they presented themselves to him in experience. Whether the Greek theory was known to him is quite uncertain; the probability is that it was not. But, even if it had been, it is not at all likely that it would have had any attractions for him, as his interest in the matter involved was nowise speculative but wholly ethical and religious. Nay, the probability is that, on ethical and religious grounds, he would have regarded the theory with aversion and disfavour. Some solid reasons can be given for this statement.

1. The theory that matter or flesh is essentially evil is decidedly *un-Hebrew*. The dualistic conception of man as composed of two natures, flesh and spirit, standing in necessary and permanent antagonism to each other, is not

to be found in the Old Testament Scriptures. It is true, indeed, that between the close of the Hebrew canon and the New Testament era the leaven of Hellenistic philosophy was at work in Hebrew thought, producing in course of time a considerable modification in Jewish ideas on various subjects; and it is a perfectly fair and legitimate hypothesis that traces of such influence are recognisable in the Pauline doctrine of the σάρξ. But the presumption is certainly not in favour of this hypothesis. It is rather all the other way; for throughout his writings St. Paul appears a Hebrew of the Hebrews. His intellectual and spiritual affinities are with the psalmists and prophets, not with Alexandrian philosophers; and if there be any new leaven in his culture it is Rabbinical rather than Hellenistic.

2. A second consideration bearing on the question at issue is that, whereas, according to the Greek view the flesh ought to be *unsanctifiable*, it is not so regarded in the Pauline Epistles. Sometimes, indeed, it might seem as if the apostle did look on the flesh, or the body, as incurably evil; as when, in a text already quoted, he speaks of killing the deeds of the body,[1] or when he employs such a phrase as "the body of this death,"[2] or represents the body as "dead on account of sin."[3] But, in other places, the body is represented as the subject of sanctification not less than the soul or spirit. Not to mention 1 *Thessalonians* v. 23, where the apostle prays that the whole spirit, soul, and body of his brethren may be preserved blameless unto the coming of the Lord Jesus Christ, there is the important text in 1 *Corinthians* vi. 19, 20, where

[1] *Rom.* viii. 13. [2] *Ibid.* vii. 24. [3] *Ibid.* viii. 10.

the body is represented as the temple of the Holy Ghost, and it is set forth as a duty arising directly out of the consciousness of redemption to glorify God in the body,[1] in the special sense of keeping clear of sexual impurity. Another very important text in this connection is 2 *Corinthians* vii. 1, where it is inculcated as a Christian duty to cleanse ourselves from all defilement of the flesh and spirit; of the flesh as well as the spirit, of flesh not more than the spirit, there being the same possibility and the same need of sanctification in both. It is true, indeed, that the genuineness of this text has been called in question by Holsten, one of the strongest advocates of the Hellenistic character and source of the Pauline idea of the flesh.[2] One can very well understand why upholders of this view should desire to get the text in question out of the way. It teaches too plainly what their theory of necessity negatives, the sanctifiableness of the flesh. They have no objection to the sanctification of the *body* taught in 1 *Corinthians* vi. 19, because "body" is a mere *Formbegriff*; but sanctification of the *flesh*—impossible, if, with the Greeks, St. Paul held the flesh, like all matter, to be inherently evil. And so, as that is held to be demonstrable, there is nothing for it but to pronounce 2 *Corinthians* vi. 14–vii. 1, a spurious insertion. It is a violent critical procedure, but it serves the one good purpose of amounting to a frank admission that the exhortation to purify the flesh is not compatible with the theory advocated by the critic.

Before passing on to another point, it may be well

---

[1] The point of the exhortation is very much blunted by the addition in T.R. καὶ ἐν τῷ πνεύματι.

[2] *Zum Evangelium des Petrus und des Paulus*, p. 387.

here to reflect for a moment on the unsatisfactoriness of the distinction taken between "body" and "flesh" in reference to the topic of sanctification. The body we are told is sanctifiable, because it is an affair of form; the flesh, on the contrary, is unsanctifiable because it is an affair of substance. We are to conceive of St. Paul solemnly exhorting the churches to which he wrote to this effect: "By all means take pains to sanctify the organic form called the body, but as for the flesh, wherein lies the seat and power of sin, it must be given up as past sanctifying." Can we imagine an earnest man like the apostle trifling with his readers in so serious a matter, by giving them an advice at once frivolous and absurd? Sanctify what does not need sanctifying; hope not to sanctify what most urgently needs sanctification! There is nothing wrong with the bodily form; it is graceful and beautiful; what is wanted is power to curb the fleshly desire which its beauty awakens, or the carnal wish to use that beauty as a stimulus to concupiscence.[1]

3. A doctrine teaching a dualistic opposition between flesh and spirit, and implying that flesh as distinct from spirit is essentially evil, ought to be accompanied by a Pagan *eschatology*, that is to say, by the doctrine that the life after death will be a purely disembodied one. If all sin spring from the body, or if nothing but evil can spring from it, then the sooner we get rid of it the

[1] *Vide* on this point Wendt, *Die Begriffe Fleisch und Geist*, p. 108. Wendt professes his inability to conceive how a man can begin to make his bodily form, apart from the matter of the body, the object of an ethical and religious sanctification, and protests against ascribing to the apostle a counsel amounting to nothing more than empty words.

better, and once rid of it let us be rid for ever, such riddance being a necessary condition of our felicity. Not such, however, was the outlook of the apostle. The object of his hope for the future was not the immortality of the naked, unclothed soul,[1] but the immortal life of *man*, body and soul. The fulfilment of his hope demanded the resurrection of the body: only when that event had taken place would the redemption of man in his view be complete.[2] To one holding this view, a theory involving that the soul in the future state should be unclothed could not fail to be repulsive. It is true indeed that the body of the eternal state, as the apostle conceives it, is not the corruptible, mortal, gross body of the present state, but a "spiritual body" endowed with incorruptibility, and apparently resembling the heavenly bodies radiant with light rather than this "muddy vesture of decay."[3] The point to be emphasised, however, is that the apostle demands that there shall be a body of some sort in the eternal state, even though conscious of the difficulty of satisfying all the conditions of the problem. You may say if you please that the problem is insoluble, and that the expression "spiritual body" is simply a combination of words which cancel each other. It is enough to remark, by way of reply, that that was not St. Paul's view, and the fact sufficiently proves that he lived in a different thought-world from that of the Greeks.

While I say this, I am perfectly aware that the Pauline anthropology is by no means free from difficulties and obscurities. The phrase "a spiritual body" is of

[1] *Vide* 2 *Cor.* v. 4. [2] *Rom.* viii. 23. [3] *Cor.* xv. 45-50.

itself sufficient to show the contrary. The two words "spiritual" and "body" seem to point in opposite directions, and to imply incompatible speculative presuppositions. A similar lack of theoretic coherence seems to confront us in other utterances on the same topic. Thus in 1 *Cor.* xv. the resurrection body is represented as differing not only from our present mortal body but even from that of the first man. "The first man is of the earth earthy."[1] These words not unnaturally suggest the view that Adam's flesh and our flesh are in all respects the same, both alike unfit for the kingdom of God and the eternal state, both alike mortal, corruptible, and even sinful. This accordingly is the construction put upon the words by the advocates of the theory now under discussion. But, on the other hand, it is not difficult to cite texts from the Pauline literature which seem to imply that mortality and sinfulness were not natural and original attributes of human nature, but accidents befalling it in consequence of Adam's transgression. *Rom.* v. 12 seems to point in this direction; so also does *Rom.* viii. 21–23, where the corruptibility of the creation generally is called a bondage, and the body of man is represented as sharing in the general bondage and looking forward to redemption from it. The whole train of thought in this passage seems to imply that the present condition of things is something abnormal, something not belonging to the original state of creation, something therefore which it belongs to Christ as the Redeemer to remove. The same idea is suggested even by the statement in *Rom.* vii. 14, one

[1] Ver. 47.

of the texts on which chief reliance is placed for proof of the thesis that the Pauline anthropology is based on Greek dualism. "I am made of flesh (σάρκινος), sold under sin." Assuming that the writer speaks here not merely for himself, but as the spokesman of the race, we get from these words the doctrine that wherever there is human flesh there is sin, which seems to be the very doctrine imputed to the apostle by such theologians as Holsten and Baur. Yet the very terms in which he expresses the fact of universal human sinfulness suggest another theory as to its source. "*Sold* under sin." The words convey the notion that the sinful proclivity of man, while universal, is accidental, a departure from the normal and original state of things, therefore not irremediable. Were it a matter of natural necessity it were vain to cry, "Who shall deliver me?" No man or angel could deliver. Only death, dissolving the unhappy union between νοῦς and σάρξ, could come to the rescue.

On these grounds it may be confidently affirmed that the metaphysical dualism of the Greeks could not possibly have commended itself to the mind of St. Paul. An ethical dualism he does teach, but he never goes beyond that. It is of course open to anyone to say that the metaphysical dualism really lies behind the ethical one, though St. Paul himself was not conscious of the fact, and that therefore radical disciples like Marcion were only following out his principles to their final consequences when they set spirit and matter, God and the world, over against each other as hostile kingdoms. But even those who take up this position are forced in candour to admit that such gnostic or Manichæan doctrine was not in all the apostle's thoughts.[1]

An *ethical* dualism, however, of a decided character St. Paul does teach. If we cannot agree with those who impute to him Greek metaphysics, as little can we sympathise with those who in a reactionary mood go to the opposite extreme, and endeavour, as far as possible, to assign to the word σάρξ in his Epistles the innocent sense of creaturely weakness, as opposed to divine power, without any necessary connotation of sin. This is the view of Wendt, as expounded in his able tractate on the notions Flesh and Spirit. He tries to show that the Hebrew word for "flesh" bears this sense in all passages in the Old Testament in which the term is charged with a religious significance, and this result he brings as a key to the study of Pauline texts in hope that it will open all doors. One cannot but admire his ingenuity in the attempt, but as little can one resist the feeling that he is guilty of exaggeration not less than those whose theory it is his aim to refute. Of course he is not so blinded by bias as to be unable to see that St. Paul does frequently ascribe to the creaturely weakness of man both intellectual and moral aberration. But then he tells us that these adverse judgments on the flesh are "*synthetic*" not "analytic"; that is, state something concerning the flesh not involved in the notion of it. "I am of flesh, sold under sin" is a synthetic proposition which proclaims not the origin of sin out of an essentially evil flesh, but the tyrannic power, somehow acquired, of sin in an originally innocent

[1] *Vide* Hausrath, *Neutestamentliche Zeitgeschichte*, ii. 468.

flesh. It may be so; nevertheless we cannot but note that for the writer the synthesis seems to have become so firmly established that to say "I am σάρκινος" is all one with saying, "I am sold under sin." To such transformation of the synthetic into the analytic, human speech is liable. Consider the original etymological meaning of the word Jesu-it(e), then reflect what a word of evil omen it is now, and what damnatory judgments, no longer "synthetic," but grown very "analytic" indeed, it suggests to the average Protestant mind! "Flesh" seems to have become for the apostle Paul a term of not less similar import than "Jesuit" is for us. Whence this transmutation of the creaturely weakness of the Old Testament into the wicked carnality of the Pauline Epistles? If Hellenism does not explain it, as little does Hebrewism as interpreted by Wendt. The Pauline conception of the flesh seems to be a *tertium quid*, something intermediate between Hellenism and Hebrewism, the creation of a very intense religious experience, and of a very pronounced moral individuality.[1]

Thoughts having such a genesis are not wont to be expressed in the colourless measured terms of scholastic theology; and if a certain element of exaggeration, onesidedness, morbidity, enter into the language in which they are clothed, there is no cause for surprise. Can any such element be discerned in St. Paul's statements concerning the flesh? Those who are disposed to find a

[1] Such is the view taken by Harnack of St. Paul's doctrine as to Christ's pre-existence, and it involves a similar view of the apostle's doctrine as to the "flesh." *Vide* his *Dogmengeschichte*, vol. i. pp. 755-764, 3d Aufl.

tinge of pessimism in this part of his teaching might refer in proof, not merely to the peculiarity of his religious history, but to the high-strung enthusiasm of his Christian life, to the artificial condition of enforced celibacy under which he prosecuted his apostolic vocation, and to his expressed preference for the single state as the best not only for himself but for all, especially in view of the near approach of the world's end.[1] It is certainly not easy to maintain a perfect balance of judgment in such circumstances, and perhaps at this point the great apostle falls short of the calm, tranquil wisdom of the greater Master. But it were a serious mistake to set aside his stern utterances as mere rhetorical extravagances not worthy of our earnest attention. Here, as elsewhere, his statements, however startling, are in contact with reality. It would be well for us all to lay to heart the humbling word: "In me, that is, in my flesh, dwelleth no good thing," not by way of extracting comfort from the thought that it is only in the flesh the evil lies, but rather of realising that the flesh is ours, and of making ourselves fully responsible for the evil to which it prompts. No man who fails to do this has any right to express an opinion on the question how far St. Paul in his doctrine of the flesh is true to fact and to right Christian feeling.

Before passing from this subject, we must consider a text which has given rise to much controversy in its bearing thereon, *Romans* viii. 3. This, however, must be reserved for another chapter.

[1] 1 *Cor.* vii. 29-31.

CHAPTER XV

THE LIKENESS OF SINFUL FLESH.

THE text, *Romans* viii. 3, has already been considered in connection with the Pauline doctrine concerning the significance of Christ's death. We then found reasons for coming to the conclusion that the text does not, as is usually supposed, properly refer to Christ's death, but rather alludes to the redeeming virtue of Christ's holy life in the flesh, showing, as it does, that subjection to the flesh is no inevitable doom, and giving promise of power to believers living in the flesh to walk after the Spirit. Such I still hold to be the true import of the words: "God, sending His own Son in the likeness of sinful flesh and with reference to sin, condemned sin in the flesh." But it is obvious that these words raise questions on which we have not yet touched—questions having an important bearing on the Pauline doctrine of the flesh. God sent His Son in the flesh. Was Christ's flesh, in the apostle's view, in all respects the same as ours? Would he have applied to it the epithet "sinful" as he does to the flesh of ordinary men in the expression "flesh of sin" ($\sigma a \rho \kappa \grave{o} \varsigma\ \dot{a} \mu a \rho \tau \acute{\iota} a \varsigma$)? There have always been theologians ready to answer these questions in the affirmative. And along with this view of what St. Paul believed concerning the flesh of Christ goes usually, if not by any logical necessity, a certain theory as to what he meant to teach in reference to the atoning function of the Redeemer. In discussing the apostle's doctrine concerning Christ's death, I judged it best to make no reference to that theory, and to confine myself to a positive statement of what seemed to me to be the gist of his teaching on that subject. But an opportunity now offers itself of making some remarks on the theory in question, which may help to confirm results already arrived at, and throw some additional light on the apostle's whole way of conceiving Christ's earthly experience in relation to the problem of redemption.

The answer to the question concerning the moral quality of our Lord's flesh depends, or has been thought to depend, on the interpretation of the expression "in the likeness of sinful flesh" (ἐν ὁμοιώματι σαρκὸς ἁμαρτίας). Opinion is much divided here. There are two debatable questions—(1) Is the emphasis in the word ὁμοιώματι to be placed on the likeness, or on an implied unlikeness? (2) Do the words σαρκὸς ἁμαρτίας constitute a single idea, implying that sin is an essential property of the σάρξ, or are the two words separate, so that ἁμαρτίας expresses only an accidental, though it may be all but universal property of the flesh? Either of the alternatives may be taken in either case, yielding four different interpretations. The second alternative under (1) is combined with the first under (2) by Baur, Zeller, and Hilgenfeld, and the resulting interpretation is as follows: St. Paul regarded sin as an essential property of the flesh, but he hesitated to ascribe to Christ sinful flesh, therefore he said not that God sent Him in sinful flesh, but that God sent Him in *the likeness* of sinful flesh, meaning likeness in all respects, *sin excepted*. Others, among whom may be specially mentioned Lüdemann,[1] combine the two first alternatives; and, while agreeing with the fore-mentioned writers in taking sinful flesh as one idea, differ from them by holding that it is the apostle's purpose to teach that God furnished His Son with a flesh made exactly like ours, like in this respect that it too was a flesh of sin. Not that the apostle meant thereby to deny the sinlessness of Jesus. For though ἁμαρτία was immanent in the flesh of Christ as in that of other men, it was only objective sin, not subjective; it never came to παράβασις; it was prevented from doing so by the Holy Spirit, who guided all Christ's conduct, and kept the flesh in perfect subjection. A third class of interpreters, such as Hofmann, Weiss, etc., combine the two second alternatives, treating σὰρξ and ἁμαρτία as separate ideas, and taking ὁμοίωμα as implying limitation of likeness in respect of the sinfulness of ordinary fallen human nature. Finally, Wendt combines the first alternative under (1) with the second alternative under (2), and takes out of the words the sense: Christ's creaturely nature was exactly the same as ours, to which sin adheres only *per accidens*, and the sinfulness of our flesh is referred to not to indicate *wherein* Christ was like us, but *wherefore* He was made like us.

None of these diverse interpretations can be considered exegetically self-evident. They are all, from the point

[1] *Die Anthropologie des Apostels Paulus*, 1872.

of view of verbal exegesis, legitimate, and our decision must depend on other considerations. The view supported by Baur has a good deal of *primâ facie* plausibility; but assuming his interpretation of ἐν ὁμοιώματι to be correct, it appears to me to be an argument in favour of the separability of the ideas of flesh and sin. For why should it be supposed that the motive of the limitation is mere shrinking in reverence from applying a principle to Christ which is firmly held by the writer as a necessary truth? If the apostle believed that where σάρξ is there is, must be, sin, ἁμαρτία at least, if not παράβασις, would he who was so thoroughgoing in all his thinking have hesitated to ascribe it to Christ also? Would he not rather have done what, according to Lüdemann, he really has done, viz. ascribed to Christ's flesh ἁμαρτία, and then sought to guard His personal sinlessness by emphasising the indwelling of the Divine Spirit as the means of preventing objective sin, ἁμαρτία, from breaking out into παράβασις? Surely he was much more likely to do this than to adopt the weak expedient of covering over a difficulty with a word.

The first alternative under (1) is therefore decidedly to be preferred. The emphasis lies on the likeness, not on an implied unlikeness. This conclusion is confirmed by the construction I have put on the didactic significance of the whole passage. If the apostle's aim was to insist on the redemptive value of Christ's successful transit through a curriculum of temptation, then he had a manifest interest in making the similarity of the conditions under which Christ was tempted to those in which we are placed as great as possible. The battle with sin must be very real for Christ as well as for us —not a sham fight. If in order to that it was necessary that Christ's flesh should be the same as ours in all respects, why then so it must be. Whether it was necessary or not is a difficult question, on which opinion may differ. Was that question present to St. Paul's mind, and if it was did he mean to pronounce an opinion upon it? It is commonly assumed that the problem was in his view, and that we here have his solution. Is this really so?

That so deep a thinker had asked himself the question: What about our Lord's flesh, was it wholly like ours? is probable. But that he was prepared to dogmatise on the question is not so likely. What if he was in a state of uncertainty about it, feeling the delicacy of the question, and the pressure of two contrary religious interests, each vitally important: on the one hand, the necessity of guarding the sinlessness of Jesus; on the other, the equal necessity of making His curriculum of temptation most thoroughly, even grimly, real? I do not think it matters much for the ascertainment of the apostle's mind on this point whether we take the expression "sinful flesh" as analytic, with Baur, or as synthetic, with Wendt. Synthetic or not, the two ideas "flesh" and "sin" had become, as we saw, very coherent in his thought. For all practical purposes "sinful flesh" had assumed for him the character of a single indissoluble idea, at least with reference to ordinary men. And just on that account he could not well get past the question: Was Christ's flesh an exception? was there in His case no law in the members warring against the law of the mind? But it does not follow that he was ready with his answer. The question is a puzzle to us, why should it not be to him? And if it was, what could he do but say, "Christ came in the likeness of sinful flesh, *to the extent of being subject to very real temptation to sin and all that that may involve?*" That is what, when the previous context is taken into account, he in effect does say in this much contested passage.

And so it results that the true interpretation of the text, *Romans* viii. 3, after all does not enable us to answer the question propounded, but leaves it an open question for theologians. As such, however, the most representative theologians of the Church have not treated it. The decided tendency of orthodox theology has ever been to regard the question as closed, to the effect of holding that Christ's flesh differed from that of ordinary men in being free from that law in the members warring against the law of the mind, whereof the apostle complains.[1] But there have never been lacking some Christian thinkers who have been unable

[1] In an article on the phrase ἐν ὁμοιώματι σαρκὸς ἁμαρτίας in *Zeitschrift für Wissenschaftliche Theologie* (1869), Overbeck remarks that from Marcion to Baur interpreters have assigned to ὁμοίωμα a negative sense, similarity as opposed to likeness, in relation to ἁμαρτία. He characterises the history of the interpretation of this word as that of the almost uncontested reign of an exegetical *monstrum* of patristic controversial theology. The question has recently been discussed, What is the precise lexical meaning of ὁμοίωμα? Holsten makes it signify the visible image. With this view Overbeck generally agrees, dissenting only from the notion that *visibility* is an essential part of the meaning. He makes ὁμοίωμα=essential identity. Cremer, *Biblisch theologisches Wörter-*

to acquiesce in this decision. The grounds of dissent have been such as these: If Christ's personal sinlessness be loyally maintained, the interests of faith are sufficiently safeguarded. The more difficult it was for Christ to be sinless, the more meritorious. The utmost that can be said against the flesh in any case is, that it makes holiness difficult by supplying powerful sources of temptation. That is all that is meant by the expression, "objective sin." Properly speaking, what the apostle calls "flesh of sin" is not sinful. Sin and sinlessness belong to the person and not to the nature.[1] The flesh as such is in no case bad. It is the inversion of the right relation between flesh and spirit that is sin.[2] Only in case the flesh as we inherit it made perfect holiness impossible, would it be necessary for Christ the sinless One to have a flesh uniquely endowed. But the apostle's view is not that perfect holiness, blameless walking in the Spirit, is impossible for Christians. He exhorts church members to perfect holiness by cleansing themselves from all defilement of flesh and spirit,[3] and treats Christ's moral triumph over temptation as a guarantee for the fulfilment of the righteousness of the

buch, 7th Aufl. (1893), gives as the radical sense *das Gleichgemachte, Bild, Abbild*. With reference to New Testament use, he remarks that abstractly considered ὁμοίωμα might signify the same thing as ὁμοίωσις, *similarity*, but in none of the texts where it occurs does he think this sense called for. The meaning which suits them all is *Gestalt, form*, not in the abstract but in the concrete. The word occurs four times in the Epistle to the Romans, i. 2, 3 ; v. 14 ; vi. 5; viii. 3.

[1] So Porcher du Bose, *The Soteriology of the New Testament* (1892), p. 202.
[2] So Beyschlag, *Neutestamentliche Theologie* (1892), vol. ii. p. 41.
[3] 2 *Cor.* vii. 1.

law in Christian men walking not after the flesh but after the Spirit.¹ If that be possible in us, with the flesh as we have it, it was possible *à fortiori* in Christ, even in a flesh in all respects like ours. Finally, by what means could Christ's flesh be made different from ours? By the power of the Holy Ghost? But moral effects cannot be produced by mere physical power. "The function of the Holy Ghost is influence and never mere power,"² and its proper sphere is the will, not the material frame.³

I proceed now to make some observations on the theory of atonement which is usually associated with this "heterodox" view as to the flesh of Christ. I have been accustomed to call it the theory of "Redemption by sample."⁴ The name, though not accepted by the advocates of the theory, sufficiently indicates the principle. That principle is, that Christ did for Himself first of all what needs to be done for us, and did it by living a perfectly holy life in a human nature in all respects like ours. He sanctified the sample of human nature which He assumed, and so laid a sure foundation for the sanctification of humanity at large. Christ on this view was at once the thing to be redeemed, its redemption, and the thing redeemed,⁵ and His work was "through His own self-perfection to perfect us."⁶ A

---

¹ *Rom.* viii. 4.   ² Du Bose, *Soteriology,* p. 208.
³ Among the theologians belonging to this school fall to be classed Dr. Jamieson of Aberdeen. His views are set forth in *Profound Problems in Theology and Philosophy* (1884); *Discussions on the Atonement, is it vicarious?* (1887); and *A Revised Theology* (1891).
⁴ Vide *The Humiliation of Christ,* pp. 47, 253 ff.
⁵ Du Bose, *Soteriology.* p. 227.   ⁶ *Ibid.* p. 286.

peculiar significance is attached to the death of Christ by some exponents of the theory. What took place in the crucifixion was, that sin in Christ's own flesh was judicially condemned and executed, and so the power of sin in the flesh in principle overcome and abolished for all Christians.

Before making critical remarks on this theory, it may be proper here to point out the precise relation in which it stands to the view of Christ's flesh, with which it is associated. The state of the case I take to be this. The theory of atonement in question demands that Christ's flesh be in all respects like ours, but holding this view does not necessitate adoption of the theory. Redemption by sample requires that Christ's flesh be a sample of the corrupt mass to be redeemed. But Christ's flesh might be that, and yet redemption proceed on another principle. The identity of the Redeemer's flesh with ours would fit in to the theory of redemption by *self-humiliation* quite as well as to the theory of redemption by self-redemption. It would mean simply that Christ's temptations would be very fully assimilated to ours, and so become a very strong ground of hope. Possibly Christ's experience of temptation would sufficiently resemble ours without such identity. In that case, the theory of redemption by *self-humiliation* could afford to leave the question as to Christ's flesh open. On the other hand, the theory of redemption by self-redemption cannot allow the question to be open. Hence the relevancy of a criticism on that theory in this place. We criticise a theory which excludes our view as to the vagueness of St. Paul's statement that God sent His Son in the likeness of sinful flesh.

This theory, then, seems very open to criticism in the construction it puts on the crucifixion. In the first place, if the ἁμαρτία in Christ's flesh was a thing which could be completely kept under by the holy will of Christ (as is admitted on all hands), was it not morally insignificant, and therefore not a thing calling for judicial condemnation and execution? Is there not something theatrical in this pouring out of the vials of divine wrath on the flesh of Christ for the objective sin latent in it? It is impossible to read the eloquent declamations on this topic, in the writings of Edward Irving,[1] *e.g.*, without feeling that the whole affair is utterly unreal, without any fact-basis, a pure theological figment. Then, on the other hand, one fails to see how the judicial condemnation on the cross of potential sin in Christ's flesh is to benefit us in the way of preventing the vicious bias in our flesh from breaking out into transgression. For though the objective sin of the flesh in Christ's case happily proved innocuous, it is far enough from being harmless in our case, *teste* St. Paul. How, then, are we to be benefited? How will the condemnation of Christ's flesh in His death deliver us from our body of death? Shall we say to ourselves: In that death my flesh was crucified? Alas! the faith-mysticism will not help us here. The faith-mysticism may act on the imagination and the heart, but hardly on the flesh.

[1] Vide *The Doctrine of the Incarnation Opened* (Collected Writings, vol. v.), and the account of his view in *The Humiliation of Christ*, p. 254.

It will remain as obstinately as ever opposed to all good, for anything the condemnation of Christ's flesh on Calvary effected. Instead of faith-mysticism, then, must we have recourse to sacramental magic, and say that in the Lord's Supper the Lord's resurrection-body, purged from potential sin by the fire of the cross, passes into our bodies and becomes there a transforming influence, spiritualising, sublimating our carnal frames into the likeness of Christ's risen humanity? That certainly was the way Irving's adventurous spirit took in carrying out his pet theory. It seems the only course open, and it is the *reductio ad absurdum* of the theory.

If the stress of Christ's work be placed, as perhaps on this theory it ought to be, on the life rather than on the death of the Redeemer, then the redemptive value of our Lord's experience lies in His heroic struggle to maintain perfect holiness in spite of the sinful flesh. Now here at least we are in contact with a fact. The condemnation of Christ's flesh on the cross has all the appearance of being a pure figment, but Christ's battle with temptation was an indubitable, stern reality, to which value must be assigned in every true theory of redemption. The only question is, How can it be made to tell for our advantage? The apostle's answer to this question, so far as I can make out, is this: Christ's holy life in the flesh shows that for men living in the flesh bondage to sin is not the natural and inevitable state; it is a judgment on the actual condition of bondage as what ought not to be and need not be. Further, as the whole of Christ's earthly experience was in the view of the apostle an appointment of God for a redemptive purpose, that sinless life is a promise and guarantee of divine aid to holy living for all who believe in Jesus. Jesus walked in the Spirit while in the flesh, and to those who believe in Him, God will communicate His Spirit to enable them to do the same. Finally, the culmination of Christ's victorious life in the Spirit, in a resurrection into pneumatic manhood from which all gross fleshliness has disappeared, gives us a sure ground of hope for the ultimate redemption of our body out of the natural into the spiritual, out of the corruptible into the incorruptible. An objective sentence of illegitimacy on the reign of sin in the flesh, an incipient and progressive emancipation therefrom through the strengthening of the spiritual powers, with the prospect of completed emancipation hereafter,—surely these together constitute a not inconsiderable boon! It is difficult to see what more we could have on any theory, unless it were some physical process of transformation carried on in the flesh even now.

Just this the advocates of the theory of redemption by sample seem to think their theory secures. Their way of thought is so different from mine that it is with diffidence I attempt to expound it, but the position taken up is something like this. Christ is not now in process of redemption; the process is complete so far as He is concerned, and the fact must tell for our advantage. Christ and we are organically one. He is one with us, and we are one with Him—one with Him risen, not in hope only, but somehow even at the present time. The risen Christ has it in His power to make us now what He Himself is. And by what means? By sacraments, especially by the sacrament of baptism. Once more the sacramental *Deus ex machinâ*. The links of thought here are not easily traceable. It may be due in part to the fact that the prominent exponents of the theory are connected with churches deeply tinged with sacramentarianism that so much stress is laid on ritual in connection with the process of salvation. Be that as it may, the logic of sacramentarianism is too subtle for me. That the completely self-redeemed Christ should be able in the case of Christians to hasten the process of redemption through the exceptional powers He has attained is conceivable. According to the apostle, He is eventually to change our vile body into the likeness of His glorious body, and for anything we know the process might conceivably begin before death, or at the moment when a man becomes by faith a new creature in Christ Jesus. But why should baptism be the instrument in this miraculous process? How comes it that a mere rite possesses such tremendous significance as to be "an integral part of the divine act or process of incarnation,"[1] whereby the individual incarnation of Christ becomes gradually the collective incarnation of redeemed humanity? The reply may be: We cannot tell; it is enough for us that such is the fact as declared in Pauline texts, like *Romans* vi. 3, 4, and still more remarkably in the Lord's great commission to His apostles before His ascension: "All power is given unto Me in heaven and on earth. Go ye therefore and teach all nations, *baptizing* them." What is this but an intimation from the risen One, that He is at length in possession of a power to raise

[1] Du Bose, *Soteriology*, etc., p. 358.

humanity up to God, to impart His own risen humanity to men, and that the instrument by which He is to effect that great result through the agency of His disciples is *baptism* ?[1] We are not here concerned with the exegesis of supposed proof-texts, but simply with the point of view in support of which they are adduced. Practically the outcome is salvation by *sacraments*. This is what redemption of men by the self-redemption of Christ ends in. Christ fought a battle with the flesh, unaided save by the Holy Spirit who dwelt in Him in all possible fulness. His victory makes the struggle easier for us, not merely by ensuring for us the aid of the Divine Spirit through whom He conquered, but by introducing into the very flesh, which is the seat of our foe, the mysterious powers of His heavenly humanity through the use of consecrated spiritualised matter in the forms of water, bread, and wine. This recourse to sacramental grace as the mainstay is, in my view, a confession of failure. It is the mountain labouring and bringing forth a ridiculous birth. It is more and worse. The *reductio ad absurdum* of a certain theory of redemption, it is at the same time a melancholy perversion and caricature of Christianity.

[1] *Vide* Du Bose, *Soteriology*, etc., p. 354.

CHAPTER XVI

THE LAW

THE negative side of St. Paul's doctrine of justification was, we have seen, that a God-pleasing righteousness is not attainable through the keeping of the law. "Apart from law, a righteousness of God has been manifested."[1] The negative thesis is not less startling than the positive one, that righteousness comes through the imputation of faith. One who breaks so completely with tradition is in danger of going to extremes. A temper of indiscriminate depreciation is apt to be engendered, under the influence of which the innovator, not content with setting existing institutions in their own proper place, is tempted to refuse them any legitimate place and function. On a superficial view it might appear that some traces of this temper are discernible in the Pauline Epistles, and especially in the earliest of them, the Epistle to the Galatians. The tone in which the law is spoken of in that Epistle is certainly depreciatory, in comparison with that which pervades the Epistle to the Romans. The expression "weak and beggarly elements,"[2] whatever its precise reference, applies at least generally to the Jewish law, and conveys the opposite of an exalted conception

[1] *Rom.* iii. 21. [2] *Gal.* iv. 9.

of its use and value. In the later Epistle, on the other hand, the law appears as embodying the moral ideal, as holy, just, good, spiritual, as only realised, not transcended, by the highest attainments of the Christian life. The difference is due in part to the fact, that in the Epistle to the Romans the apostle writes in a non-controversial, irenical spirit, while in the Epistle to the Galatians his attitude and tone are vehemently polemical. But besides that it has to be noted, that in Galatians he has chiefly in view the ritual aspect of the law, while in Romans it is the ethical aspect as embodied in the Decalogue that is mainly before his mind. And, as showing that the contrast between the two Epistles in this connection is only on the surface, it must further be pointed out, that when in the earlier Epistle the writer has occasion to refer to the ethical side of the law, his manner of expressing himself is not a whit less reverential than in the later. "The whole law is fulfilled in one word, even in this, Thou shalt love thy neighbour as thyself." [1]

It was indeed not possible for a man of St. Paul's mental and moral calibre to become under any provocation a reckless critic of so venerable and valuable an institution as the Jewish law. A clever but comparatively superficial, flippant man, like Marcion, might play that rôle, but hardly the great apostle of Gentile Christianity, with his religious earnestness, moral depth, and intellectual affinity for great, comprehensive views of history. However decisive the reaction brought about by the spiritual crisis he passed through when he became a

[1] *Gal.* v. 14.

Christian, he must continue to believe in the divine origin of the law of Moses, and therefore in its immense importance as a factor in the moral education of the world. That it had a real, vitally significant function remained for him a matter of course; the only question requiring reconsideration was, What is the true function of the law?

We know what the converted Pharisee's answer to that question was. The law, said St. Paul, was given to bring the knowledge of sin, to provoke latent sin into manifestation, to breed despair of salvation through self-righteousness, and so to prepare the despairing for welcoming Christ as the Redeemer from the dominion of sin. It was a grave, serious answer to a weighty question. It cannot be said that in giving such an answer the apostle trifled with the subject, or assigned to the Jewish law a function unworthy of its alleged divine origin. But three questions may legitimately be asked with reference to this part of the Pauline apologetic: (1) Is the Pauline view of the law in accordance with the function assigned to it in the Hebrew Scriptures? (2) Are the functions the apostle ascribes to the law real, and recognised in the Old Testament? (3) Is the account he gives of the law's functions in the four Epistles exhaustive, or does it need supplementing?

1. To the first of these three questions, Dr. Baur's reply was a decided negative. His view of the matter is in substance as follows: In the great controversy between Judaists and himself the apostle was naturally led to make the antithesis between law and faith as

broad and distinct as possible. Hence the "works of the law" in his anti-Judaistic dialectics mean works of a purely external character into which right motive and disposition do not enter, and the position of the Judaist is supposed to be that by such external works a man may make himself just before God. Faith, on the other hand, is emptied of all ethical contents, in so far as it is viewed as the instrument of justification, a mere empty form, in itself nothing and receiving any contents it has from its object. But the legal works and the faith of the Pauline polemics are both alike mere abstractions, or controversial exaggerations, to which there is nothing answering in the world of realities or in Old Testament Scriptures. Especially is this true of the works of the law, which as they appear in the Hebrew Scriptures are not purely external, but the fruit of pious, God-fearing dispositions, and as such acceptable to God. Moreover, as the works of Old Testament saints are not pharisaical in character, neither are they pharisaical in spirit. They are not wrought by men who imagine that they stand in no need of divine forgiveness. The Old Testament saint knows full well that he comes short of perfection, that he needs divine mercy; and he believes that there is forgiveness with God, and believing this he serves God hopefully and gratefully, striving to do God's will in all things with a pure heart, and trusting thereby to please God. And according to these Scriptures it is possible so to please God. A pious man can do substantially the things prescribed by the law, and he that doeth them is blessed in his deed, pleases God, and wins His favour. And the law was given for that end, that it might be kept, and that so men might attain unto the blessedness of the righteous.

Dr. Baur further maintained that even St. Paul himself seemed to regard the antithesis between works of the law and faith as a mere affair of controversial dialectics, and to be only half in earnest about it; the proof of this being that, when not actually engaged in polemics, he forgets his hair-spun distinctions, and speaks of works as the ground of the divine judgment on men, just as any ordinary Jew might have done. The texts cited to substantiate this statement are *Romans* ii. 6; 1 *Corinthians* iii. 13; 2 *Corinthians* v. 10; *Galatians* vi. 7.

The account given by Dr. Baur, of the Old Testament attitude toward the law and legal righteousness, is not entirely baseless. It is the fact that Old Testament saints confessed sin and trusted in God's mercy, and had no thought of being able to do without it. It is further true that they practised works of righteousness in accordance with the law, and hoped by these to please God, and are represented as actually pleasing God thereby. It is furthermore true that these works, proceeding from the love of God and a genuine passion for righteousness, were not merely externally good works of the Pharisaic order, but works such as God who looketh on the heart could regard with complacency. All this is broadly true of the piety depicted in the Hebrew sacred books, even though a certain deduction may have to be made from the estimate on account of the influence of the incipient legalism traceable in some of the later additions to the collection.[1] But all this the apostle knew as well as we, and his quarrel was not with Old Testament piety, or with the Old Testament itself. He was in accord with the *prophetic* spirit, out of accord only with the *Judaistic* spirit. He believed that the truly representative men of the Old Testament —Abraham, David, etc.—were on his side. His very position is, that his gospel of justification by faith is that which best interprets the Hebrew Scriptures, is true to their deepest spirit, and that the men who oppose him do not understand these sacred books, but read them with a veil upon their faces. He believes himself to be in close touch with the spirit of the ancient worthies, and doubts not that had they lived in his time they would have been in cordial sympathy with him. Was this assuming too much? Is it going too far to say, that had all the Christians of the apostolic generation been like-minded with the authors of the 51st, 103rd, 116th, 130th Psalms, the Judaistic controversy would never have arisen? In that case faith in Christ and reverence for the law in its essential elements might have co-existed peaceably in the consciousness of the Church as a whole, as of St. Paul himself in particular. But unhappily the righteousness of the time was not a righteousness like that of prophets and psalmists, but rather a righteousness like that of scribes and Pharisees, the sinister growth of the post-exilian time. The apostle knew it well, for he had been tainted with the disease himself. It was a leaven of that kind, combined with a nominal Christianity, that

[1] *Vide* on this my *Apologetics*, pp. 321-336.

gave rise to the great controversy about the law. The manner in which the apostle speaks of his opponents proves this. They appear in the four Epistles, not as men whose general moral and religious character commands respect, but rather as men who have their own ends to serve, and make zeal for the law a cloak for self-seeking. Of course it is a plausible suggestion that this is their character not in truth, but only as seen through the distorting medium of polemical prejudice. But the fact probably is that there is little or no distortion, but merely genuine character, shown with the unreserve of a time of war, when the interests at stake demand the suspension of the conventional rules of courteous speech. Such men having found their way into the Church, controversy of the most determined kind was inevitable. The apostle will have to fight over again with them the battle he has already fought with himself, and to formulate for the guidance of the Church the principles his own religious experience made clear to his mind many years previously. For it was there the dialectic began, and it is in that region it may best be understood. The individual man, Saul of Tarsus, was a mirror of his time, and the process of his religious consciousness was but the rehearsal on a small scale of the conflict through which the Church attained to an understanding of its own faith. Thence we understand why the works of the law, spoken of in the Judaistic controversy, are not works like those of Old Testament saints, but either ritual performances, or works of any sort done from impure motives. The reason is, that it was only with such works Saul the Pharisee had been occupied. By reflection on the same experience, we further understand whence came the doctrine that the law itself was not given for the attainment of righteousness. When Saul the Pharisee began to see into the spiritual inwardness of the law, through the contact of his conscience with such a precept as, "Thou shalt not covet," he knew that there was no hope for him save in the mercy of God, and he drew the conclusion: By the law at its best, as a spiritual code of duty, comes not righteousness as I have hitherto been seeking it, *i.e.* as a righteousness with which I can go into the presence of a merely just God, and demand a verdict of approval. By the law comes rather the consciousness of sin, and through that a clear perception that the only attitude it becomes me to take up is that of one who prays, "God be merciful to me." The apostle's doctrine concerning the law must be read in the light of this experience. When he says, righteousness comes not by the law, he means, righteousness such as I sought when a Pharisee, the approval of God *as pharisaically conceived*. This doctrine was an axiom to the man who wrote Psalm 130. But it was not an axiom to Saul of Tarsus, nor to the Judaistic opponents of Paul the apostle. Therefore it needed to be affirmed with emphasis, as in the controversial Epistles. It is not a new doctrine. It is a commonplace, proclaimed with vehemence by one who discovered its truth only after a momentous struggle to men who altogether or to a great extent ignored it. The doctrine rests on two propositions which the truly good have believed in all ages—that man is sinful and that God is gracious. No man, therefore, who has self-knowledge, and who cherishes a Christian idea of God, will have much quarrel with the doctrine, or fall into the mistake of imagining that Paulinism at this point is in conflict with the general spirit of the Old Testament.

As to the alleged inconsistency of the apostle's utterances concerning the law, two things must be borne in mind. First, his *whole* doctrine as to faith's function. Faith in the Pauline Epistles is by no means the empty form it is sometimes represented to be. It is not only an attitude of receptivity to God's forgiving grace, but an energetic, ethical principle working towards personal holiness. Secondly, it has to be remembered that, according to the apostle's doctrine, faith works by love. The good works of his justified man are done in a filial spirit, spring out of the consciousness of redemption, and as such are acceptable to God here and hereafter, as truly good in quality, though not necessarily free from all defect. Hence the apostle's conception of the final judgment is not the same with that of the Pharisee. The two conceptions agree, in so far as both make judgment proceed on the basis of works. They differ as to the character of the judge, and of the works judged. The judge of the Pharisaic creed is the God of mere justice; the judge of St. Paul's creed is the God of grace, for the gracious character is indefeasible, and underlies the work of judgment. Then the works judged, as conceived by Pharisaism, are works done not in the consciousness of redemption and the spirit of sonship, but in the mercenary spirit of a hireling, or in the fear-stricken spirit of a slave. The apostle's conception of the judgment is in affinity with that of Christ. It is the judgment of the God of love, making the great test of character the presence or absence of His own spirit of charity. This we may say in all fairness, while freely acknowledging that the judgment programme in *Matthew* xxv. 31–46 reaches a high-water mark of Christianised ethics, not touched by any utterance in the Pauline Epistles. Here, as in many other respects, the disciple comes behind the Master. It is not easy altogether to escape from the system under which one has been reared. Some traces of Rabbinism may cling to one who has made the most radical revolt from Rabbinism.

2. Our second question is: Are the functions St. Paul ascribes to the law real, and are they recognised in the Old Testament? Now, there can be no question that the functions ascribed to the law in the Pauline letters, as enumerated on a previous page, were based on actual results of the law's action in the apostle's own case. And on careful consideration it appears that the same result followed from the discipline of law in the history of the Jewish people. By the law came to that people a deepened consciousness of sin, an intensified keen-visioned moral sense. There came, also, an enhanced sinfulness. The Jewish people not only knew themselves to be sinners better than other men, but they were greater sinners than other men. For the law, though it showed them their duty, did not incline them to do it, rather provoked reaction, and made their sin more criminal by putting them in the position of sinning against the light. Despair and longing for redemption

were the natural results of those two effects on all the better minds in Israel, as is apparent from the utterances of the prophets, very specially from Jeremiah's oracle of the new covenant. The only point, therefore, on which there is room for doubt is: Whether the results of the law's action, as unfolded in Israel's history, were those contemplated from the first as the design of the law-giving, or whether they were not rather the proof that the law had failed of its end. Now, here a distinction may be taken between the divine end of the law, and the end which was consciously present to the instruments of revelation, *e.g.*, Moses. From the view-point of theistic teleology, as conceived by the Hebrew mind, the apostle's doctrine of the law is unassailable. The ultimate result reveals the initial divine aim.[1] On this principle it is true, as St. Paul taught, that what God had in view from the first was the promise, and that the law entered to prepare for the reception of the promise, to be a pedagogue, a gaoler, a tutor to make Christ and the era of grace, liberty, and love welcome. In philosophical language, the law was a lower stage in the development of humanity preparing for a higher, in presence of which it lost its rights, though the good that was in it was taken up into the higher, and united to the initial stage of the promise to which it stood in opposition. As to the view taken of the end of the law by those who lived in the early time, without doubt it

[1] This principle must be applied with caution, else it will lead to some unwelcome conclusions: *e.g.*, that God created man that he might fall, and the lost that they might be condemned; and that Christ taught in parables expressly in order to make His insusceptible hearers spiritually blind.

was very different from that of St. Paul. They looked with hope on an institution which was destined to end in failure. The commandment which the apostle found to be unto death, they regarded as ordained unto life. They did not see to the end of that which was to be abolished. There was a veil upon their faces in reference to the law. But as time went on the veil began to be taken away by sorrowful experience. Spirit-taught men began to see that the law was given, not so much for life and blessedness, as for the knowledge of sin and misery, and that if any good was to come to Israel it must be through the supersession of the Sinaitic covenant by a new covenant of grace. That by the law is the knowledge of sin he understood who asked: "Who can understand his errors?" That the law was an irritant to transgression, Jeremiah understood when he said in God's name: "Which my covenant they brake, and I loathed them." And the very prophecy of a new covenant is a witness to the despair of any good coming out of the old one. It is an anticipation of the apostle's cry of anguish: "Wretched man, who shall deliver me?"

We can now answer the question, How far are the functions assigned to the law in the Pauline theology recognised in the Old Testament? There is not a little in the Hebrew Scriptures which might lead one to think that the law's functions, as conceived by men of the older time, were very different from those assigned to it in that theology in the light of history. In the initial period, antecedent to experience, the tone was naturally hopeful. From the law they expected life and blessing, not death and cursing. But there were thoughts in God's heart which men at first did not understand, and that could be revealed only in the course of ages. At length these deeper thoughts did dawn upon devout minds and find utterance in prophetic oracles, though to men of another temper living in the "night of legalism" they remained hidden. The prophets were on Paul's side, if Moses and Ezra seemed to be on the side of his opponents. The dispute between him and them as to the purpose of the law is one which might be raised in reference to any epoch-making event or institution. What, *e.g.*, was the purpose of the American civil war? If the question be regarded as referring to the aims of men, the answer might be, It was a fight on one side for independence, on the other for unity. But if the question be taken as referring to the design of Providence, the answer might be, It was a struggle designed to issue in the emancipation of oppressed bondsmen. How many, as the struggle went on, were earnestly on the side of Providence who had little sympathy either with north or with south! Even so in the case of the great debate regarding the Jewish law. Our sympathies go with Providence and with St. Paul, though we admit that the prosaic Judaistic constitutionalist might be right in his views as to the aims of Moses the legislator and of Ezra the scribe.

3. One question more remains to be considered. Is the account of the law's function given in the anti-Judaistic Epistles exhaustive, or does it admit of supplementing? Our reply must be that that account, while true and valuable so far as it goes, stands in need of

supplement in order to a complete view of the subject. The remark of course applies to the ritual law. On the ethical side the apostle's doctrine leaves nothing to be desired. The law summed up in love, and truly kept only when the outward commandment is transformed into an inward spirit of life—this is teaching thoroughly in sympathy with the mind of Christ, to which nothing needs to be added. It is otherwise with the representations of the law's functions and value in which the ritual aspect is mainly in view. Here the apostle's attitude is chiefly negative. Yet even for apologetic purposes in connection with the Judaistic controversy, a positive conception of the law's function might usefully have been presented—that, viz., according to which it was a sort of rudimentary gospel during the pre-Christian time, setting forth spiritual truths in emblems, as pictures are employed in the training of children. This is the view actually set forth at length in the Epistle to the Hebrews, and epitomised in the motto: "The law a shadow of good things to come."[1] On this view, priests, sacrifices, festivals, the tabernacle and its furniture were emblems of the spiritual verities which came with Christ and Christianity, the final eternal religion. By the adequate exposition of this idea, the author of that Epistle rendered an important apologetic aid to the Christian faith in a transition time. One naturally wonders why St. Paul did not employ it for the same purpose in his conflict with the legalist party, and that all the more that even in the letters provoked by that controversy there are not wanting indications that the

[1] *Heb.* x. 1.

point of view was not altogether foreign to his system of thought.[1] It has been suggested that he was prevented from doing so by the fact of the allegorical or symbolic method of interpreting the Levitical ritual having been previously employed in a conservative interest. But it is not easy to see why such a reason should have weighed with him any more than with the author of *Hebrews*. The true reason why St. Paul did not adopt the typical method of justifying the abrogation of the law, while assigning to it an important function in its own time and place, doubtless is, that he had not himself arrived at the revolutionary conclusion along that road. His manner of viewing the law was determined for him by the part it had played in his religious history. It may be assumed that a similar explanation is to be given of the point of view adopted in the Epistle to the Hebrews, and that its author gained insight into the transient character of the Levitical religion, and the glory of the New Testament religion, not through a fruitless attempt at keeping the law with Pharisaic scrupulosity, but through a mental discipline which enabled him to distinguish between symbol and spiritual reality, shadow and substance. In other words, while St. Paul was a moralist, he was a religious philosopher; while for St. Paul the organ of spiritual knowledge was the conscience, for him it was devout reason. With this difference between the two men was associated a corresponding difference in temper—the apostle, impetuous, passionate, vehement; the unknown author of *Hebrews* calm, contemplative, leisurely. The diversity of spirit is so markedly reflected in their re-

[1] *Vide* Note at the end.

spective styles as writers, that to accept *Hebrews* as a Pauline writing is out of the question.

Yet the apostle was not disqualified for writing that Epistle by any radical contrariety of view. As already hinted, there are indications of the idea that the law had a symbolical function in his anti-Judaistic writings, although he did not think fit to make use of it for controversial purposes. Such an indication might be discovered even in the depreciatory phrase, " weak and poor elements." It suggests an educational view of the law, and specially of the ritual portion of it, which is in advance of the merely negative view of its function. It likens the Levitical ritual to the alphabet arranged in rows ($\sigma\tau\circ\iota\chi\epsilon\hat{\iota}a$) which children were taught when they first went to school. The comparison implies, that in the ancient ritual might be found all the elements of the Christian religion, as in the alphabet all the elements of speech. This educational view of the ritual law is applied to the whole Mosaic law, by the figure of the heir under tutors and governors. The work of a tutor is not merely negative; it is not merely to make the ward acquainted with his faults, or to dispose him to rebel against irksome restraints, or to discourage him by a discovery of his ignorance, and by all these effects to awaken in his breast a hearty desire to be rid of an unwelcome yoke. It is also to train him in moral habits, from which he will reap benefits all the days of his life. By implication it is taught that Israel derived a similar benefit from the discipline of law. In this great apologetic word concerning the heir, it is recognised that the discipline of external law forms a necessary stage in the education of mankind, good while it lasts, and fitting for a higher stage, when the heir, arrived at length at maturity, can be trusted to himself, because he has within him the eternal law of duty, the reason firm, and temperate will, the self-regulating spirit of a manly life.[1]

[1] A particular instance of the typical mode of viewing the Levitical ritual may be found in 1 *Cor.* v. 7, where Christ is called, "our Passover" (τὸ πάσχα ἡμῶν). The idea in general form finds expression in one of the later Christological Epistles, that to the *Colossians* (ii. 17), in the identical terms used in *Hebrews*: "a shadow of things to come."

CHAPTER XVII

THE ELECTION OF ISRAEL

WE have now to consider the Pauline apologetic in relation to the last of the three topics on which it bears —*the Election of Israel*. The materials available for our purpose are contained in the ninth, tenth, and eleventh chapters of the Epistle to the Romans.

The subject is very abruptly introduced. There appears to be no connection between the close of chapter eighth and the beginning of chapter ninth. And there is indeed no *logical* connection, but there is a very close *emotional* one. The subject is suggested to the writer's mind on the principle of contrast. He has been expatiating with impassioned eloquence on the peace-giving faith and inspiring hope of believers in Christ. But when he has ended his song of triumph and paused for a moment to recover breath, the bitter reflection suddenly suggests itself—in all this peace and joy of faith and hope most of my countrymen have no share. It is a reflection most painful to his feelings as a Jew who loves his race, and takes pride in their national prerogatives and privileges. But the fact that Israel is prevalently unbelieving is more than a source of personal grief to Paul the Jew; it is a serious difficulty for him to grapple with as the apostle of the Gentiles, and the advocate of a universal gospel independent of Judaism, and as one whose mission among the Gentiles had been greatly successful. For did not the unbelief of Israel, taken along with the extensive reception of the gospel by Gentiles, signify the cancelling of Israel's election, the rejection of the Jews and the substitution of the Gentiles in their place as the objects of divine favour? Or, if it did not signify this, was it not an argument against his gospel to this effect: The Pauline gospel cannot be true, for it is rejected by the mass of the elect people? Thus does the apostle appear placed in a dilemma, on neither horn of which he will care to be impaled. How does he get out of the dilemma?

He deals with the hard problem in two ways, in both of which he successfully escapes the dreaded inference that his gospel is illegitimate. First he reckons with the facts on the assumption that they signify an absolute final cancelling of Israel's election, striving to show that even in that case there is no presumption against his gospel. The argument of his opponents being: "If you are right in your view of Christianity, then God has rejected His chosen people; but such a rejection is impossible, therefore you are wrong;" his reply in the first instance is: "Such a rejection is not impossible." This is the line of defence pursued in the ninth and tenth chapters. But the apostle is not content with this line of defence. He proceeds next to consider more carefully whether the facts do necessarily amount to a final absolute rejection of Israel, and comes to the conclusion that they do not, so, of course, again evading the unwelcome inference of the falsity of his Gentile gospel. This is the train of thought in the eleventh chapter. This two-sided apologetic argument we have now to consider in detail.

I. The argument as adjusted to the hypothesis of a cancelled election.

The apostle guards against unfavourable inferences from this construction of the facts by three distinct arguments. The first of these is, that there was always an election within the election; the second, that in election God is sovereign and not under law to the elect; the third, that if Israel was rejected it was her own fault: she had brought it upon herself by a habit of disobedience and unbelief for which she had had a bad reputation all through her history.

1. *There was always an election within the election.* This is the gist of ix. 6–9. What the apostle says here is in substance this: It is certainly a serious thing to speak of Israel's election as cancelled, for that would seem to amount to saying that God's word declaring Israel to be His peculiar treasure had been made void. But we must distinguish between election and election. There is an election that is cancellable, and an election that cannot be cancelled, an outer circle that may be effaced, and an inner circle that is ineffaceable. There always have been these two elections, the outer and the inner, an Israel of God within the Israel after the flesh, a seed of Jacob the child of promise within the seed of Abraham. The two elements can be traced all along the course of Israel's history; they are very recognisable now. There is an Israel after the flesh, and an Israel

after the promise at this hour. And it is of the former only that cancelling of election can be predicated. The election within the election stands, for this inner circle is to be found within the Christian Church. It cannot, therefore, be said now that the word of God calling Israel to be a chosen race has been rendered void, except in a sense in which the same thing could have been said at any time in Israel's history, *e.g.*, in the time of Elijah.

2. *In election God is sovereign.* This is the import of ix. 10–24. The leading thought in this section is, that in electing acts God is free; that as no people has a claim to be elected, so no people has a claim to the continuance of its election; that what God sovereignly begins He may sovereignly end. There may be good reasons why God should not end what He has solemnly begun, but they are to be found in God, not in man. The apostle, having in view to beat down Jewish pride, which thought that the elect race had a claim to a monopoly and to the perpetual enjoyment of divine favour, asserts the sovereignty of God in the business of election in a very absolute and peremptory manner. Going back to the commencement of Israel's history, he shows how conspicuously God's sovereignty asserted itself even there, inasmuch as it determined which of the two sons about to be borne by Rebecca was to be the heir of the promise before the children were born, therefore before anything in the conduct of the two sons had emerged to make the election turn on personal merit. The elder, it was announced beforehand, was to serve the younger, so excluding not merely personal character, but civil law and custom as a ground of choice. This might

seem arbitrary and even unrighteous, but the apostle is not careful to repel such a charge. The point he insists on is the matter of fact; arbitrary or not, so stands the history. And he goes on to show that it was not a solitary instance of sovereign action, pointing out that God claimed the right of so acting in all cases in the words, " I will have mercy on whom I will have mercy, and I will have compassion on whom I will have compassion," then citing the case of Pharaoh in proof that God acts on that principle not merely to the positive effect of sovereignly exercising mercy but also to the negative effect of hardening unto destruction. An extreme position which naturally suggests the objection: What room under this doctrine for the imputation of guilt, for who hath resisted His will? Had this difficulty been stated by a devout inquirer, anxious to maintain an equilibrium between divine sovereignty and human responsibility, the apostle would doubtless have taken pains to soften, modify, and adjust his statements. Of this they certainly stand in need, for the assertion that God hardens men to their destruction is unquestionably capable of most mischievous perversion, to the detriment of both piety and morality. Had St. Paul been in the mood to pursue an apologetic line of thought, with a view to reconciling divine sovereignty with divine love on the one hand, and with human responsibility on the other, he could easily have found materials for the purpose even in the history of God's dealings with the king of Egypt. For what was the natural tendency of the signs and wonders wrought in the land of Ham? Surely to soften Pharaoh's heart, to the effect of letting

Israel go. God hardened Pharaoh's heart by means fitted and intended to have the opposite effect. And the fact is so in all cases. The means of hardening are ever means naturally fitted to soften and win. The apostle knew this as well as we, but he was not in the mood to indulge in such a strain of explanatory, conciliatory remark. He was dealing with proud men who thought the election of their fathers gave them a prescriptive right to divine favour. Therefore, instead of softening down hard statements he goes on to make harder statements still; representing God as a potter and men as clay, out of which God can make such vessels as He pleases, one to be a vessel of mercy, another to be a vessel of destruction, to be dashed to pieces at the maker's will. As against human arrogance it is a legitimate representation, but as an exact complete statement of the relation between God and man it cannot of course be regarded. So viewed, it would be simple fatalism.

3. How far the apostle was from intending to teach fatalism appears from his third argument under the first alternative, the object of which is to *throw the blame of Israel's rejection on herself.* This argument forms the leading contents of chapter x. He here brings against Israel the grave charge of not submitting to the righteousness of God. Fully recognising the good side of the national character, zeal for righteousness as popularly conceived, he nevertheless holds his countrymen responsible for the great miscarriage of their election, finding in their passion for righteousness not only a lack of knowledge or spiritual insight, for which they might

be pitied, but a culpable spirit of self-will. He ascribes to them the ambition to establish a righteousness which they can regard as their own achievement. They are too proud to be debtors to God. They desire to be able to say: "God, I thank Thee, I am not as other men." Hence the gospel of pardon to the sinful has no attraction for them. Its very simplicity is an offence to their pride. They are unbelievers, not because they have not heard the gospel, or have not understood its meaning. They have heard enough, and they have understood too well. And the present unbelief is but the reproduction of a standing feature in the character of the race in all its generations, which provoked the remonstrances of God's messengers from Moses to Isaiah. Moses said, "I will provoke you to jealousy by a no-nation, by an unwise nation will I anger you," thereby hinting a threat of degradation from the position of the elect race. Isaiah still more outspokenly revealed such a divine purpose of disinheritance by signalising on the one hand the honour God had received among the outside peoples, and on the other hand the indifference and even hostility with which His messages by the prophets had been treated by the chosen nation. The drift of the citations is: Unbelief and disobedience have been features of the Jewish national character all through her history, provoking God to repent of His choice, and to threaten disinheritance. The same features reappear in the living generation, in exaggerated form, in reference to the mission of Jesus; till now at length the divine patience is all but exhausted, and the oft-repeated threat is on the point of becoming an accomplished fact.

II. But at this point the thought of the apostle takes a new turn. He recoils from the idea of an absolute and final disinheritance; nay, as we shall see, he finds even in the prophetic oracles which threaten such a disaster a bit of solid ground whereon patriotic hope can plant its foot. Looked at broadly, the relative oracles do seem to point at complete rejection; therefore, the question inevitably arises whether that is really what was intended and what is now actually happening. The apostle does not shirk the question. He plainly asks it, and as plainly answers it, and that in the negative.

"I say, then, hath God thrust away His people? God forbid!" He speaks vehemently, and he has a good right. For he too is an Israelite, of the seed of Abraham, of the tribe of Benjamin. And he speaks confidently, again with good right. For he remembers his own history, that of one who also had been unbelieving and disobedient, and he cannot but hope that God, who had mercy on him, has grace in store for his countrymen, notwithstanding all their provocations. Moved at once by patriotism, and by the hope inspired by his own conversion, he sets himself to put as encouraging a construction on the facts as possible. In the first place, he lays stress on the mere fact of the election. "God hath not thrust away His people whom He foreknew."[1] He has indeed already combated the idea that the act of election gives the elected a claim to perpetual enjoyment of the privilege. But quite compatibly with that position, he holds that an act of election may bring God under obligation to Himself, that an act of that kind

[1] *Rom.* xi. 2.

once solemnly performed cannot lightly be recalled without loss of dignity. It is therefore, in his view, a strong point in favour of any people that God hath foreknown or chosen it to any signal position in history. The dignity of the divine character is on the side of continuance. From this point of view it may be affirmed that "the gifts and the calling of God are without repentance."[1] Next the apostle extracts comfort from the consideration that now, as in Elijah's time, there are doubtless more faithful ones than at first appears; that the remnant, the inner circle of the elect, is not by any means so inconsiderable a body as in hours of depression one is apt to suppose. When Elijah thought he stood alone in a faithless, apostate time, there were seven thousand men who had not bowed the knee to Baal,—a small number compared with the whole nation, but a great number compared with one man. So now the sad-hearted apostle would bear in mind that there were not a few believing Israelites in all the churches. "So then also in the present time there is a remnant according to the election of grace."[2]

Still the sad fact remained, that the great majority of the Jewish nation were unbelievers. What is to be said of them? In the first place, it must be sorrowfully acknowledged that they have been blinded by inveterate prejudice, in accordance with Scripture representations.[3] The picture of a blind, decrepit old man, bowed down with age and infirmity, suggested by the concluding words of the quotation from the Psalter, is a very pathetic representation of a people in a state of religious senility.

[1] *Rom.* xi. 29.   [2] *Ibid.* xi. 5.   [3] *Ibid.* xi. 7-10.

When a people gets to this senile condition in religion, its inevitable fate, one would say, is to stumble and fall; for blind, feeble old age can neither see obstacles in the way, nor recover its balance when it strikes its foot against a stone.

What then ? Is Israel's doom to stumble and fall and die, and disappear from the face of the earth, like an aged man when the powers of physical nature fail ? That is the question the apostle has to face. "I say then, did they stumble (over the Christian faith) that they might fall (finally and irretrievably)?"[1] Not this either can he believe. He repels the idea with another energetic μὴ γένοιτο. But is it that he simply will not believe it ? or has he any shadow of a reason for taking up this position ? It must be confessed that the prospect of discovering such a reason is at first sight not encouraging; for what can befall blind, tottering old age but death and burial? It is easy to see that the apostle is conscious of having a stiff piece of argument on hand. His "I say then's," and his "God forbid's," are the sure index of laborious effort. But a patriotic heart can discern a "bit of blue sky" where other eyes can see nothing but dark clouds. The apostle finds the bit of blue sky even in the threatening words quoted from the song of Moses, "I will provoke you to jealousy by them that are no people"; and backs up his μὴ γένοιτο by the remark: "But by their fall salvation to the Gentiles, unto the provoking of jealousy in them."[2] Paraphrased, his reasoning is to this effect: "The facts do not mean final, irretrievable rejection; the construction I,

[1] *Rom.* xi. 11.   [2] *Ibid.* xi. 11.

taking encouragement from the words of Moses, put on the facts is this: That which has been the occasion of stumbling to unbelieving Jews, Christ crucified, has brought salvation to the Gentiles; and salvation has come to the Gentiles to make unbelieving Jews feel envious at the loss of privileges that have fallen to the lot of others, and desirous to recover them." It is an ingenious turn of thought; but, for St. Paul, it is more than that—a deep conviction firmly rooted in his mind, and influencing his whole conduct. For even when he is busy evangelising the Gentiles, he has his countrymen in view, hoping to reach them in a roundabout way through the conversion of heathens to the Christian faith. When we see him turning his back on the Jewish synagogue, and addressing himself to Pagans, we might think he is abandoning the Jews to their fate in a huff, and that he is not going to trouble himself any more about them. But it is not so. He is only changing his tactics. Having failed to win Jews to Christ by direct preaching of the gospel, he is trying to *spite* them into faith. "Inasmuch as I am an apostle of the Gentiles, I magnify mine office, if by any means I may provoke to emulation my flesh, and may save some of them."[1] That is, "I do my utmost to convert the non-elect peoples that the elect people may be made jealous, and at length accept the grace of God in the gospel it has hitherto despised." Such is the apostle's *modus operandi*, and such his motive; and he expects his Gentile readers to sympathise with him both in method and in motive. They will lose nothing, he assures them, by such generous

[1] *Rom.* xi. 14, 15.

conduct. If they have benefited by the fall of the Jews, they will benefit still more by their rising again. The ultimate union of Jew and Gentile in one commonwealth of religious faith will be as life from the dead to a world long cursed with alienations between man and man, race and race.

The foregoing thought, that the rejection of the Jews in favour of the Gentiles was not an absolute rejection, but only a new way of working beneficially on the Jewish mind, possesses genuine biographic interest as the utterance of a noble man animated by the invincible optimism of Christian patriotism. But it is also of value as throwing light upon St. Paul's way of thinking on the subject of *election*. These chapters of the Epistle to the Romans have been, by scholastic theology, put to uses for which they were never intended. They are not a contribution to the doctrine of the eternal predestination of individuals to everlasting life or death. Their theme is not the election of individuals, but of a people. And the point of view from which the principle of election is contemplated is historical. The writer treats of divine choices as they reveal themselves in this world in the career and destiny of nations. But still more important is it to note that in these chapters election is not conceived of as an arbitrary choice to the enjoyment of benefits from which all others are excluded. Election is to *function* as well as to favour, and the function has the good of others besides the elect in view. As the Jews, according to the Hebrew Scriptures, were chosen to be a blessing eventually to the Gentiles, so, according to the apostle, the Gentile no-nations were chosen in turn to be God's people, for their own good doubtless, but also for the spiritual benefit of the temporarily disinherited Jews. It is unnecessary to point out that this view is in accordance with the uniform teaching of Scripture, and very specially with the teaching of Christ, in which the elect appear as the light, the salt, and the leaven of the world. It is a vital truth strangely overlooked in elaborate creeds large enough to have room for many doctrines much less important, and far from sufficiently recognised, as yet, even in the living faith of the Church, though the missionary spirit of modern Christianity may be regarded as an unconscious homage to its importance.

Before passing from this topic it may be worth while to note the figures employed by the apostle to denote the function of the elect in reference to the world. Whereas our Lord employed for this purpose the emblems of light, salt, and leaven, St. Paul uses the analogies of the first-fruits of a harvest presented as an offering to God and so sanctifying the whole crop, and of the roots of a tree as determining the character of the tree and of its produce.[1] The former analogy assigns by implication to the elect a representative character. They are the ten men in Sodom whose presence saves the whole guilty community. The latter analogy ascribes to the elect a vital influence in society. They are the roots of the social tree, from which rises up through trunk and branches a spiritual sap, to be ultimately transmuted into Christian deeds and virtues.

The apostle expresses his belief that Israel will at length be provoked to jealousy; in other words, that the

[1] *Rom.* xi. 16.

now unbelieving elect race will one day be converted to Christianity. This cheering hope occupies the principal place in his thoughts throughout the remainder of the eleventh chapter.[1] Here again he has recourse to metaphor to aid him in the expression of his views with regard both to the present and to the future. His figure this time is taken from the process of grafting. What has happened is, that some branches of an olive tree have been broken off, and a wild olive slip, the Gentile Church, has been grafted in their place. The branches were broken off for unbelief, but it is hoped that their unbelief will not be final, that on the contrary the severed branches will be engrafted on the tree.[2] The parable is in some respects defective. The disciple here comes far behind the Master, whose parabolic utterances were so true to nature. The process of grafting a wild slip on a good olive is in the natural sphere useless, and the process of regrafting broken-off branches impossible. But St. Paul's idea is clear enough. He expects a time when Jew and Gentile shall be united in one Church. He cannot believe in the final unbelief of Israel. As little can he believe in the utter rejection of Israel. The character of God, as he conceives it, forbids the thought. God must be consistent with Himself, stable in His ways of action, therefore it must be held firmly as a great principle that His gifts and calling are without repentance; always, of course, without prejudice to the divine independence and freedom, which must ever be strenuously asserted against pretensions to perpetuity of privilege on the part either of Jew or of Gentile. For while God

[1] *Rom.* xi. 23-36.   [2] *Rom.* xi. 17-23.

owes nothing to man He owes something to Himself. It is God-worthy to be unchanging, and on this firm foundation rests the great word: ἀμεταμέλητα τὰ χαρίσματα καὶ ἡ κλῆσις τοῦ θεοῦ.

It is well to note here the relativity of biblical utterances, and the necessity of balancing one statement against another. In a sentence going before the one just quoted, the apostle ascribes ἀποτομία to God, in the Authorised Version rendered "severity," the literal meaning being propensity to prune or lop off. In this sentence, on the other hand, he ascribes to God just the opposite quality, a propensity to continue privileges once conferred. It is an antinomy, but not one of the kind which some have found in the apostle's writings, antinomies which he makes no attempt to reconcile, nay, does not even seem to be conscious of. He is conscious of the antinomy in this case, and offers a solution. His solution is to treat the pruning, the cutting off, or, to revert to a previous form of expression, the blinding or hardening, as partial and temporary. "All Israel shall be saved,"[1] he boldly avers, taking courage from Old Testament texts which seem to point that way. The mystery of the past shall be matched by a mystery to be revealed in the future. The mystery of the past, hid *in* God, not from Him, only from men till the time of manifestation, was the admission of the outside nations to participation in the Messianic salvation. That mystery, of old a secret known only to the initiated few, inspired prophets and poets, is now a fact patent to all the world, a mystery no longer. The other mystery, the mystery of the future, is the ultimate

[1] *Rom.* xi. 26.

softening of Israel's hard, impenitent heart, so that she shall be willing to be united with converted pagans in one grand fellowship of faith and hope and worship. St. Paul expects this, because Israel, though hostile to Christianity, is yet beloved of Providence for the sake of devout forefathers, who trusted God, served Him faithfully, and received from Him promises of eternal friendship.[1] He even expects it on the ground of equity, or what we may call poetic justice. As Gentiles have benefited from Jewish unbelief, receiving the offer of what Israel had refused, as the beggars in the highway were invited to the supper which well-to-do people had politely declined, so it was meet and fair that Jews should benefit from the mercy shown to Gentiles and at length share it with them.[2] So the final issue will be: all alike guilty in their turn of unbelief, and all alike partakers of divine mercy; no room for envy, and to God all the glory.[3]

"God hath shut up all unto disobedience, that He might have mercy upon all." Such is the last word of this magnificent apology at once for Paulinism and for divine Providence. Like all great generalisations, it suggests more than it expressly teaches, fascinating the imagination by its vagueness and provoking questions which it does not answer. It breathes the spirit of optimism, and encourages the larger and even the largest hope, yet one knows not how far he may with certainty infer therefrom the final salvation of all men or even the conversion of the Jews. It looks as if St. Paul himself had been led on by the resistless logic of his great argument, and by the inspiration of the Divine Spirit, to pen a

[1] *Rom.* xi. 28.   [2] *Ibid.* xi. 30, 31.   [3] *Ibid.* xi. 32.

sentence whose depths he felt himself unable to fathom. And so argument gives place to worship, apologetic to admiration of the inscrutable wisdom of God, to whom be the glory for ever. Amen.[1]

[1] *Rom.* xi. 33, 36.

CHAPTER XVIII

CHRIST

IT may appear a grave defect in our treatment of Paulinism that so important a theme as this should be taken up at so advanced a stage. Its postponement may be deemed the more reprehensible that there is nothing binding us to a particular order in the arrangement of topics, and that one might begin the presentation of the Pauline conception of Christianity with any of the great cardinal categories of the system, and therefore with the person of Christ.[1] But there are advantages to be gained by assigning to this august theme a position near the end of our discussions. For one thing, we thereby raise the topic out of the region of controversy into the serener atmosphere of calm contemplation. The formulation of Pauline theology had, as we now know, a polemical origin, and from first to last we have been pursuing our studies under the shadow of Judaistic antagonism. But now at length we come into the sunshine, and can contemplate the Lord of the Church as He appears in the pages of

[1] Weizsäcker remarks that, in endeavouring to present in a connected view the doctrinal utterances in St. Paul's Epistles, "we can start just as well from his doctrine of Christ as from that of the means of salvation, or, to go a step further back, from that of sin." —*The Apostolic Age of the Christian Church*, vol. i. p. 141.

the apostle, not as the subject of a theological debate, but as the object of tranquil religious reverence. Another advantage resulting from taking up the present theme at this late stage is, that we bring to the study of it all the light to be obtained from acquaintance with the Pauline system of thought in general, and in particular with his *doctrine of redemption*.[1]

For it is beyond doubt that St. Paul's conception of Christ's dignity was closely connected with his faith in Christ as the Redeemer. Jesus was for Him the Lord because He was the Saviour. The title Lord frequently occurring in the Pauline Epistles means "the One who by His death has earned the place of sovereign in my heart, and whom I feel constrained to worship and serve with all my heart and mind."[2] The doctrine of Christ's Person in these Epistles is no mere theological speculation; it is the outgrowth of religious experience, the offspring of the consciousness of personal redemption.

But the connection between the two topics of Christ's Person and work in the apostle's mind is not merely æsthetic. His whole manner of conceiving Christ's redemptive work rendered certain conceptions concerning the Redeemer's Person inevitable. To see this we have only to recall the lessons we have learned in our past studies on the former of these topics.

By the vision on the way to Damascus, Saul of Tarsus

[1] R. Schmidt in his *Die Paulinische Christologie* (1870) strongly insists on this order of treatment. "The question as to the connection of the doctrine of Christ's Person with the apostle's distinctive doctrine of salvation is indispensable" (p. 4).

[2] Such is the connection of thought in such texts as *Gal.* vi. 14 and *Rom.* v. 1.

became convinced that Jesus was the *Christ.* From this conviction the inference immediately followed, that Jesus must have suffered on the cross not for His own sin but for the sin of the world, the choice, on the convert's view of the connection between sin and death, lying between these two alternatives. The crucified Christ for the converted Pharisee became a *vicarious* Sufferer. But this character of vicariousness could not be confined to the Passion. It must be extended to the whole earthly experience of Jesus. That experience was full of indignities, beginning with the circumcision of the Child, if not before, and ending with the bitter pains of the cross. These indignities one and all must be conceived of as vicarious, and therefore redemptive collectively and separately. Christ became a Redeemer by subjection to humiliation, and each element in His humiliation made its own contribution to redemption, procuring for men a benefit corresponding to its nature—redemption from legalism, *e.g.*, by the Redeemer's subjection to law. Christ's experience of humiliation was an appointment by God. But it was also Christ's own act. He humbled Himself; His whole earthly experience was a long course of *self-humiliation*, and the redemption he achieved was *a redemption by self-humiliation*.

If this be, as I believe it is, St. Paul's theory of redemption, then it inevitably involved one other step—a step out of time into the eternal. The whole earthly life of Christ was a self-humiliation in detail. But how did it begin? In a divine mission? Doubtless: God sent His own Son. But to make the conception of Christ's earthly experience as a humiliation complete, is it not necessary to view it as a whole, and regard it as resulting from a foregoing resolve on the part of Christ to enter into such a state? If so, then the necessary presupposition of the Pauline doctrine of redemption is the *pre-existence* of Christ, not merely in the foreknowledge of God, as the Jews conceived all important persons and things to pre-exist, or in the form of an ideal in heaven answering to an imperfect earthly reality, in accordance with the Greek way of thinking, but as a moral personality capable of forming a conscious purpose.[1]

This great thought finds classic expression in the Epistle to the Philippians,[2] as to the authenticity of which little doubt exists even among the freest critical inquirers. But we do not need to go outside the four great Epistles for traces of the idea. It is plainly hinted at in the words: "Ye know the grace of the Lord Jesus Christ, that though He was rich, yet for your sakes He became poor."[3] Nothing more than a hint is needed, for in view of the apostle's doctrine of redemption, the conception of a great Personality, high in dignity but lowly and gracious in spirit, freely resolving to enter into a state of humiliation on earth, almost goes without saying. It is what we expect, and it does not require

---

[1] On the difference between the Pauline idea of pre-existence and the notions entertained by Jews and Greeks, *vide* Harnack's *Dogmengeschichte*, vol. i. pp. 755-764, 3te Aufl., consisting of an appendix on the idea of pre-existence. For the religious value of St. Paul's view on this point *vide* Weizsäcker's *Apostolic Age*, p. 146. Neither of these writers has any doubt that St. Paul believed in and taught the pre-existence of Christ.

[2] Chap. ii. 5-9.   [3] 2 *Cor.* viii. 9.

a multitude of very explicit texts to overcome scepticism and convince us that it really entered into the Pauline system of thought.

This conception of the pre-existent Christ immediately raises other questions. In what relation does this Being who humbled Himself stand to man, to the universe, and to God? Materials bearing on all these topics may be found in the letters which form the chief basis of our study.

1. The apostle says that Christ was made of a woman,[1] and that He was sent into the world in the likeness of sinful flesh.[2] That is, He came into the world by birth, like other men, and He bore to the eye the aspect of any ordinary man. But though Christ came in the likeness of the flesh of sin, He was not, according to the apostle, a sinner. He " knew no sin."[3] The mind that was in Him before He came ruled His life after He came. He walked in the Spirit while on this earth, the Son of God according to the Spirit of holiness. Yet St. Paul conceived of the resurrection as constituting an important crisis in the experience of Christ. Thereby He was declared to be, or constituted, the Son of God with power. Thereafter He became altogether spiritual, even in His humanity the *Man from Heaven.*[4] The expression suggests that Christ, as St. Paul conceived Him, was human even in the pre-existent state, so that while on earth He was the Man who had been in heaven, and whose destination it was to return thither again. This view would seem to imperil the reality of the

[1] *Gal.* iv. 4. [2] *Rom.* viii. 3.
[3] 2 *Cor.* v. 21. [4] 1 *Cor.* xv. 47.

earthly state as something inadequate, phantasmal, transitory, and a mere incident in the eternal life of a Being not of this world; not a true man, though "made in the likeness of men," and "found in fashion as a man."[1] But the soteriological doctrine of the apostle demanded that Christ should be a real man, and that His human experience should be in all respects as like ours as possible. Even in respect to the flesh of sin, the likeness must be close enough to insure that Christ should have an experience of temptation sufficiently thorough to qualify Him for helping us to walk in the Spirit.

Among the realistic elements in the Pauline conception of Christ's humanity may be reckoned the references to the Jewish nationality and Davidic descent of our Lord. These occur in the Epistle to the Romans,[2] which is irenical in aim, and might therefore not unnaturally be regarded as indicating the desire to conciliate rather than the religious value they possessed for the writer's own mind. Such references are indeed not what we expect from the apostle. His interest was in the universal rather than in the particular, in the human race rather than in any one nation, even if it were the privileged people to which he himself belonged. Then it is not easy to conceive of him as attaching vital importance to Davidic descent, in the strictly physical sense, as an indispensable condition of Jesus being the Christ and the Saviour of the world. He rested his own claims to be an apostle on spiritual rather than on technical grounds, and we can imagine him holding that Jesus might be the Messiah though not of the seed of

[1] *Phil.* ii. 7–8.   [2] *Rom.* i. 3; ix. 5.

David, just as the author of the Epistle to the Hebrews maintained that Jesus was a priest of the highest order though not belonging to the tribe of Levi. Instead of reasoning from Davidic descent to Messiahship, St. Paul might invert the argument and say: "Because Christ, therefore David's seed"; just as he said of believers in Christ: "If ye be Christ's, then are ye Abraham's seed";[1] "seed" in both cases being understood in an ideal not in a literal sense. But, all the more just on that account, it is significant that he does think it worth while to state that Jesus was "of the seed of David according to the flesh." It may be taken as indicating two things: that St. Paul believed in Christ's descent from David as a matter of fact, and that he regarded it as a fact of some interest. The statement occurs in a passage at the commencement of his most important Epistle, in which he carefully indicates his Christological position, and it may therefore legitimately be regarded as counting for something in that position. Obviously the divine Sonship is for him the main concern, but it does not follow that the other side is for him a thing of no moment. And wherein lies its value? Why say Christ is a Jew and a son of David when stating a truth which eclipses these facts and reduces them apparently to utter insignificance, viz., that He is the Son of God? Because he desires to affirm the reality of Christ's humanity, not in an abstract form, but as a concrete, definitely-qualified thing: Jesus a real Man; a Jew with Hebrew blood in His veins, and possessing Hebrew idiosyncracies, physical and mental; a descendant of

[1] *Gal.* iii. 29.

David with hereditary qualities inherited from a long line of ancestors running back to the hero-king. Such seems to have been St. Paul's idea, and it is worth noting as a thing to be set over against any traces of apparent docetism in his Epistles, and against the notion that he regarded Christ's earthly life in the flesh as possessing no permanent significance—a mere transitory phenomenon that might with advantage be forgotten.[1]

Yet nationality and definite individuality, while not irrelevant trivialities, were far from being everything or the main thing for St. Paul. For the enthusiastic apostle of Gentile Christianity, the universal relation of Christ to mankind was of much more importance than his particular relation to Israel or to David. And, as was to be expected, he had a name for the wider relation as well as for the narrower. The Son of David was for him, moreover and more emphatically, "the *second Man*."[2] The title assigns to Christ a universal, representative significance analogous to that of Adam. It is not merely a title of honour, but a title indicative of function. It points out Christ as one who has for His vocation to undo the mischief wrought by the transgression of the first man. Hence He is called in sharp antithesis to the Adam who caused the Fall the last

---

[1] There is nothing decisive in the Pauline Epistles concerning the miraculous birth of Christ. The expression ἐκ σπέρματος Δαυεὶδ κατὰ σάρκα might even be held to exclude it, except on the assumption that Mary, as well as Joseph, was of the line of David. If connection with David depended on Joseph only, Jesus might be more exactly described as Son of David κατὰ νόμον than κατὰ σάρκα. The expression γενόμενον ἐκ γυναικός fits into, but does not prove, birth from a virgin.

[2] 1 *Cor.* xv. 47.

Adam made into a *quickening spirit*.¹ As the one brought death into the world, so the other brings life. "As in Adam all die, so in Christ shall all be made alive." ²

2. That in a system of thought in which Christ stands in a vital relation to the whole human race He might also be conceived as occupying an important position in relation to the universe it is not difficult to believe. It is well known that in the Christological Epistles ascribed to St. Paul, especially in the Epistle to the Colossians, a very high cosmic place is assigned to Christ. He is there represented as the First-born of all creation, nay, as the originator of the creation, as well as its final cause; all things in heaven and on earth, visible and invisible, angels included, being made by Him and for Him.³ This goes beyond anything to be found in the four leading Epistles. But even in these we find rudiments of a doctrine as to the cosmic relations of Christ which might easily develop into the full-blown Colossian thesis under appropriate conditions. For St. Paul, as for Jesus, it was an axiom that the universe had its final aim in the kingdom of God, or in Christ its King. This truth finds expression in several familiar texts, as when it is said: "All things work together for good to them that love God";⁴ or again: "All things are yours, and ye are Christ's, and Christ is God's." ⁵ The groaning of the creation in labour for the bringing forth of a new redeemed world is a graphic pictorial representation of the same great thought.⁶ It is only the complement of this doctrine that Christ should be represented as having

---

¹ 1 *Cor.* xv. 45.   ² *Ibid.* xv. 22.   ³ *Col.* i. 15, 16.
⁴ *Rom.* viii. 28.   ⁵ 1 *Cor.* iii. 22, 23.   ⁶ *Rom.* viii. 22.

the control of providence, or as the Mediator of God's activity in the world. This is done when it is stated that God "hath put all things under His feet";[1] and still more explicitly in another text from the same Epistle, where Jesus Christ is described as the one Lord by whom, or on account of whom, are all things.[2] The reading varies here. If it were certain that δι' οὗ is the correct reading, we might find in this passage the doctrine of a mediatorial action of Christ in creation, and not merely in providence, while from the reading δι' ὅν the latter only can be inferred. But indeed, in any case, from providential power to creative is only one step. He who directs providence in some sense creates. He furnishes the divine reason for creation, and is the Logos, if not the physical cause, of the universe. And in this point of view, the doctrine of Christ's creative activity is thoroughly congruous to the Christian faith, and altogether such as we might expect a man like St. Paul to teach. The *rationale* of that doctrine is not the idea of divine transcendency, which, in the interest of God's majesty, demands that all His action on and in the world be through intermediaries. It is rather an ethical conception of the universe, which demands that all things shall exist and be maintained in being for a God-worthy purpose.

3. In passing to the question as to the relation of Christ to God as set forth in the Pauline Epistles, I remark that the titles most commonly applied to Christ by the apostle in his other Epistles are just those we found in use in the Primer Epistles: the *Son of God*

[1] 1 *Cor.* xv. 27.   [2] 1 *Ibid.* viii. 6.

and *the Lord*!¹ We find both combined in the Christological introduction to the Epistle to the Romans, where we have reason to believe the writer is expressing himself with the utmost care and deliberation: " His Son, Jesus Christ our Lord." If we inquire in what sense the former of the two titles is to be understood, another phrase occurring in the same place might lead us to conclude that the sonship of Jesus is ethical in its nature. The apostle represents Christ as from or after the resurrection declared or constituted the Son of God in power, *according to the Spirit of holiness*, as if to suggest that Jesus was always worthy to be called the Son of God because of the measure in which the Holy Spirit of God dwelt in Him, and that His claim to the title became doubly manifest after the resurrection, whereby God set His seal upon Him as the Holy One, and made such doubts about His character as had existed previous to His death for ever impossible. And unquestionably this is at least one most important element in St. Paul's conception of Christ's sonship: sonship based on community of spirit. It is a sonship of this nature he has in view when further on in the same Epistle he represents Christ, God's Son, as a type to which the objects of God's electing love are to be conformed, and as occupying among those who have been assimilated to the type the position of first-born among many brethren, that is a position of pre-eminence on a basis of generic identity.² Yet that there was something unique in Christ's sonship, as St. Paul conceived it, we might infer from the expression, " His own

¹ *Vide* Chap. I. ² *Rom.* viii. 29.

Son" occurring at the beginning of the same section of the Epistle in which the brotherhood of sons is spoken of;[1] His own Son," not merely the first begotten in a large family, but the only begotten in some sense. And this aspect of solitariness or uniqueness is even more strongly suggested in the text in 1 *Thessalonians*, in which Christians are described as waiting for God's Son from heaven.[2] There is indeed no ἑαυτοῦ there to lend emphasis to the title. The emphasis comes from the juxtaposition of the title with words in which conversion to Christianity is made to consist in turning to the true God from *idols*.[3] How significant the application to Jesus, in such a connection, of the title Son of God! Finally we may note, as pointing in the same direction, the statement in 2 *Corinthians* iv. 4, that Christ is the image of God,[4] taken along with that in *Romans* viii. 29, that the destiny of believers is to be conformed to the image of God's Son. The ideal for Christians is to bear the image of Christ; for Christ Himself is reserved the distinction of being the image of God. We are but the reflection of that in Him which is the direct radiance of God's glory (ἀπαύγασμα τῆς δόξης), the copy of that which constitutes Him the express image of God's essence (χαρακτὴρ τῆς ὑποστάσεως).

In an important passage in 1 *Corinthians* viii. the title *Lord* gains equal significance to that which *Son* bears in 1 *Thessalonians* i. 10, from its position in a similar context. In some cases, as already hinted, the title might be regarded as the generous ascription of

[1] *Rom.* viii. 3.
[2] 1 *Thess.* i. 9.
[3] *Ibid.* i. 10.
[4] ὅς ἐστιν εἰκὼν τοῦ Θεοῦ.

religious honour to Christ as Redeemer, proceeding from a heart too warm to be exact in its use of language. But in 1 *Corinthians* viii. St. Paul is thinking as well as feeling, and he is thinking on a difficult and delicate problem, viz., the place to be assigned to Christ in view of pagan polytheism. In that connection he makes this statement: "For though there be that are called gods, whether in heaven or in earth; as there are gods many and lords many, yet to us there is one God, the Father, of whom are all things, and we unto Him; and one Lord Jesus Christ, through whom or for whom are all things, and we through Him."[1] The apostle here sets one real θεὸς over against the many θεοὶ λεγόμενοι of Paganism, and one real lord over against its κύριοι πολλοί. And one cannot fail to feel that the title Lord ascribed to Jesus in such a connection is charged with great significance. It seems as if the apostle meant thereby to introduce Christ into the sphere of the truly divine, urged on thereto by the imperious exigencies of his religious faith, and against his prejudices as a Jew in favour of a strict abstract monotheism inherited from his forefathers. And the title Father attached to the name of God seems to suggest that He finds room for Christ within the divine, under the title Son.

From what we have now ascertained as to St. Paul's way of thinking concerning Christ, it might seem to follow that he would have no hesitation in calling Christ God. Has he then done this in any of his Epistles, more especially in those which are most certainly authentic? There is one passage in the Epistle to the Romans which,

[1] 1 *Cor.* viii. 5 and 6.

in the judgment of many, supplies a clear instance of the ascription to Christ of the title Θεός. It is the well-known text, *Romans* ix. 5 : ὧν οἱ πατέρες καὶ ἐξ ὧν ὁ Χριστὸς τὸ κατὰ σάρκα, ὁ ὢν ἐπὶ πάντων Θεὸς εὐλογητὸς εἰς τοὺς αἰῶνας. Ἀμήν. The construction of this sentence which most readily suggests itself, at least to minds familiar with the doctrine of Christ's divinity, is that which places a comma after σάρκα, and takes the following clause as a declaration concerning Christ that He is God over all, blessed for ever. Another arrangement and interpretation, however, are possible, viz., to put a full stop after σάρκα, and to regard the last clause as a doxology, or ascription of praise to God the supreme Ruler: "May God who is over all be blessed for ever." Thus read, the text contains no ascription of deity to Christ. Here, it may be observed in passing, we have an instance showing how much may depend on punctuation, and what a serious defect from the point of view of a mechanical theory of inspiration is the absence of punctuation from the autograph text. In connection with so important a subject as the Person of Christ it would certainly have been a great advantage to have had from the apostle's own hands a carefully punctuated text. Had this existed, and had it been found to contain a sign of the value of a comma after σάρκα, it would have left little room for doubt that St. Paul meant to speak of Christ as God over all. As the case stands we are left to determine the question whether this was indeed his intention by other considerations, and at most we can arrive only at a probable conclusion on either side of the question. As was to be expected the passage has given rise to an immense amount of discussion, in which, of course, exegesis has been to a considerable extent influenced by dogmatic bias. Into the history of the interpretation I cannot here enter; I cannot even attempt to state in detail the grounds on which the decision of the point at issue turns. Let it suffice to state that among the considerations which have been urged in support of the view that the claim refers to Christ are these: that whenever an ascription of blessing to God occurs in the Hebrew or Greek Scriptures εὐλογητὸς precedes Θεὸς, that if the clause in question were a doxology referring to God as distinct from Christ the ὤν would be superfluous, and that such a doxology coming in where the clause stands would be frigid and senseless. These and other arguments, however, have not been deemed unanswerable; and, on the whole, in spite of personal predilection, one is constrained, after perusal of learned monographs, to admit that the bearing of this famous text on the deity of Christ is by no means so certain as at one time he may have been disposed to think.[1]

[1] Amongst the most thorough discussions of the passage may be mentioned the article on the Construction of *Romans* ix. 5, in *Critical Essays*, by Ezra Abbot (George H. Ellis, 1888), pp. 332–438, which gives a very full account of the literature of the topic. Prof. Abbot distinguishes no fewer than seven different ways in which the text may be and has been punctuated and interpreted. Among the orthodox theologians who have pronounced against the reference to Christ may be named Dr. Agar Beet. *Vide* his *Commentary on the Epistle to the Romans*, p. 271. Weizsäcker, *Das Apostolische Zeitalter*, p. 580, refers to *Romans* i. 25, 2 *Corinthians* xi. 31, as instances of interjectional doxologies interrupting the train of thought similar to the one in *Romans* ix. 5, assuming that the reference is to God.

One other text of great importance in its bearing on Christ's relation to God may here be noticed. It is the benediction at the close of the Second Epistle to the Corinthians: Ἡ χάρις τοῦ κυρίου Ἰησοῦ, καὶ ἡ ἀγάπη τοῦ Θεοῦ, καὶ ἡ κοινωνία τοῦ ἁγίου πνεύματος, μετὰ πάντων. We have here a Trinity, not, however, to be forthwith identified with that of the formula framed by the Council of Nice. The apostolic benediction does not run as a dogmatic theologian, having in view the interests of Trinitarianism, might desire. Dogmatic bias would suggest at least two changes: the transposition of the first two clauses, and the addition of the word πατρός after Θεοῦ, lest the use of the latter term absolutely should seem to imply that Christ while Lord was not God. Yet, notwithstanding these peculiarities—defects they might be called from the dogmatic point of view—this benediction of St. Paul implies surely a very high conception of Christ's person and position. One would say that he could hardly have used such a collocation of phrases as the grace of the Lord Jesus, the love of God, and the fellowship of the Holy Spirit, unless Christ had been for him a divine being—God. All the three Beings named in the sentence must possess in common divine nature. The second and third certainly do. It has been questioned whether for St. Paul the Holy Spirit was a divine *Person*, or merely a divine *Power*, but He was certainly either the one or the other. The Holy Spirit, if not a distinct Person in the Godhead, was at least God's—God's energy, therefore practically a synonym for God. What, then, are we to think but that the Lord Jesus, being named together with God and the energy of

God as a source of blessing, is also God, and that all the three august Beings here spoken of are bound together by the tie of a common divine nature?

While this appears to be the just interpretation of the apostolic benediction, it must be owned that in the Pauline Epistles a certain position of subordination seems to be assigned to Christ in relation to God. The most outstanding text in this connection is that in 1 *Cor.* xv. 28, where the winding up of the drama of redemption is made to consist in the resignation by the Son of God of His mediatorial power into the hands of His Father, that God may be all in all. This is one of those grand comprehensive statements with which the apostle is wont to conclude important trains of thought. Like all other statements of the same type, it rises to the oratorical sublime; but while inspiring awe it leaves us in doubt. The spoken word makes us feel how much is unspoken. We are taken in spirit to the outermost circle of revelation, whence we descry all around an infinite extent of darkness.

CHAPTER XIX

THE CHRISTIAN LIFE

The title of this chapter is somewhat vague, but what I have in view is to consider such questions as these: How does the apostle conceive the Christian life in reference to its beginning? How far does he recognise the idea of growth as applicable to that life? What features of that life occupied the place of prominence in his mind?

1. The leading Pauline Epistles contain various forms of representation, bearing on the first of these questions. One of the most important and striking occurs in the earliest of the four. I refer to the statement in *Galatians* vi. 15: "Neither circumcision is anything, nor uncircumcision, but a *new creation*" (καινὴ κτίσις). A certain controversial colouring is discernible here. The supreme importance of the new spiritual creation is asserted against those who set value on rites. As against these, St. Paul says in effect: "The one thing needful is the new creation; without a share in it the rite of circumcision will do you no good, and if you possess it the want of circumcision will do you no harm." It is easy to see that the antithesis gives much sharpness and point to the thought expressed by the phrase καινὴ κτίσις. The

apostle conceives of Christianity as a new world ushered into being by the divine fiat, and taking the place of an old world worn out and doomed to dissolution. To his opponents he says in effect: "God has created a new world in Christ which is entitled to assert to the full its right of existence. Speak to me no more of circumcision and uncircumcision, Jew and Gentile; these distinctions belong to the old world which, by the very advent of the new, has received notice to pass away." Thus viewed the new creation refers not so much, at least directly, to the religious life of the individual Christian, as to the whole comprehensive social phenomenon denoted by the term Christianity. But there is little room for doubt that the individual reference was also present to the apostle's mind. For the very antithesis between the new creation and ritual implies that the former is ethical. The new creation is a moral creation, and it is such for the Church collectively, because it is such for each member of the Church. It consists of a community of men who have become partakers of a new life through faith in Christ, and it is because it is so constituted that the καινὴ κτίσις is the marvellous thing it is represented to be. Accordingly we find that, immediately after mentioning this new creation, St. Paul goes on to speak of individual members of the Christian commonwealth in these terms: "As many as walk by this rule, peace be upon them and mercy, even upon the Israel of God." The members of the mystic Israel are thus represented as persons who walk by the rule, or have for their watchword—circumcision nothing, uncircumcision nothing, the new creation everything; and the adoption of this motto is possible only for those who are conscious of a new spiritual life within them.

It is not surprising, therefore, to find the apostle in a later Epistle expressly stating what in the earlier he rather hints than says, viz., that every man who believes in Christ is a new creation. The important text containing the statement is 2 *Cor.* v. 17: "Wherefore if any one in Christ, a new creation; the old things passed away, behold new things have come into being." The sentence is characterised by laconic energy, and reveals intense conviction. It is an echo of the prophetic oracle: "Remember ye not the former things, neither consider the things of old. Behold I do new things,"[1] and is directed against the Judaists who were enamoured of the old. For the apostle Christianity is the new thing spoken of by the prophet, and he claims for it as only what is due to its importance that in its interest all old things, not excepting even Christ after the flesh, shall be forgotten, as they are by him for his part. But there is much more in his mind than this controversial meaning. When he speaks of a καινὴ κτίσις, he has in view a marvellous moral phenomenon that has made its appearance in every man who has truly believed in Christ. A great transformation has taken place. The believer has become in thought, feeling, aim, a new man; old characteristics have disappeared, and new ones have taken their place. If we inquire what the old things vanishing, and the new things replacing the old are, the context helps us to an answer. We find a very significant hint in these words of v. 15: "He died for all,

[1] *Isa.* xliii. 18, 19.

that the living might *no longer* live to themselves, but to Him who for them died and rose again." The μηκέτι implies that those who believe did formerly live for themselves, and the change that has come over them consists in their resolving to do so no longer. The new creation then, for one thing, signifies selfishness giving place to self-sacrifice for Christ's sake.

Passing from the Epistle to the Corinthians to the Epistle to the Romans, we find the idea of a new creation recurring under slightly altered forms of expression. In the sixth chapter the apostle speaks of *an old man* (παλαιὸς ἄνθρωπος), implying, of course, a new; and he represents Christians as called to walk in *newness of life*.[1] The same chapter gives us additional information as to what the newness consists in. In the sequel Christians are exhorted thus: "Let not sin therefore reign in your mortal body that ye should obey its desires."[2] The new man, that is, is one who is free, or at least strives to assert his freedom from the dominion of fleshly desire, and who seeks to make all his members instruments of righteousness. At the commencement of chapter xii., where begins the hortatory part of the Epistle, the same truth is suggested by the exhortation to Christians to present their bodies a living sacrifice characterised as a rational service (λογικὴ λατρεία), in tacit contrast to the ritual service of the Levitical system under which brute beasts were offered in sacrifice. The exhortation is virtually a summons to mortify the lusts of the flesh, so that the life in the body may be pure and holy. And he is a new man who so puts to death unholy desire and

[1] *Rom.* vi. 4-6.   [2] *Ibid.* vi. 12.

lives a temperate life. The same exhortation recurs in *Romans* xiii., accompanied with some details as to the things to be shunned.[1] Here the doctrine of the new life is stated in altered terms, being represented as a *putting on of Christ Jesus*, Christ being conceived as a new garment to be worn by the Christian in place of an old one. The figure suits a connection of thought in which believers are exhorted to a change of bodily habits; for habits are a garment of the soul. It also supplies us with a link of thought wherewith to connect the two characteristics of the new creation which have come under our notice—self-sacrifice and self-control in reference to personal habits ($\dot{\epsilon}\gamma\kappa\rho\acute{a}\tau\epsilon\iota a$).[2] That link is Christ. Christ by His redeeming love supplies the motive to self-sacrifice; by the same love, and by the purity of His life, He furnishes the motive to temperance. It is true that, in exhorting to put on Christ, the apostle makes no express allusion either to Christ's love or to His holiness. But the exhortation plainly implies that Christ is the model. To put on Christ is to have Christ's habits, to be Christlike. It further implies that Christ is a power within which generates a new moral habit; and if it be asked, Whence has He this power? the answer may be found in another place, where the apostle says: "Ye are not your own, for ye are bought with a price; therefore glorify God in your body."[3] The implied truth is that temperance, Christian

---

[1] *Rom.* xiii. 13. [2] *Gal.* v. 23.
[3] 1 *Cor.* vi. 20. Note the δὴ after δοξάσατε. It implies that to glorify God in the body is the self-evident duty arising out of the consciousness of redemption.

sobriety and purity, not less than self-sacrifice, naturally spring out of the sense of redemption. They are a debt of honour we owe to Christ, the Saviour of men.

Comparing the teaching of St. Paul with that of our Lord on the present topic, we find in both the doctrine that the Christian life begins with a decisive change, but expressed in different terms. In the Synoptical Gospels, Jesus speaks of repentance and conversion, and in the Fourth Gospel the change of mind denoted by the words, μετάνοια, ἐπιστροφή, is figuratively described as a new birth. The apostle's name for the same experience is, as we have seen, a new creation. The name is well chosen to convey an idea of the greatness of the change, and on that account it commended itself to the mind of one whose experience amounted to nothing short of a mighty religious revolution. The phrase is the reflection of a momentous spiritual history. It was further welcome to the apostle as applicable not only to individual experience, but to the collective body of phenomena which owed their existence to the gospel. Conscious of a new creation in himself, he also saw a new creation all around him, and he applied to it a title which was at once a claim and an argument for the recognition of a great and startling novelty. Finally, we cannot doubt that another recommendation of this name to him was the implied ascription of the revolution it denoted, whether in the individual or in the community, to God as its author. It was meant to suggest that He who at the beginning made the heavens and the earth had in the end of the world uttered the fiat: "Let the new heavens and the new earth be." An express recognition of the creative causality of God, in the apostle's own experience, occurs in the remarkable words of 2 *Cor.* iv. 6 : " It was the God who said, ' out of darkness let light shine,' who shined in our hearts, giving the illumination consisting in the knowledge of the glory of God in the face of Christ."

It is obvious that while well fitted to express the phenomenal aspect of the new life, as presenting to discerning eyes a great startling change, the figure of the new creation, much less aptly than the figure of the new birth, expresses the nature of that life and its relation to what went before. The latter figure conveys the thought that the new life is not a creation out of nothing, having no relation to antecedent conditions, but rather a manifestation in power of what was there before in germ, the divine element in human nature made dominant. This relation, so far from being suggested, might rather seem to be negatived by the Pauline phrase. The apostle, however, did not mean to deny the existence of a divine element in what theologians call the "natural" man. On the contrary, he expressly recognises it in *Rom.* vii. under the name, *the law of the mind.*

2. We pass now to the second topic, viz., how far the idea of growth is recognised in the Pauline literature in connection with the Christian life. In the synoptical representation of Christ's teaching, the idea of growth in the kingdom of God is very strikingly and adequately stated in the parable of the blade, the green ear, and the ripe corn.[1] The thought therein suggested is, that in the kingdom of God, as in the natural world, life is subject

[1] *Mark* iv. 26–29.

to the law of gradual development, proceeding towards the ultimate state of maturity by regular well-defined stages, which must be gone through successively. It must be admitted, perhaps not without a feeling of disappointment, that we search in vain for a similarly clear conception in the Pauline Epistles. In none of these, not even in the later Christological Epistles, can we discover any such distinct and significant recognition of a law of growth; and if we confine our attention to the four leading Epistles, we can find no sufficient ground for the assertion that St. Paul represents the Christian life as an organic process of growth. On the other hand, it would be going too far to say that, in the Pauline mode of conceiving the matter, the Christian life springs into existence complete from the first, undergoing no subsequent change, and needing none because fully answering to the ideal.[1] This view might indeed be held compatibly with the admission that there are texts which suggest another mode of regarding the matter. The theory of a new life, complete from the first, is not justified by experience; it was not justified by St. Paul's experience any more than by ours. He found no perfect Christians in the churches to which he wrote letters, very much the reverse. Hence the frequent occurrence of texts containing exhortations, encouragements, reproaches, threatenings, suggesting the idea that the new life is at first a rudimentary imperfect thing requiring improve-

[1] So Reuss in his *Theology of the Apostolic Age.* Pfleiderer takes the opposite view, at least in the first edition of *Paulinismus.* I have not noticed any modification of his opinion in the second edition.

ment, a tendency rather than an attainment, a struggle rather than a victory achieved. Notwithstanding such passages, however, it has been maintained that the notion of a new life complete from the first is involved in some Pauline utterances, and a protest has been taken against attempts at harmonising the two sets of texts by the construction of a dogma of gradual sanctification, according to which regeneration should be merely the point of departure for the new life, to be followed by a progressive amelioration, an increasing power over the flesh. The Pauline ideal, it is contended, is a new life in Christ, perfect from the first, a death to sin and a resurrection to holiness, accomplished not gradually but *per saltum*. If the reality fall short, the ideal is not to be sacrificed or lowered; the reality is rather to be regarded as a fault to be corrected, the ideal being kept constantly before the eye in its uncompromising grandeur and unearthly beauty as a stimulus to the task of self-correction.[1]

The one thing I seriously object to in this representation is the assumption that St. Paul regarded the Christian ideal as realisable at the outset. That he might invest the beginning of the Christian life with an ideal significance, representing it as a death to sin and a resurrection to a new life (ideas both excluding lapse of time), is very conceivable; that he did this in fact I believe. But that it was a surprise to him that nowhere did he find young Christians in whom the ideal significance of faith was fully realised, is not so easy to

[1] *Vide* Reuss' whole chapter on Regeneration in his account of the Pauline theology, *Theologie Chrétienne*, vol. ii. p. 135.

believe. It might have been a surprise to him when he was himself a young Christian, as it is apt to be to all beginners. For in the blossom of the new life, Christians feel as if their spiritual being were already complete, and the advent of the green fruit is a surprise and a disappointment to them, and hence it is commonly construed wrongly as a lapse or declension. But twenty years' experience must surely have helped to correct such crude ideas, and taught the apostle to cherish moderate sober expectations in reference to beginners, and to recognise, if not with full understanding of its *rationale*, at least virtually, that the divine life is not a momentary product, but a process, a problem to be worked out, an organic growth.

Such a conception accordingly we do find, though mainly in the later Epistles. The exhortation, "Work out your salvation," suggests the idea of a problem to be solved.[1] The comparison of the Church to the human body, growing up to the stature of manhood, suggests the idea of organic growth.[2] The metaphorical expression, "rooted in love,"[3] suggests a comparison of the Christian life to a tree planted in a good soil, and growing from a small plant to the dimensions of a forest tree.

Rudimentary hints of a doctrine of growth are not wanting even in the four leading Epistles. The idea of growth is clearly recognised in regard to humanity at large, if not in reference to the individual, in the comparison of the law to tutors and governors who have charge of an heir during the time of his minority.[4] The

[1] *Phil.* ii. 12. [2] *Eph.* iv. 11–15.
[3] *Ibid.* iii. 17. [4] *Gal.* iv. 1, 2.

word καρπὸς, in the text where the apostle sets the *fruit* of the Spirit over against the *works* of the flesh,[1] readily suggests to us the idea of gradual growth, knowing as we do that ripe fruit is the slow product of time. Yet it is doubtful if this thought was present to the apostle's mind. Equally doubtful is it whether we are entitled to lay stress on the word "soweth" in the text: "He that soweth to the Spirit shall of the Spirit reap life everlasting,"[2] as it is probable that the whole earthly life is here regarded as the seed time, the harvest falling in the life hereafter. The surest indication of a doctrine of growth in grace to be found in the Epistle to the Galatians is contained in chap. v. 5, where the Christian is represented as waiting for the hope of righteousness. Assuming that the righteousness referred to is to be taken subjectively, we find in this text the idea that personal holiness is an object of hope and patient expectation. The ideal is thus projected into the future, and we are by implication taught not to fret because it is not at once realised. We are to wait for the realisation of the ideal in a mature spiritual manhood, with the patience of a farmer waiting for the harvest, who knows that growth is gradual, there being first the blade, then the green ear, and only then the full corn in the ear.

Among the hints of a doctrine of growth in the other Epistles belonging to the main group may be mentioned the following :—

In 1 *Corinthians* the apostle describes the members of the Church as νήπιοι to whom he could give only milk,[3] while he claims to be in possession of a wisdom which

[1] *Gal* v. 22. [2] *Ibid.* vi. 8. [3] 1 *Cor.* iii. 2.

he could teach to the more advanced, denominated τέλειοι.[1] But as showing that the full significance of the doctrine was not present to his mind, it has to be noted that he speaks of the infantile state of the Corinthian Church as something blameworthy, associating with the epithet "babes" the attributes of unspirituality and carnality.[2] The tone here is markedly different from that of the words put into the mouth of Jesus in the Fourth Gospel: "I have yet many things to say unto you, but ye cannot bear them now,"[3] which tacitly recognise that spiritual children cannot be expected to have the understanding of spiritual men. It resembles rather the tone of the writer of the Epistle to the Hebrews when he complains of his readers as being destitute of manly intelligence, and like children having need of milk. Only there was this difference between the Corinthian and the Hebrew Christians, that the latter were in their second childhood, and they had become as children, while the Corinthians were in their first childhood, and had only recently become converts to Christianity. Blame in the case of second childhood, spiritual dotage, was certainly called for, but ought not much allowance to be made for beginners?

In 2 *Corinthians* iii. 18, the apostle represents Christians as undergoing transformation through contemplation of the glory of the Lord Christ. "We are being changed into the same image from glory to glory." The present tense suggests a process continually going on. The expression "from glory to glory" may also point to a steady gradual advance, though it may mean from glory in Him to glory in us.

[1] 1 *Cor.* ii. 6.   [2] *Ibid.* iii. 1.   [3] *John* xvi. 12.

In *Romans* vi. 14, the apostle remarks: "Sin shall not reign over you, for ye are not under law, but under grace." This statement does not teach a doctrine of gradual sanctification, but it leaves room for it. Sin dethroned may still attempt to regain its lost sovereignty, and we know that when a change of dynasty takes place in a country there is generally a more or less protracted period of trouble, during which members of the degraded royal family endeavour to get themselves restored to power. Sin dethroned, therefore, may continue to give trouble as a pretender. In the 12th chapter of the same Epistle occurs this exhortation: "Be ye not conformed to this world, but be ye transformed in the renewal of the mind, to the effect of your proving what is the will of God, the good, and acceptable, and perfect." This transformation of character and this proving of the divine will, so as to verify its characteristics, imply a gradual process, lapse of time, a thing done bit by bit, a progressive experience enlightening the mind in the knowledge of God's will, and bringing our life more and more into conformity with it. A process of growth is equally implied in the text, chap. v. 3: "We glory in tribulation, knowing that tribulation worketh out patience, and patience attestation, and attestation hope." The working out of patience is a process involving time, and, what is still more to our present purpose, the result of the process, patience, and the consciousness of being tested and attested, whence come self-reliance and calm assurance, is something we could not possess antecedent to experience. That is to say, these are Christian virtues developed by the discipline of trial which no beginner can possess.

The result of our inquiry, on the whole, is this. In the Pauline letters, and especially the controversial group, there is no formulated doctrine of growth enunciated with full consciousness and deliberate didactic purpose. But there is a doctrine of growth latent in these letters; there are germs which we may use in the construction of such a doctrine. Moreover, there are facts in the life of the Churches alluded to in these letters which we may employ in verification of the doctrine, though not so used by the apostle himself. For example, there is the lapse of the Galatian Church into legalism, and of the Corinthian Church into various sorts of errors in opinion, and the contentions prevailing therein, and there is the scrupulosity about meats and drinks spoken of in the Epistle to the Romans. We may use the phenomena as helping us to form a vivid idea of the characteristics of the green ear, or let us call it the stage of the crude fruit in the divine life, between the blossom and the ripe fruit. St. Paul dealt with them as faults. But are they not more than faults accidentally occurring; are they not phenomena which reappear regularly with all the certainty of a fixed law? As sure as after the blossom comes the green crude fruit, come there not in the experiences of Christians, after the time of first enthusiasm is past, such features as these: joylessness, a religion of legal temper and mechanical routine, scrupulosity, opinionativeness, censoriousness, quarrelsomeness, doubt? Then, on the other hand, what is that spirit of adoption whose presence and influence within the Churches to which he writes the apostle misses and so greatly desiderates but one of the most outstanding characteristics of Christian maturity, of the stage of the ripe fruit in Christian growth, when a believing man at last begins to have some conception of the true character of the new life and some practical acquaintance with its blessedness? The advent of that spirit St. Paul viewed as the sign that the world at large, humanity, had arrived at its majority, and it is an equally sure sign of the arrival of the same important epoch in the spiritual life of the individual. Thus might we find valuable material for the construction of a doctrine of gradual sanctification, advancing through well-marked stages, not merely or even chiefly in the didactic statements of the apostle, but very specially in his complaints against and exhortations to the Churches to which he addressed his Epistles.

3. The last point we proposed to consider refers to the salient features of the Christian character as conceived by St. Paul. Two of these, sobriety and devotion to Christ, have already been mentioned as among the moral phenomena of the new creation. To these has now to be added charity, ἀγάπη, which makes the list of the cardinal virtues in the Pauline ethical system tolerably complete. It might seem due to the prominence given to it in the First Epistle to the Corinthians that a fourth should be added to the number, viz., spiritual knowledge or insight. The apostle there claims for the pneumatical man, as against the psychical, knowledge and appreciation of the things of the Spirit of God.[1] Such knowledge he evidently regarded as an outstanding mark of

[1] 1 *Cor.* ii. 14-15.

distinction between the two classes of men, one of the prominent phenomena of the new creation. The man of the new creation knows the mind of God; the man who is outside this creation is not able to know. The psychical man has the five senses of the soul, but not the sixth sense of the Spirit. Of this St. Paul was doubtless strongly convinced. Yet it would be contrary to the whole spirit of his teaching to mention anything of the nature of gnosis, even though it be spiritual gnosis, alongside of charity, as if of co-ordinate importance. In the same Epistle further on he expressly represents knowledge as of no account in comparison with charity. "If I know all mysteries and all knowledge and have not charity, I am nothing."[1] In another place he remarks: "Knowledge inflates, charity edifies."[2] The knowledge thus depreciated relates to divine things, but that does not prevent the apostle from assigning to it a place of secondary importance. Gnosis, theological gnosis especially, is very good in its own place, but it tends to make a man think more highly of himself than he ought. No fear of that in the case of love; it builds up a solid structure of real, not imaginary Christian worth.

Very significant of the sovereign place which ἀγάπη occupied in St. Paul's esteem is the fact that in his enumeration of the fruit of the Spirit he names it first,[3] not without a controversial reference to the religious contentions which vexed the Churches of Galatia. Yet charity, in the sense of love to the brethren, is not the absolute first for him. Devotion to Christ takes precedence. Witness the stern word: "If any one love not

[1] 1 *Cor.* xiii. 2.   [2] *Ibid.* viii. 1.   [3] *Gal.* v. 22.

the Lord, let him be anathema." St. Paul's charity is great; he loves weak brethren, and out of regard to their scruples denies himself the use of his Christian liberty.[1] He loves even those in the Churches who regard him with distrust as a dangerous revolutionary, setting aside the divine law, changing venerable customs, as is shown by his diligence in making collections for the poor disciples in Jerusalem, though fully aware what hard thoughts they cherish regarding him there. His charity rises superior to party divisions, and embraces all who belong to the Israel of God, strong or weak, Jew or Gentile, friendly or hostile to himself. He loves, moreover, all without, and yearns to do them good as he has opportunity, especially to bring to them the good tidings, that they also may believe. But there is one class of men whom he can regard only with abhorrence: those who have had opportunity of knowing Jesus Christ in His goodness, wisdom, and grace, yet love Him not, but think and speak evil of Him. That for St. Paul was the unpardonable sin. He can love all but those who, knowing what they do, dislike Jesus. And in further proof that devotion to Jesus is the supreme virtue for him, it may be added that he loves all men, but these, for Christ's sake. He considers the scruples of the weak, because Christ died for them. He loves the poor in Jerusalem because, though they distrust him, they are disciples of Jesus, though very imperfectly understanding His teaching. He loves the honest-minded among his opponents, because they are fighting for what they consider to be the truth in Jesus. He loves the whole

[1] 1 *Cor.* viii. 11, 13.

world, because he believes all mankind have a place in Christ's Saviour sympathies. It is not meant by these statements to insinuate that St. Paul exercised charity by calculation, and after deliberate reflection on motives. His Christianity was too vigorous and healthy for that. I mean that Christ had so possessed his soul as to become the inspiration of his whole life, the latent source of all his impulses, the supreme end of all his actions.

CHAPTER XX

THE CHURCH

It is natural that one should desire to know what is taught in the Pauline letters, and especially in the controversial group, on the subject of the Church, and in what relation the Pauline idea of the Church stands to the idea of the kingdom of God, so prominent in the teaching of Christ as reported in the Synoptical Gospels.

As to the latter topic, for we may begin with it, it is to be noted that both ideas—Church and Kingdom, and the terms corresponding—occur both in Synoptic Gospels and in Pauline Epistles, but in an inverse order of prominence. The Kingdom is the leading idea in our Lord's teaching; the Church is named only twice in the evangelic narratives, and the question has been discussed whether Jesus ever used the word at all, or even contemplated the thing. The Church, on the other hand, is the leading category in St. Paul's Epistles; the kingdom of God is mentioned only five times in the four great Epistles, while the terms "Church" and "Churches" occur many times. From these facts the natural inference might seem to be that in the view both of Jesus and of Paul, the Kingdom and the Church were practically equivalent, the Church being the ideal of the Kingdom realised; from Christ's point of view the ideal to be realised in the future, therefore rarely mentioned, from St. Paul's point of view the ideal already realised, therefore most frequently spoken of. Broadly viewed this is the truth. Yet the statement must be taken with qualification, for neither in the teaching of our Lord, nor in that of St. Paul, do the two conceptions exactly cover each other. For both the Kingdom possesses a certain transcendental character not belonging to the Church. This amounts to saying that it is a pure ideal hovering over the reality, or in advance of it, a goal which the Church seeks to approximate but never overtakes. Along with this transcendental character goes an *apocalyptic* aspect, revealing itself in evangelic and Pauline representations of the Kingdom. These two attributes of transcendency and futurity are very recognisable in the passages referring to the Kingdom in the Pauline letters. The eschatological aspect is apparent in the texts, *Galatians* v. 21; 1 *Corinthians* vi. 9, 10; 1 *Corinthians* xv. 50; in the two former of which it is declared, concerning men guilty of certain specified sins, that they shall not inherit the Kingdom, while in the latter the same declaration is made concerning *flesh* and *blood*—that is, our present mortal corruptible bodies. The transcendent character of the Kingdom is plainly implied in the remaining two texts in which it is mentioned, 1 *Corinthians* iv. 20 and *Romans* xiv. 17. "Not in word," says the apostle in the former place (is) "the kingdom of God, but in power." It is clear that for the writer of such a sentence, at the moment, the

Kingdom is not identical with the Church, but something rising far above it in ideal purity and beauty and dignity. For the statement quoted could not have been made concerning the Church as represented by the Christian community in Corinth. The very opposite was the truth as regarded it. The Church at Corinth was in word not in power. It was a society wholly given up to talk, to oratory, to prophesying, to speaking with tongues. The one phenomenon visible there was a universally diffused talent for speech; there was a sad dearth of all that tends to give a religious community spiritual power, of wisdom and charity, or even common morality. A state of things like that would compel one to distinguish between Church and Kingdom, and to think of the latter as exalted above the former as far as heaven is above the earth. Similar observations apply to the other text which runs: "The kingdom of God is not meat and drink, but righteousness and peace and joy in the Holy Spirit." The obvious meaning is, that in the Kingdom ritual cleanness and uncleanness are of no account, nothing is of value there that is merely ceremonial, nothing but the moral and spiritual; the qualification for citizenship is not eating or abstaining from eating a given sort of food, but possessing a righteous, loving, sunny spirit. The men to whom belongs the Kingdom are those who have a passion for righteousness, who are peacemakers, and who can rejoice even in tribulation, because they have chosen God for their *summum bonum*.

The very fact that the apostle thought it needful to make the observation just commented on proves that the Church of Rome was far enough from realising the idea of a community in which questions about meats and drinks were nothing, and righteousness, peace, and joy in the Spirit everything. There were in it, on the one hand, many whose consciences were enslaved by petty scruples, and, on the other, many who treated such scruples with contempt; consequently, there prevailed a great forgetfulness in opposite directions of the great things of the law—justice, mercy, and faith. Such a state of matters is a disappointing and depressing spectacle wherever exhibited, and the soul of a good man naturally takes to itself wings of a dove and flies away in quest of a refuge from despair and scepticism to the fair kingdom of heaven where nought but what is noble and benignant and bright finds entrance. It is well for one who lives in evil times to be able thus mentally to see the transcendent commonwealth. It is his salvation from unbelief, his quietive amid disgusts, his consolation amid disappointments and disenchantments; a temple wherein he may behold the beauty of the Lord, when there is nowhere else anything beautiful to look upon; a pavilion in which he can hide himself in the time of trouble. There is no other refuge than the *Church transcendent*. However disappointing any particular religious society may be, it is not worth while to leave it for any other. The Church at Corinth was bad, but the Church at Rome was also far from perfect. In the one was licentious liberty, in the other religious narrowness and petty scrupulosity. Therefore, a truly Christlike man, whose lot was cast in either, might well say: "I had rather bear the ills I have than fly to others that I know not of." St. Paul's comfort in reference to both was to lift up his thoughts to the transcendent kingdom of God.

It thus appears that in the mind of the apostle the divine Kingdom was by no means immediately identical with the Christian Church. Yet while this is true, it is at the same time also true that in his writings we observe a constant effort to contemplate the Church in the bright light of the ideal, and not merely in the dim disenchanting light of vulgar reality. He desired ever to invest the Church with the attributes of the divine Kingdom, and loved to think of it as a glorious Church, without spot of defilement, or wrinkle of age, holy, free from blemish as became the bride of Christ.[1] Various traces of this idealising tendency are discoverable in the leading Epistles. First we may note the generalising conception of the Church as a *unity*. Sometimes the apostle speaks of Churches in the plural, as in *Galatians* i. 2, where he salutes "the Churches of Galatia," and in i. 22, where he states that he was unknown to "the Churches of Judea." The Churches in these texts are little communities of Christians in different towns who associated together as believers in Jesus, and met in one place for divine worship. In other texts the apostle uses the word "Church" collectively, to denote the whole body of believers, as in *Galatians* i. 13, where he penitently refers to the time when he persecuted "the Church of God," and in 1 *Corinthians* x. 32, where he counsels the Christians in Corinth to give no occasion of stumbling to Jews or to Greeks, or to the

[1] *Eph.* v. 27; the Epistle, whether one of St. Paul's or not, utters here genuinely Pauline sentiment.

Church of God, where it is clear from the reference to Jews and Greeks that he has a wide public in view; the whole world in fact divided into three classes: the Jews, the Gentiles represented by the Greeks (these two embracing all unbelievers), and the Church embracing all believers.

Another indication of the tendency to invest the Church with the ideal attributes of the divine Kingdom may be found in the representation of the Church as a society in which all outward distinctions are cancelled, and the sole qualification for membership is purely spiritual union to Christ by faith. The conception of the new humanity in which Christ is all and in all occurs chiefly in the later Epistles, especially in that to the Ephesians, but it is found also in the earlier, very distinctly in *Galatians* iii. 27, 28. "As many of you as were baptized into Christ put on Christ. There is (in Him) neither Jew nor Greek, there is neither slave nor freeman, there is neither male nor female; for ye are all one in Christ Jesus." Here is sketched a spiritual society in which nothing is taken into account but the personal relation of each member to the common object of faith. While the attribute of spirituality is accentuated the kindred attribute of universality is plainly implied. There is neither Jew, Greek, bond, free, male, female, because all are there together. This new society of the apostle's, like the kingdom of Jesus, is open to all comers, just because it negates all distinctions, and insists only on the one condition of faith, possible for all alike. It may here be noted that the expression "the Israel of God" used in the close of the Epistle to the Galatians shows how closely the ideas of the Church and the Kingdom were connected in the writer's mind. The new creation presented to view in the Christian Church was for him the ideal commonwealth, whereof the theocratic kingdom of Israel was an adumbration.

One other indication of this idealising tendency is to be found in the high moral attributes ascribed by St. Paul to the members of the Church. Though not unaware of the prevalent shortcoming in faith and life, he nevertheless speaks of the members of the various churches as "saints," sanctified, holy. Even the Corinthian Christians are saluted as "sanctified in Christ Jesus,"[1] and the title "saints" is extended to all Christians in the province of Achaia.[2] This might seem to be a mere matter of courtesy did we not find in the body of the First Epistle to the Corinthians a deliberate statement to the effect that the members of the Church were a body of sanctified men, a statement rendered all the more emphatic by the plainness with which the apostle indicates that the Corinthians had been the reverse of holy before they became converts to the Christian religion. "Such were some of you, but ye were washed, but ye were sanctified."[3]

From the foregoing discussion we have obtained a sufficiently clear general idea of the Christian Church as conceived by St. Paul. It is a society of men united by a common faith in Jesus Christ as the Saviour, and a common devotion to Him as their Lord, gathered together from all classes, conditions, and races of men. It does not need to be said that the members of such a society would have very close fellowship with each other. There is no brotherhood so intimate and precious as one based

[1] 1 *Cor.* i. 2. [2] 2 *Cor.* i. 1. [3] 1 *Cor.* vi. 11.

on a pure religion sincerely professed. It may be taken for granted that those who belong to such a brotherhood will avail themselves of all possible opportunities of meeting together for the interchange of thought and affection in mutual converse, and for united worship of the common object of faith, and for ministering to each other's wants and comforts. The Westminster Confession says: "Saints by profession are *bound* to maintain an holy fellowship and communion in the worship of God, and in performing such other spiritual services as tend to their mutual edification; as also in relieving each other in outward things, according to their several abilities and necessities."[1] In the initial period of fresh enthusiasm Christians would do all this instinctively without needing to be told it was their duty.

Accordingly, we are not surprised to find in the letters of St. Paul to the Churches he had planted traces of a very lively fellowship in worship, religious intercourse, and mutual benefit prevalent among those bearing the Christian name. They met together in public assembly, how often does not appear, but certainly at least once a week, and on the first day of the week; and when they met they prayed, sang, prophesied for mutual edification. They also ate together, and while doing so they set apart a portion of the bread and wine to be memorials of Christ's death, and partook of these with reverent, grateful thoughts of Him who died for them, and in token of mutual love to each other as His disciples.[2] At first,

[1] Chapter xxvi. sect. 2.
[2] The question has been discussed, whether the celebration of the Lord's Supper took place at the meeting for general worship or at a

apparently, all members of the community took part indiscriminately in the religious exercises. Everyone had his psalm, his doctrine, his revelation, or his still more mysterious utterance called a tongue (γλῶσσα), or his interpretation of a brother's tongue. All were on a level, there was perfect equality of privilege, unrestricted liberty of speech for the common good. It is easy to see that in a city like Corinth, among an excitable race like the Greeks, a religious meeting conducted in this manner would be more lively than orderly. It would not be long before a need for some little measure of order and organisation would be felt, a need for dividing the Church into two classes: those on the one hand who would best serve the brotherhood by silence, and those on the other whose special business it should be to contribute to the common benefit by speech. The question who were to be silent and who were to speak would settle itself by a process of natural selection. It would be seen by degrees who could speak to profit and who could not, and means would be found for silencing the unprofitable speaker, and for giving those who could speak profitably the position of recognised teachers. In a similar way spontaneous differentiation would take place in reference to other gifts, and certain persons would gradually come to be recognised as possessing the charism of healing, of succouring the needy, of government, and so on. Recognition would follow experimental proof of possession of the function. The honour of recognition would be the reward of service

separate meeting. *Vide* on this Weizsäcker, *Das Apostolische Zeitalter*, pp. 546–583, where the second of these alternatives is on strong grounds advocated.

actually rendered. For in the primitive Church the law enunciated by Christ, distinction to be reached through service, was thoroughly understood and acted on. The law is clearly proclaimed in St. Paul's Epistles. He represents the Church as an organism like the human body, wherein each part has a function to perform for the good of the whole, and in which if one part has more honour than another, it is because of its serviceableness.[1]

How far the process of differentiation into distinctiveness of function, and of corresponding recognition of fitness for distinct functions, had been carried at the time the four great Epistles were written it is not easy to determine. It seems pretty certain that by that time an order of teachers had arisen, but it is not so clear that all the communities were furnished with an order of rulers. No certain trace of such an order can be discovered in the sources of information concerning the Churches of Galatia and Corinth. One might indeed suppose that 1 *Cor.* xvi. 15, 16, contained a reference to something of the kind. "I beseech you, brethren (ye know the house of Stephanas, that it is the first fruits of Achaia, and that they gave themselves for service to the saints), that ye also be in subjection to such and to every fellow-worker and labourer." But this is too vague an exhortation to serve as a proof-text, especially when it is remembered that in connection with the case of immoral conduct in the Corinthian Church the apostle does not anywhere summon church rulers to exercise needful discipline, but simply appeals to the congregation to purge themselves of complicity with the sin. A more reliable

[1] 1 *Cor.* xii. 12-26.

indication of the existence of a ruling function in rudimentary form is to be found in what we have reason to regard as the earliest of the Pauline Epistles, the first to the Thessalonians. In that Epistle (v. 12) the apostle exhorts the Thessalonian Church to know those that laboured among them and *were over them in the Lord* (προϊσταμένους) and admonished them. A real authority is doubtless here pointed at, only we are not to conceive of it as of an official character originating in ecclesiastical ordination. It arose naturally and spontaneously, probably out of priority in faith, or from the fact that the προϊστάμενοι held the meetings of the congregation in their own houses and with the expenditure of their own means.[1]

As regards *teachers* on the other hand, distinct allusions to such an order occur in the leading Epistles. The apostle thus exhorts the Galatians: "Let him that is taught in the word—the catechumen—communicate with him that teacheth (τῷ κατηχοῦντι) in all good things." The exhortation seems to imply not only the existence of

[1] *Vide* on this Weizsäcker's *Apostolic Age*, p. 291. The reader may also consult two articles by Heinrici in the *Zeitschrift für wissenschaftliche Theologie*, 1876, 1877, on "Die Christengemeinde Korinths und die religiösen Genossenschaften der Greichen," and "Zur Geschichte der Anfänge Paulinischen Gemeinde." Heinrici's view is that the Gentile Churches founded by St. Paul were not modelled on the Jewish synagogue, but assumed the characteristics of the religious associations of the Pagan world. These, as they existed in Greece, according to Heinrici, bore a purely republican character. All members possessed the same rights, all were expected to show equal zeal. All were alike sovereign and alike responsible. The collective body ruled, resolved, rewarded, punished (*Zeitschrift für wissenschaftliche Theologie*, p. 501). The προϊστάμενος mentioned in 1 *Thess.* v. 12 and in *Romans* xii. 8, Heinrici compares to the *Patronus* of an association, who, as a person of influence, guarded its legal rights.

teachers, but of teachers who gave their whole time to the work, and therefore needed to be supported by the Church. In Corinth the position of teacher was occupied by Apollos, to whom reference is made in 1 *Cor.* iii. 4. That Apollos was more than an occasional speaker, even a regular instructor, is evident from the terms in which the apostle speaks of him. Claiming for himself the function of planter, he assigns to Apollos the function of watering, a task which, in its nature, requires to be performed systematically. In 1 *Cor.* iv. he describes both Apollos and himself as servants of Christ and stewards of the mysteries of God, phrases implying that both exercised functions of great importance, the one as a founder of churches, moving about from land to land, the other as a stationary instructor in a particular church.

But the passage which beyond all others shows that an importance and dignity belonged to the teaching ministry in St. Paul's esteem is that in 2 *Corinthians* where he describes himself as a fit servant of the New Testament.[1] It is implied that it is no small matter to be a fit minister of the Christian religion. That this is the thought in the apostle's mind is proved by the fact that, having claimed for himself to be such a minister, he goes on to pronounce an eulogium on the Christian dispensation in impassioned language, describing it as the religion of the Spirit, the dispensation of life, the ministration of righteousness, and in virtue of these attributes as the abiding perennial religion, as opposed to the transient religion of the old covenant. He claims for himself fitness for the service of this new order of things,

[1] 2 *Cor.* iii. 6.

basing his claim on his ability to appreciate the distinctive excellence and glory of the New Testament, an ability for which he is indebted to his whole past religious experience. And the service which he has in view is just the preaching of the gospel; for in the foregoing context he repudiates all complicity in the acts of those who huckster the word of God, and in the following he protests that if his gospel be hid it is hid from them that are lost. So, then, it is the word of God that is concerned in this New Testament service, it is the preaching of the gospel in which the service consists.

But it may be thought that this eulogy of the New Testament, and, by implication, of its ministry, affects only the preaching of an apostle, and cannot legitimately be extended to an ordinary gospel ministry. This inference, however, is contrary to the spirit, I may say even to the language, of the passage in question. For it is observable that the apostle employs the plural pronoun throughout, as if, while asserting his own importance against assailants,[1] with express intent to include others, like Apollos, Titus, and Timothy, in his eulogy. Then it is to be noted that at the end of the chapter the expression " we " is replaced by " we all,"[2] in which the writer certainly has in view more than himself. But indeed no one who enters into the drift of the argument throughout can possibly imagine that St. Paul is thinking merely of his own apostleship when he speaks of the ministry of the New Testament. The kind of argument he uses to define his

[1] For the bearing of the whole passage on the defence of St. Paul's apostolic standing against the Judaists, *vide* Chap. IV
[2] 2 *Cor.* iii. 18.

apostleship is such as to serve a wider purpose, viz., to legitimise the ministry of all who, with unveiled face, see the glory of Christ and of Christianity. For him the ultimate ground of a right to preach is insight into the genius of the New Testament religion. That carries with it the right of everyone who has the insight. Whoever has the open eye and the unveiled face may take part in the ministry. "The tools to him that can use them" was a principle for St. Paul as well as for Napoleon. He that had the open eye was, in his judgment, not only entitled but bound to take part in the New Testament ministry. God made the sun in order that it might shine, and He gives the light of the knowledge of the glory of God in the face of Jesus to Christian men that they in turn may be lights to the world.

There is another thing in this great passage which clearly shows that, in the writer's view, a teaching or preaching ministry was a most congenial and fitting feature of the New Testament dispensation. It is the remark about $παρρησία$, "Seeing then that we have such hope, we use great plainness of speech."[1] The frankness with which the apostle is wont to utter himself as a preacher he here connects with the hopeful character of the faith he preaches, which is a feature naturally rising out of all the others previously mentioned. The religion of the Spirit, of life, and of righteousness, cannot but be a religion of good hope. But a religion of good hope is sure to be a religion of free speech. For it puts men in good spirits; it gives them heart to speak; it makes them feel that they have good news to tell. Who would

[1] 2 Cor. iii. 12.

care to be a preaching minister of a religion of condemnation and despair and death? But how pleasant to be the messenger of mercy, the publisher of good tidings! How beautiful are the feet of them that preach a gospel of peace! beautiful because they move so nimbly and gracefully, as no feet can move but those of him that goes on a glad errand. It may be taken for granted that under a religion of good hope great will be the company of preachers characterised by παρρησία, boldness, frankness. The more the better St. Paul would have said, provided they be of the right kind, men in sympathy with the new era of grace and the genius of the New Testament; hopeful, outspoken, eloquent, as only those can be who are at once sincere and happy. To men of another spirit, gloomy, reserved, prudential, he would have said, "You are not fit for this ministry; you are fit only for a ministry like that of Moses, who put a veil on his face. You are living not in the new era but in the old one, which I for my part am glad to be done with. Go and take service under the Levitical system; you are of no use in the Christian Church."

The upshot of what has been said is that evangelism—frank, fervent speech about the common faith—may be expected as a prominent feature of organised Christianity in proportion as the organisation is filled with the spirit of St. Paul and of the apostolic age. Whether a systematically trained class of professional preachers be a legitimate development out of such evangelism is a question of grave concern for all the Churches in the present time. Preaching is a very outstanding feature in our church life, and all the modern Churches have with more or less decision adopted as their ideal "a learned ministry." Is the ideal justified by results? In reply I have to say that my sympathies are very strongly with the advocates of a learned ministry. In my view, what we have to complain of is, not that the Churches have adopted this as their ideal, but that the ministry turned out of their theological seminaries can only by courtesy be described as learned. What we need is not less learning, but a great deal more and of the right sort. At the same time, it has to be acknowledged that the programme involves dangers. Learning may kill enthusiasm, and transform the prophet into a rabbi. That will mean decay of the evangelic spirit, lapse into legalism. This is the form in which the legal temper is apt to invade Churches which magnify the importance of the preacher. The bane of other Churches is sacramentarianism and priestcraft, under which prophetic $\pi\alpha\rho\rho\eta\sigma\iota\alpha$ disappears, and mystery takes its place. The bane to be dreaded by Churches not sacramentarian in tendency, is a rabbinised pulpit, offering the people scholastic dogmas or philosophic ideas in place of the gospel. Religious teachers ought to know theology, and to be deep, earnest thinkers; but in the *concio ad populum* the prophet should be more prominent than the theologian, and the poet than the philosopher.

One other topic remains to be noticed briefly, the view presented in the Pauline Epistles of the Church's relation to Christ. In the Christological Epistles the Church is conceived as the body of Christ, He being the Head. This idea is found also in the controversial letters, more especially in 1 *Corinthians*. It is stated with great distinctness in the words, "But ye are the body of Christ and members individually" (ἐκ μέρους);[1] well paraphrased by Stanley: "You, the Christian society, as distinct from the bodily organisation, of which I have just been speaking, you are, collectively speaking, the body of Christ, as individually you are His limbs." The value of this idea is the use made of it in assigning a *rationale* for the diversity of gifts in the Church. In order to a complete Church, such is the apostle's thought, there must be a great variety of gifts, just as there is a great variety of members in the human body. It would not be well if all had the same gifts, any more than if the whole body were an eye or an ear. There must be differentiation of function: apostles, prophets, teachers, gifts of healing, talent for administration, the power of speaking with tongues. The diversity need not create disorder. It finds its unity in Christ. "There are diversities of services, and the same Lord."[2] A splendid ideal, if only it were wisely and conscientiously worked out. But alas, to carry out the programme, there is wanted a spirit of self-abnegation and magnanimity such as animated the apostle Paul. We are so apt to imagine that our function is the only important or even legitimate one, and to regard men of other gifts as aliens and rebels. It is so hard to realise our own limits, and to see in our brethren the complement of our own defects; and to grasp the thought that it takes all Christians together, with all their diverse talents and graces, to shadow forth, even imperfectly, the fulness of wisdom and goodness that is in Christ.

[1] 1 *Cor.* xii. 27. [2] *Ibid.* xii. 5.

CHAPTER XXI

THE LAST THINGS

On no subject, perhaps, was St. Paul, in his way of thinking, more a man of his time than on that of eschatology. And on no subject is it more difficult for one influenced by the modern spirit to sympathise with, or even to understand, the apostle. For modern modes of thought in this connection are very diverse from those of the Jews in the apostolic age. Not only our secular but even our religious interest centres largely in the present; theirs looked to the future. We desire to possess the *summum bonum*, salvation, life as it ought to be, here and now; for them it was something that was coming in the end of the days. And if we still believe in a final consummation, it is for us indefinitely remote, a goal so distant that we can leave it practically out of account, and conceive of the present order of things as going on, if not quite for ever, at least for a long series of ages. For the Jew, for St. Paul, the end was nigh, might come any day; probably would come within his own lifetime. The last time, indeed, had already come; Christ Himself, even at His first coming, was an eschatological phenomenon, and His second advent could not be separated from His first by much more than a generation.

All this now seems so strange that the subject of the eschatology of the New Testament in general, and of St. Paul in particular, is apt to appear the reverse of inviting, a theme to be passed over in respectful silence. But, in connection with an attempt to expound the Pauline system of thought, such a procedure is inadmissible. The prominence of the eschatological point of view in the Pauline letters forbids evasion of the topic, simply because it may happen to be difficult or distasteful. For eschatology in these letters does not mean merely the discussion of some curious, obscure, and more or less unimportant questions respecting the end of this world and the incoming of the next. It covers the whole ground of Christian hope. Salvation itself is eschatologically conceived. We had occasion to observe this fact in connection with the earliest of the Pauline Epistles, in which Christians are described as waiting for Christ from heaven;[1] but the remark applies more or less to all the Epistles.[2]

Those who wait for a good greatly desired are naturally impatient of delay. Hence the second advent, in the apostolic age, was expected very soon. The apostle Paul expected it in his lifetime. To us now this may appear surprising, not so much on account of the complete ignorance as to the future course of things the explanation implied, as by reason of the indifference it seemed to show to the working out of the end for which Jesus Christ came into the world. How, we are inclined to ask, could a man who, like St. Paul, regarded the

[1] 1 *Thess.* i. 10.
[2] *Vide* on this Kabisch, *Die Eschatologie des Paulus*, pp. 12–70.

gospel as good news for the whole world, desire the speedy termination of the present order of things? Why not rather long and pray for ample time wherein to carry on missionary operations? In cherishing a contrary wish, was he not preferring personal interests to the great public interest of the kingdom of God? Surely it was desirable that all men should hear the good tidings! That end was not accomplished by preaching the gospel in a few of the principal centres of population in Asia and Europe. True, the faith might spread from town to country, and the evangelisation of Corinth might be regarded as in germ the Christianisation of Greece. But that meant a process of gradual growth demanding time. And if time was not to be allowed for that process, was it really worth while contending so zealously for the cause of Gentile Christianity? Why not let the Judaists have their way if the end was to be so soon? If the programme, a gospel of grace unfettered by legalism for the whole human race, was worth fighting for, surely its champion ought in consistency to wish for time to work it thoroughly out! The Jewish day of grace had lasted for millenniums; was the pittance of a single generation all that was to be thrown to Gentile dogs? To us it certainly seems as if the bias of St. Paul, as the advocate of Christian universalism, ought to have been decidedly in favour of a lengthened Christian era, and an indefinitely delayed παρουσία; unless by the latter he meant Christ coming not to judge the world, but to resume the gracious work He had carried on in Palestine, adopting the larger world of heathenism as His sphere, and to quicken by His presence the energies of His servants, so that the process of converting the nations might go on at a tenfold speed.

A trace of the conception of a protracted Christian era may be discovered in the words of *Ephesians* iii. 21: "To Him be glory in the Church, and in Christ Jesus, unto all the generations of the age of the ages." But for critics this fact might simply be an additional argument against the authenticity of the Epistle. Turning to the Epistles more certainly Pauline, we find in two of them indications of a change of view to some extent in reference to the second coming. In *Philippians* the apostle represents himself as in a strait between two alternatives, one being to live on in this present world, in spite of all discomfort, for the benefit of fellow-Christians, the other to die (ἀναλῦσαι) and to be with Christ.[1] We see here the apostle's generous heart leaning to the side of postponement of the end. But the event to be postponed is not the second coming of Christ, but his own departure from this life. And the change in his mind does not consist in thinking that the advent will not happen so soon as he had once expected, but rather in thinking that death will overtake himself before the great event arrives. He had hoped that Jesus would come during his lifetime. He cherishes that hope no longer, because the prospect before him is that his life will be cut short by an unfavourable judicial sentence. In 2 *Corinthians* v., the same mood prevails, possibly for a different reason. "We know," writes the apostle, "that if the earthly house of our tabernacle be dissolved, we

[1] *Phil.* i. 23.

have a building from God, a house not made with hands, eternal in the heavens."[1] This is in a different key from those words in the first Epistle to the same Church: "Behold, I tell you a mystery: we shall not all sleep, but we shall all be changed."[2] In the earlier Epistle, written not long before, the apostle seems to hope to be alive when the Lord comes; in the later, he writes like a man who expects to die, and who comforts himself by thoughts of the felicity awaiting him beyond the grave. Whence this altered mood within so brief an interval? It may be due to failure of the physical powers, through sickness and hard conditions of existence, premonitory of dissolution at no distant date. The preceding chapter is full of hints at such a breaking down. The phrases "earthen vessels" (iv. 7), "the outward man wasting" (iv. 16), "the lightness of our present affliction" (iv. 17), are significant, implying bodily affliction by no means light, but *made* light by the buoyant spirit of the writer, and by the hope of the glory which awaits him when life's tragic drama is ended.

This change in the apostle's personal expectation was likely to have one consequence. It might lead him to reflect more than he had previously done on the state of the dead, intermediate between the hour of death and the resurrection. As long as the second advent was expected within his lifetime, the intermediate state would not be a pressing question for him, and as far as appears he does not seem to have thought much about it. The phrase he uses in 1 *Thessalonians* to denote the dead is "those who sleep,"[3] a vague expression conveying no

[1] 2 *Cor.* v. 1.   [2] 1 *Cor.* xv. 51.   [3] 1 *Thess.* iv 13, 14.

definite idea, or suggesting an idea analogous to that entertained by the ancient Hebrews, according to which the life of the departed was a shadowy, unreal thing, compared with the life of those living on earth. In 2 *Corinthians* this vague phrase is replaced by much more definite language. The apostle expects at death to exchange the frail tabernacle of his mortal body for a permanent dwelling-place in heaven, and by this house from heaven he seems to mean a body not liable to corruption. It is to be put on as a garment ($\dot{\epsilon}\pi\epsilon\nu\delta\acute{\upsilon}\sigma a\sigma\theta a\iota$) fitting close to the soul. The word "naked" ($\gamma\upsilon\mu\nu o\grave{\iota}$) in ver. 3 points in the same direction. The nakedness shrunk from is that of a disembodied spirit. The apostle does not wish to enter the world beyond as a bodiless ghost—that seems to his imagination a cold, cheerless prospect; he simply desires to exchange the body that is mortal for a body that is endowed with the power of an endless life.

If this be the apostle's meaning, the question arises: How is this idea of a body in heaven to be put on at death to be reconciled with the doctrine of the resurrection? To what end a resurrection body, if there is a body awaiting the deceased to be put on immediately after the corruptible one is put off? Or if the resurrection is to be held fast, is this body which the soul puts on as a new garment at death to be viewed as a temporary body, not an $o\grave{\iota}\kappa\eta\tau\acute{\eta}\rho\iota o\nu$, or house after all, but a tabernacle also, like the mortal body, only perchance of finer mould? This curious notion of a temporary body, to be worn in the intermediate state, has actually been resorted to by some interpreters, as a hypothesis wherewith to reconcile St. Paul's various statements about the future life. But it is a very questionable way of getting out of a difficulty. It is better to hold that the apostle had no clear light on the subject of the intermediate state, no dogma to teach, but was simply groping his way like the rest of us, and that what we are to find in 2 *Corinthians* v. is not the expression of a definite opinion, far less the revelation of a truth to be received as an item in the creed, as to the life beyond, but the utterance of a wish or hope. One cannot but note the contrast between the confident language of the first two verses and the hesitating tone of the next two. "We know," says the apostle in ver. 1; "if being clothed we shall not be found naked," "we wish not to be unclothed, but clothed upon," are the phrases he employs in vers. 3 and 4. It would seem as if in the first sentence of the chapter the writer's mind contemplated the future state as a whole, without distinction between the pre-resurrection and the post-resurrection states, and that then the intermediate state occurring to his mind led to a change of tone.

Passing from this obscure topic to the more important subject of the resurrection, several grave questions present themselves for consideration, such as these, Whom does the resurrection concern? What is the nature of the resurrection life and of the resurrection body, and what the relation between the second advent, the resurrection, and the final consummation of the end?

1. As to the first of these questions, we are accustomed to take for granted that in the New Testament generally, and in the Epistles of St. Paul in particular, the resurrec-

rection of course concerns all men. To one whose mind is preoccupied with the belief in a general resurrection, both of the just and the unjust, of believers and unbelievers alike, it seems easy to find traces of the doctrine in 1 *Corinthians* xv. The words "as in Adam all die, even so in Christ shall all be made alive"[1] seem to express it plainly, and the end spoken of in ver. 24 is naturally taken to mean the end of the resurrection process, accomplished in three stages: Christ the first-fruits, then those who belong to Christ rising at His second coming, then finally, after an interval, the resurrection of all the rest of the dead. But an imposing array of interpreters dispute this view of the apostle's meaning, restricting the "all" who are to be made alive in Christ to those who before death were in living fellowship with Him, and seeing in the "end" not a reference to the concluding stage of the resurrection, but rather to the final stage of Christ's mediatorial work, when He shall deliver up His kingdom to the Father. It is conceivable, of course, that the apostle might have nothing to say on the subject of the general resurrection in a particular passage, while yet believing in it, and even teaching it in other parts of his writings. But there are those who would have us believe that St. Paul knew nothing of a general resurrection, or of a life beyond for the ungodly and the unbelieving, and that his programme for the future was— life perpetual for all who believe in Jesus, for all the rest of mankind total extinction of being after death. It is even contended that the precise object of the Christian hope, according to St. Paul, was continuance of life, in

[1] 1 *Cor.* xv. 22.

the literal physical sense, after death, and the privilege of the Christian as compared with other men, that in his case this hope will be realised.[1]

To those accustomed to other ways of thinking, these views are startling and disconcerting; and, apart altogether from the discomfort connected with the unsettling of preconceived opinions, it is disappointing to meet with so much diversity of view as to the interpretation of texts whose meaning had previously appeared so plain. But it is idle to indulge in querulous reflections. The wise course is to adjust ourselves to the situation, and to recognise once for all that the eschatological teaching of St. Paul is neither so simple nor so plain as we had imagined, and that the whole subject demands careful reconsideration. The result of a new study may, not improbably, be to convict such a discussion as that of Kabisch of the "vigour and rigour" characteristic of so many German theories. But it were well that that should appear as the conclusion of a serious inquiry, rather than be assumed at the outset as an excuse for neglecting further examination. Meantime, it is satisfactory to find there is a large measure of agreement in regard to one fundamental point, viz., that St. Paul did earnestly believe and teach a resurrection of Christians to eternal life.

2. And yet there are those who seem not disinclined to call even this in question, or at least to rob the fact of abiding value for the Christian faith, by insisting on the *ethical* aspect of resurrection as opposed to the eschatological. The basis of this view is the manner in which

[1] So Kabisch, in *Eschatologie des Paulus*.

St. Paul seems in various places to blend together the two aspects: the resurrection now experienced in the new life in the Spirit with the resurrection of the dead. Two instances of this may be cited. In *Romans* viii. 11, we read: "If the Spirit of Him that raised up Jesus from the dead dwell in you, He that raised up Christ from the dead shall also quicken your mortal bodies by His Spirit that dwelleth in you"; and in 2 *Corinthians* v. 5: "Now He that hath wrought us for this very thing is God" (the thing referred to is the investiture with the heavenly body), "who also hath given unto us the earnest of the Spirit." In these texts the apostle seems to found, on the spiritual resurrection of the soul to a new divine life, an argument in favour of a future physical resurrection to eternal life. It is a line of argument with which we are perfectly familiar, and of which all Christians feel the force in proportion to the vigour of their own spiritual experience. But writers such as Pfleiderer and the late Mr. Matthew Arnold, acting as the mouthpieces of the modern spirit, find in these and kindred texts much more than this, even a new ethical way of thinking really incompatible with the old Jewish eschatological theory of the universe; co-existing indeed in St. Paul's mind with the latter, but destined eventually to supersede it. "The three essential terms of Pauline theology are not," writes Mr. Arnold, in *Paul and Protestantism*, "calling, justification, sanctification. They are rather dying with Christ, resurrection from the dead, growing into Christ. The order in which these terms are placed indicates the true Pauline sense of the expression, 'resurrection from the dead.' In St. Paul's ideas the expression has no essential connection with physical death. It is true popular theology connects it with this almost exclusively, and regards any other use of it as purely figurative and secondary. . . . But whoever has carefully followed St. Paul's line of thought, as we have endeavoured to trace it, will see that in his mature theology, as the Epistle to the Romans exhibits it, it cannot be this physical and miraculous aspect of the resurrection which holds the first place in his mind, for under this aspect the resurrection does not fit in with the ideas he is developing."[1] Mr. Arnold does not mean to deny that St. Paul held the doctrine of a physical resurrection and a future life. He admits that if the apostle had been asked at any time of his life whether he held that doctrine, he would have replied with entire conviction that he did. Nevertheless, he thinks that that Jewish doctrine was only an outer skin which the new ethical system of thought was sooner or later to slough off.

> "Below the surface stream, shallow and light,
> Of what we say we feel,—below the stream,
> As light, of what we think we feel,—there flows,
> With noiseless current, strong, obscure, and deep,
> The central stream of what we feel indeed."

The question thus raised is a momentous one, the full drift of which it is important to understand. It is nothing less than whether the eschatological point of view in general be really compatible with the ethical. If the question be decided in the negative, then all the eschatological ideas—resurrection, judgment, a future life,

[1] p. 260.

with its alternative states—must be given up, or resolved into ethical equivalents; the resurrection into the new life in the Spirit, the final judgment into the incessant action of the moral order of the world, and the Eternal beyond into the Eternal here which underlies the phenomenal life of men. On this theory the eschatological categories will have to be regarded as products of the religious imagination, just as the blue sky is the illusory product of our visual organs. The Judgment will become the perpetually active moral order of the world projected forward in time by conscience, as the blue sky is the environing atmosphere projected by the eye to an indefinite distance in space. Heaven and hell will be projections into the future of the rewards and punishments inseparable from right and wrong action falling within present human experience, and brought about by the natural operation of the law of cause and effect.

To these modern conceptions, we may concede cogency so far as to admit that eschatological ideas require to undergo a process of purification, in order to bring them into harmony with ethical views of human life and destiny. But it is an unfounded assertion that eschatological ideas in any form are incompatible with the ethical view-point, to such an extent, *e.g.*, as to involve the denial of the future life altogether, which is by far the most important interest at stake. The hope of a life beyond, in which the ideal to which the good devoted their lives here shall be realised, seems to be a natural element in the creed of all theists. Nor does it appear incapable of being reconciled with the doctrine of evolution in the moral world, as even Bishop Butler seems to have dimly perceived, for he endeavoured to remove from the future state the aspect of arbitrariness, and to make it the natural outcome of the present life, in accordance with the analogy of seedtime and harvest.

How time brings its revenges! Some years ago Mr. Arnold told us that St. Paul, without being aware of it, substituted an ethical for a physical resurrection, and an eternal life in the spirit here for an everlasting life hereafter. Now a German theologian tells us that St. Paul knows nothing of a figurative "life" ethical in quality, but only of a physical life; that prolongation of physical life after death is the object of his hope; that even the Spirit, in his system of thought, is physical and finely material, and communicates itself by physical means, by baptism and even by generation through a Christian parent; that the germ of the resurrection body is a spiritual, yet physical body, existing now within the dead carcase of the old body of sin; and that the essence of the resurrection will consist in the manifestation of this spiritual body by the sloughing off of its gross carnal envelope.[1] Such are the two extremes. Surely the truth lies somewhere between!

3. In comparison with the reality of the life hereafter, the nature of the resurrection body and of its relation to the mortal body laid in the grave, is a topic of subordinate interest, but a few sentences on it may not be out of place. The apostle boldly states that flesh and blood cannot inherit the kingdom of God.[2] From this it may be inferred that the resurrection body must differ in

[1] Kabisch, *Eschatologie des Paulus*, Zweiter Abschnitt, secs. 1 and 5.
[2] 1 *Cor.* xv. 50.

nature from that worn in this present life. If we inquire as to the positive character of that body, the only suggestion we can gather from the apostle's statements is that it will be composed of a light-like substance, so that it will shine like the heavenly bodies; though it is not perfectly certain that the allusion to the latter in 1 *Corinthians* xv. 40, 41, is meant to serve any purpose beyond illustrating the difference between the natural body and the spiritual body. Yet it would not be surprising if St. Paul conceived of the spiritual body as a luminous substance, for it seems to have been a current opinion among the Jews that in the life to come the righteous would have shining bodies.[1] Too much stress, however, must not be laid on this, especially in view of the fact that more than one way of thinking seems to have prevailed in rabbinical circles. According to Weber there was a spiritualistic conception of life in the future world, as a life lacking all the characteristics of the present life — eating, drinking, generation, trade; and consisting in an eternal enjoyment of the glory of the Shekinah; and there was also a materialistic conception, according to which eating and generation would continue, only the food would be exceptionally good, and the children all righteous.[2] It is difficult to decide how far such statements are to be taken seriously. The Jewish mind was realistic and sensuous in its way of thinking. Spirit was conceived of grossly, and invested with some of the properties of matter. It was a kind of thin matter, an ether endowed with the properties of per-

---

[1] *Vide* Langen, *Judenthum in Palästina zur Zeit Christi*, p. 507.
[2] Weber, *Die Lehren des Talmud*, p. 383.

manence, luminousness, and power to penetrate all things. So at least inquirers into these obscure regions tell us.[1] If these views are to be taken literally, and if St. Paul is to be regarded as sharing them, the word "body" in the expression "a spiritual body" is superfluous. A spirit is a body, and a spiritual body is just a spirit.

What connection can a body of this kind have with the body which dies and is buried in the tomb? None at all, replies such a writer as Holsten, who goes the length of maintaining that even in the case of Christ, the post-resurrection body stood in no relation to the crucified body, in the view of St. Paul; in other words, that the apostle did not think of the crucified body as rising again. This hypothesis hangs together with the dualistic interpretation of the Pauline doctrine of the flesh, according to which the flesh is radically sinful, Christ's flesh not excepted, and the atonement really consisted in the judicial punishment of sin in Christ's body which, as a criminal, was not worthy of the honour of being raised again. On this view the body in which Christ appeared to St. Paul on the way to Damascus must have been an entirely new creation. The construction thus put on the resurrection of Jesus, and on the resurrection generally, is not the one which an unbiassed consideration of the texts naturally suggests. The very words ἐγείρω and ἀνάστασις imply the contrary view, suggesting the idea of the resurrection body springing out of the mortal body, as grain springs out of the seed sown in the ground. The analogy must not be pressed too far, but it conveys this hint at least, that the new will be related to the old

[1] *Vide* Kabisch, *Die Eschatologie des Paulus*, pp. 188-228.

so as to insure identity of form if not of substance, as the grain on the stalk is the same in kind, though not numerically the same, or composed of the same particles, as the seed out of which it springs.

4. Our last question is: Is there any trace of chiliasm in the Pauline eschatology, any recognition of a period of time intervening between the second coming and the end when Christ shall resign the kingdom? An affirmative answer may plausibly be justified by a particular mode of interpreting 1 *Corinthians* xv. 22–28. Thus, there are three stages in the resurrection process: first Christ, then Christians, then the rest of mankind. With the third final stage coincides the "end." But between the second and third stages there is an appreciable interval. This is implied in the term τάγμα involving the notion of succession, and also in the words ἀπαρχή, ἔπειτα, εἶτα, which it is natural to regard as indicative each of a distinct epoch. We know that the first two stages are separated by a considerable interval, and it may be inferred that the second and third are likewise conceived of as divided by a long space of time. Another consideration in favour of this view is that, on the contrary hypothesis, Christ's reign over His kingdom in glory would be reduced to a vanishing-point. The argument has some show of reason, but the subject is obscure, and a modest interpreter must step cautiously and timidly as one carrying but a glimmering torchlight to show him the way. Perhaps the apostle's thoughts were as represented, perhaps not; perhaps, like the prophets, he had himself but a dim, vague, shadowy conception of the future, very different from the future that is to be. The

chapter on the resurrection in 1 *Corinthians* xv. is a sublime one, full of great thoughts and inspiring hopes. But beyond one or two leading statements, such as that affirming the certainty of the future life, I should be slow to summarise its contents in definite theological formulæ. I had rather read this chapter as a Christian man seeking religious edification and moral inspiration, than as a theologian in quest of positive dogmatic teaching. The spirit of the whole is life-giving, but the letter is δυσερμήνευτον, and while some interpreters feel able on the basis of it to tell us all about the millennium, and others find therein a universal ἀποκατάστασις, when God shall be all in all, and to every human spirit, I prefer to confess my ignorance and remain silent.

SUPPLEMENTARY NOTE

ON

THE TEACHING OF ST. PAUL COMPARED WITH THE TEACHING OF OUR LORD IN THE SYNOPTICAL GOSPELS.

IN the course of our study of St. Paul's conception of Christianity we have taken occasion, as opportunity presented itself, to compare the views of the apostle with the teaching of Christ as it is set forth in the first three Gospels. The comparison touches mainly four topics: the idea of righteousness [1]; the significance of Christ's death [2]; the doctrine of Sonship [3]; and the law of growth in the Christian life.[4] We found that St. Paul's conception of the righteousness of God does not occur in the Gospels. The righteousness of God spoken of there is not, as in the Pauline Epistles, a righteousness God-given, but a righteousness of which God is the centre.[5] The nearest equivalent to St. Paul's righteousness of God in the teaching of our Lord is, as has been pointed out, the free pardon of sin, which occupied a prominent place in Christ's gospel. In reference to the death of Christ, we

[1] *Vide* Chap. VII.   [2] *Vide* Chap. VIII.   [3] *Vide* Chap. X.
[4] *Vide* Chap. XVIII   [5] *Vide The Kingdom of God*, chap. ix.

had occasion to remark that the ethical view of that event set forth in the first lesson on the doctrine of the cross[1] is overlooked by St. Paul, his interest being concentrated on the religious or theological aspect. On the subject of Sonship, we found that in representing sonship as constituted by adoption, the apostle seems to give it an aspect of artificiality or unreality, contrasting unfavourably with the sonship presented to view in the Gospels, which rests on an essential identity between the nature of God and the nature of man. In so far as this contrast is real, it points to a deeper difference in the way of conceiving God. But it was pointed out that there is reason to believe that the theology of the schools has not in this connection done full justice to the thought of St. Paul. Finally, on the subject of gradual sanctification we were forced to the conclusion that the Pauline Epistles contain nothing parallel to the firm grasp and felicitous statement of the great law of growth in the kingdom of God, exhibited in the parable of the blade, the green ear, and the ripe corn.

A somewhat elaborate study on the contrast between the two types of doctrine has recently appeared from the pen of Wendt,[2] the well-known author of the work, *Die Lehre Jesu*, of which a portion has been translated into English.[3] Among the points of comparison are these: the essence of the Messianic salvation, the righteousness of the saved man, the condition of the natural man, the

---

[1] Vide *The Kingdom of God*, chap. x.
[2] *Die Lehre des Paulus verglichen mit der Lehre Jesu*, in *Zeitschrift für Theologie und Kirche*, 1894, pp. 1–78.
[3] Wendt, *The Teaching of Jesus*, 2 vols, by Messrs T. & T. Clark.

Person of the Messiah, the significance of Christ as the Mediator of salvation, and the conditions of participation in salvation.

1. In reference to the first topic, the author finds a general agreement between the Master and the apostle, in so far as both taught that the Messianic salvation came with Jesus, and consisted not in the fulfilment of Old Testament hopes of an earthly kingdom, but in a gracious relation of sonship to God, begun here and perfected hereafter. The point of difference, according to Wendt, is that in the teaching of Jesus there is no developed doctrine as to the possession by believers of the Holy Spirit, such as we find in the Pauline letters.

2. On the second topic, the righteousness of the saved man, Wendt finds in both types of doctrine, as a common element, recognition of the truth that only the ethical has real value in God's sight, and that ritual possesses no intrinsic importance. The difference lies in the ground on which this truth is made to rest. In the teaching of Christ it is the purely ethical and spiritual nature of God, and the certainty thence flowing that the only acceptable righteousness is that which is kindred to God's own moral nature. In the teaching of St. Paul the worthlessness of ritual is a deduction from the redeeming work of Christ. Christ, by being made under law, has redeemed us from subjection to law. But this redemption covers the whole law, as law, without distinction between the ethical and the ritual. Insight into the essential difference between the two is not so markedly characteristic of the apostle.

3. In connection with the third topic, the condition of

the natural man, Wendt finds a considerable difference between the two types of doctrine. Christ's view of average human nature is, he thinks, less sombre than that of St. Paul. The natural man, as he appears in the Gospels, is not doomed by the flesh to sin. Then the Gospels contain no such speculations as to the malign influence of Adam's transgression on the character and destinies of the race, as we find in *Romans* v. 12–21.

4. As to the person of the Messiah, a common element in the two types of doctrine is the idea that the Messiah-ship of Jesus rested exclusively on his filial relation to God. Neither Christ nor Paul, according to Wendt, attached any real importance to the Davidic descent. The point of contrast under this head is found in the idea of pre-existence, propounded by the apostle, but not, according to our author, to be found in the authentic utterances of Jesus.

5. The point at which the greatest difference between the two types of doctrine reveals itself is the significance of Christ as the Mediator of salvation. There is first, according to our author, the great general contrast, that whereas Christ Himself gave special, not to say exclusive, prominence to His revealing, or prophetic, or teaching function, the apostle left that very much in the background, and made all turn on the redemptive significance of Christ's death. Then there is the specific contrast between the manner in which that death is viewed in the two types. The apostle, according to Wendt, assigned to Christ's death the significance of a vicarious penal suffering, on the part of the innocent One on behalf of the guilty. He finds no such doctrine in the words of our

Lord, not even in the saying concerning the ransom in *Mark* x. 45, nor in the words spoken at the institution of the Supper. He holds that Jesus taught the doctrine of a free forgiveness to all penitent sinners unmediated by any atonement, and that this doctrine set forth in the parable of the prodigal, and elsewhere, He did not cancel or limit towards the end of His life. The words spoken at the institution of the Supper offer no justification for such a supposition. "It is," he says, "only a prejudice arising out of our dogmatic tradition, that the thought of the saving significance of Christ's death for His followers must include or presuppose the idea of a vicarious expiation. I believe that Jesus, in the words of institution, had no such thought in His mind, although He did mean to express the other idea of a saving significance attaching to His death. It was a conception naturally arising out of His certainty as to the overwhelming love and grace of God, that God would reward the loyal obedience of His Son with rich blessings, affecting not Himself only, but also those who belong to Him, even as, in the Old Testament, we find God promising to reward the truth of those who keep His covenant with benefits to thousands (*Exodus* xx. 6). But this certainty as to the greatness of divine grace did not lead Jesus to imagine that, in order to be able to forgive penitent sinners, God demanded the vicarious sufferings of His obedient Son. As Jesus did not regard earthly suffering in general simply as evil, and as penalty of sin, it was by no means a self-evident truth to Him that His innocent suffering must have a penal relation to the sin of other men. He did not regard His death as vicarious penal suffering, but only as a proof of obedience, which God in His grace would not fail to reward."[1]

The question here raised is very important. And with regard to the answer given to it by Wendt, who holds that Christ and Paul here offer two entirely different gospels, it may be frankly admitted that the two types of doctrine are certainly not coincident at this point. There is, *e.g.*, a difference as to the view to be taken of suffering. For the apostle it is an axiom that all suffering is on account of sin. And, as we have elsewhere pointed out, this axiom raises a question to which the Pauline literature offers no answer. What about the sufferings of the righteous, the prophets, for example? Did they suffer for their own sins? Then they must have been exceptionally great sinners, as Job's friends said he was. Or did they suffer for the sins of others redemptively? If neither view is adopted, what other alternative is there which goes to the root of the matter? In Christ's teaching the penal meaning of suffering is not accentuated. He spoke not merely of a suffering for sin, whether personal or relative, but also and very emphatically of a suffering for righteousness, and He undoubtedly looked on His own suffering as belonging to the latter category. But He also recognised that the sufferings of the righteous might bring benefit to the unrighteous. This is admitted in the passage above quoted. Even in Wendt's own statement, as there given, there is room for a theory of redemptive value attaching to Christ's death. God, it is admitted, gives blessings to men for Christ's sake. This general truth is of more

[1] *Zeitschrift für Theologie und Kirche*, 1894, pp. 55, 56.

importance than any special theological formulation of it. It may be possible to formulate the fundamental truth in this matter better than theologians have formulated it, or even to improve on St. Paul's statement. But the main point to notice is, that there is a fact or truth to be formulated—that God confers blessings spiritual and temporal on some men for the sake of other men. This thought is contained in the teaching of our Lord, as well as in the letters of St. Paul. And in view of this fact it cannot be truly affirmed that the doctrine of Jesus was *auto-soteric*, while that of St. Paul was *hetero-soteric*.[1] Self-salvation, salvation by another—the difference between the Master and the apostle, is not so great as that. Both teach essentially the same doctrine, that God for Christ's sake blesses the world.

How this doctrine is to be adjusted to the natural order of the universe is a problem requiring more consideration than it has yet received. How can ten righteous men save Sodom? What does such a supposition mean, translated into terms of natural law? How do prayers count, how pains, sorrows, tears, crucifixions? Theology teaches that God has a regard to these things, and because of them imputes, and does, good to the unthankful and the evil. What is the equivalent of this divine procedure, in the world of which science takes cognisance? I do not know, but I believe that the sacrificial lives of the saintly were eternally in God's view, that they are the things of value in His sight;

[1] *Vide* Macintosh, *The Natural History of the Christian Religion* (1894), where the difference between Jesus and Paul is thus put. *Vide* especially chap. xv.

that the world exists *for* them and is preserved *by* them.

6. On the last topic, little needs to be said. According to Wendt, our Lord and the apostle were at one in attaching great importance to faith as a condition of participation in salvation. But they differed in this, that while Jesus insisted also on repentance as a joint condition, St. Paul gave prominence to faith only. But, on close inspection, it will be found that in the teaching of our Lord, not less than in that of St. Paul, faith is the great watchword. Difference at this point is on the surface only.[1]

[1] Vide *The Kingdom of God*, chap. iii.

THE END.

www.ingramcontent.com/pod-product-compliance
Lightning Source LLC
Chambersburg PA
CBHW030559300426
44111CB00009B/1037